DYSLEXIA

Diagnosis and treatment of reading disorders

DYSLEXIA

Diagnosis and treatment of reading disorders

Edited by

ARTHUR H. KEENEY, M.D., D.Sc.

Professor and Chairman, Department of Ophthalmology,
Temple University School of Medicine; Ophthalmologist-
in-Chief, Wills Eye Hospital, Philadelphia, Pennsylvania

VIRGINIA T. KEENEY, M.D.

Project Coordinator, National Conference on Dyslexia,
Philadelphia, Pennsylvania

With 24 illustrations

*Sponsored by the American Committee on Optics and Visual
Physiology and the USPHS Neurological and Sensory Disease
Service Program*

THE C. V. MOSBY COMPANY
Saint Louis   1968

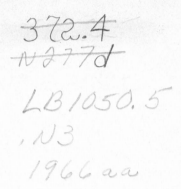

Program participants

Lauretta Bender, M.D.
Director, Research Child Psychiatry, Children's Unit, Creedmoor State Hospital, Queens Village, New York

Curtis D. Benton, Jr., M.D.
Pediatric Ophthalmologist, Ft. Lauderdale, Florida

Morton Botel, Ed.D.
Past President, International Reading Association; formerly Assistant Superintendent, Bucks County Schools, Pennsylvania; Associate Professor, Graduate School of Education, University of Pennsylvania, Philadelphia, Pennsylvania

Douglas Buchanan, M.D.
Professor of Neurology, University of Chicago, Chicago, Illinois

Macdonald Critchley, C.B.E., M.D., F.R.C.P.
Former Dean, Institute of Neurology, Queen Square, London, England, former Doyne Lecturer on Dyslexia; President, World Federation of Neurology

William M. Cruickshank, Ph.D.
Director, Institute for Study of Mental Retardation, The University of Michigan, Ann Arbor, Michigan

Herman Krieger Goldberg, M.D.
Assistant Professor of Ophthalmology, Wilmer Eye Institute, Johns Hopkins Hospital, Baltimore, Maryland

Katrina de Hirsch, F.C.S.T.
Pediatric Language Disorder Clinic, Columbia Presbyterian Medical Center, New York, New York

v

Robert J. Kirschner, M.D.
Director, Fight-for-sight Pediatric Clinic, Wills Eye Hospital;
Associate in Ophthalmology, University of Pennsylvania, Philadelphia,
Pennsylvania

John V. V. Nicholls, M.D., F.R.C.S.(C), F.A.C.S.
Associate Professor of Ophthalmology, McGill University, Montreal,
Canada

June L. Orton, M.SS.
Director, Orton Reading Center, Winston-Salem, North Carolina

Ralph D. Rabinovitch, M.D.
Neuropsychiatry; Director, Hawthorne Center, Northville, Michigan

Philip E. Rosenberg, Ph.D.
Professor of Audiology, Temple University School of Medicine,
Philadelphia, Pennsylvania

Archie A. Silver, M.D.
Chairman, Interdisciplinary Committee on Reading Problems; Psychiatrist,
New York University–Bellevue Medical Center, New York, New York

Foreword*

The National Conference on Dyslexia is jointly sponsored by the American Committee on Optics and Visual Physiology, and the U. S. Public Health Service Neurological and Sensory Disease Service Program.

The Committee, founded in 1927, is composed of three elected representatives from each of the four national ophthalmic societies: the American Ophthalmological Society, the Section on Ophthalmology of the American Medical Association, the American Academy of Ophthalmology and Otolaryngology, and the Association for Research in Ophthalmology. Members are Ph.D.'s or M.D.'s serving for periods of three years, and may be reelected without limitation. The Committee generally acts through numerous consultants and subcommittees, such as this one on dyslexia, establishing standards and definitions in such areas as color vision, low vision aids, ophthalmic lenses, lighting standards, radiation hazards, and alleged frauds. Several directed research projects have been sponsored, such as the standardization of test types, value of preschool vision screening, and value of therapy in myopia. The American Orthoptic Council was an outgrowth of action by this committee in the mid 1930's. The Committee also sponsored Paul Boder's translation of Tschermak's *Introduction to Physiologic Optics.* Evaluation and position papers are issued from time to time on such subjects as fluorescent lighting, ionizing hazards from television, and laser energy.

The Committee periodically singles out for study a subject that appears to be in flux or that has uncertain parameters. Such a subject is dyslexia.

The late Conrad Berens, of New York, was for many years chairman of this Committee. In 1961 he appointed Arthur Keeney chairman of the Subcommittee on Dyslexia of the American Committee on Optics and Visual Physiology, with Arthur Linksz, of New York City, and Kenneth Ogle, of Rochester, Minnesota, as members of the Committee. You will, I am sure, agree that this was an excellent choice when you see the manner in which this National Conference was organized. The response was most gratifying.

I am happy to express the profound gratitude of the American Committee on

---

*Adapted from the welcoming address by Hermann M. Burian, M.D., Iowa City, Iowa, Chairman of the American Committee on Optics and Visual Physiology, National Conference on Dyslexia, Philadelphia, November 18 and 19, 1966.

Optics and Visual Physiology, the Ophthalmic fraternity in general, and also of all those interested in the difficult and fascinating problems of dyslexia to Arthur and Virginia Keeney for the tremendous job they have done in preparing this conference.

Hermann M. Burian, M.D.

Preface

This volume is the product of an intensive national conference that brought together fourteen distinguished students of a currently boiling subject—dyslexia. Though the problem is receiving much attention in both lay and professional presses, truly satisfactory capabilities for either diagnosis or therapy have not been attained by any of the overlapping professions to which the public turns for help. There is currently a crescendoing cry for diagnosis, guidance, and therapy which no worker can meet even to his own satisfaction. Ophthalmic practitioners are particularly discomforted when parents, understandably feeling that a child reads with his eyes, turn to them in search of righting this dyssymbolia or strephosymbolia.

That we might assess mutual responsibilities, and interpret and apply such sparse data as are available, all participants in the conference promptly agreed to the investment of time and energy necessary to bring their studies together. Hopefully, this publication will in part make amends to the dozens of dedicated professionals who had to be turned away because of space limitations on the days of the conference.

These proceedings are directed primarily to ophthalmic and medical practitioners, though interchange with many fields such as neurology, psychiatry, audiology, education, psychology, and speech therapy is inherent in full appraisal of the subject.

Readers will note some differences of opinion in these pages. This is acknowledged by the editors and all who openmindedly address a subject where many answers are not yet at hand. Minor differences appear in the extensiveness of detail with which different investigators classify the dyslexias. At least one striking conflict emerges in the approach to therapy. The natural occurrence of remissions that plague therapeutic evaluations in many pathologic states is of relatively little significance in dyslexia. However, the role of attention, the psychology of interest, the effect of time alone on slow maturation or late bloomers, the influence of usual growth and development, plus the true value of encouragement by either the dedicated therapist or the mountebank, are factors nearly impossible to exclude in a critique of any remedial results.

This material could not have been developed without initial action of the

American Committee on Optics and Visual Physiology whose members are: Hermann M. Burian, M.D., Chairman; Goodwin M. Breinin, M.D.; Victor A. Byrnes, M.D.; Gerald Fonda, M.D.; M. Luther Kauffman, M.D.; Arthur H. Keeney, M.D.; James E. Lebensohn, M.D.; Irving Leopold, M.D.; Arthur Linksz, M.D.; Kenneth N. Ogle, Ph.D.; Louise L. Sloan, Ph.D.; and Robert L. Tour, M.D.

Counsel and financial support from the Neurological and Sensory Disease Service Program eased many of the mechanical hurdles of procedure. We wish to thank particularly the Director of Medical Education at Wills Eye Hospital, Philadelphia, Wayne L. Erdbrink, M.D., who also served as a valuable executive officer in preparation details. Miss Jacqueline Carter, Miss Patricia Campo, and Miss Nancy Skokowski have labored with both feminine grace and technical proficiency in necessary correspondence, typing and local arrangements. To these individuals, to Mr. G. Curtis Pritchard, Administrator of the Wills Eye Hospital, and to the many Wills department heads and staff workers, we wish to express sincere thanks for the cooperative efforts that have made the conference and this volume possible.

A. H. Keeney, M.D.
V. T. Keeney, M.D.

Contents

DYSLEXIA

Diagnosis and treatment of reading disorders

Chapter 1

Reading problems in children: Definitions and classifications

Ralph D. Rabinovitch, M.D.

The definitions, classifications, and incidence of dyslexia will be discussed in this chapter.

While many unanswered questions remain regarding dyslexia, there is a growing body of specific knowledge relating to reading problems in children. Ophthalmology is involved with renewed multidisciplinary interest; such involvement seems particularly important in view of the current spread of some highly questionable pseudoneuro-ophthalmologic interventions with dyslexic youngsters.

My premise is that the syndrome called "dyslexia" is a separate entity, discretely definable from many causes of reading disability.

QUESTIONS OF INCIDENCE

The incidence of reading retardation relative to mental age in children varies tremendously from community to community, with a significantly higher incidence in areas of economic deprivation and limited social opportunity. In the United States it is likely that at least 10 percent of all children are handicapped by reading incompetence before they reach seventh grade. The exact percentage of this total group who present the syndrome of dyslexia is unknown, but it is estimated that one-fourth to one-third of the group falls into this category. When these figures are projected into the total school population of the United States, we recognize that we are dealing with an enormous problem, representing one of the major educational and social challenges.

FACTORS INVOLVED IN ACADEMIC LEARNING

As a background to a discussion of reading problems in particular, some of the factors involved in academic learning in general should be examined. A major trend in child psychiatry is the attempt to move from generalization and

1

undue speculation toward clearer and more disciplined definitions of processes involved in the child's adaptation and behavior. When academic learning is considered, the following processes can be listed among those of major import:

1. General intelligence   } Verbal performance
2. Special senses   { Vision including discrimination
                       { Hearing including discrimination
3. Neurologic status   { Readiness
                         { Integration
4. Specific symbolization skills   { Verbal comprehension and expression
                                     { Visual memory and association
                                     { Auditory memory and association
                                     { Directionality
5. Emotional freedom to learn
6. Motivation   { Intrinsic
                  { Extrinsic
7. Opportunity

General intelligence. General intelligence is the capacity to abstract, to move from the concrete to the general, and to do problem solving. We are as interested in qualitative as in quantitative measures of intelligence, and we recognize the inappropriateness of overemphasis on the I.Q. scores alone. Tests such as the Wechsler Intelligence Scale for Children now permit differentiation of such factors as verbal functioning versus performance functioning, rote learning versus abstract thinking, and social identifications versus unempathic identifications. In many children with severe reading problems, we find a significant discrepancy between the performance score and the verbal I.Q. score, with functioning on performance tests higher. Because of this we now tend to ignore the full-scale I.Q. score as having little meaning, preferring to examine qualitatively the responses on the twelve subtests. Although the aforementioned exceptions exist, in general there is a close relationship between reading competence (especially comprehension) and intellectual capacity. Overexpectation must be avoided, and only reasonable pressures for learning should be imposed. We are concerned by the practice of too many clinicians to estimate intelligence of children on the basis of superficial testing in the office or by reliance on pure guesswork. All children who present learning difficulties should have full testing by a qualified clinical psychologist, with careful qualitative analysis of functioning well beyond the numerical scores.

Vision. In order for a child to utilize fully his learning capacity, his vision and hearing must be relatively intact or his disabilities corrected. The relationship of vision to reading problems is of special interest. To reiterate the findings of competent ophthalmologists and optometrists, it is relatively rare to find a child in whom a reading retardation results from vision problems per se. Certainly all children should have careful vision and hearing screening with appropriate correction if defects are found. In recent years there has been a tendency toward very loose thinking and practice in relation to vision factors in reading, with far too many children exposed to inappropriate and useless programs of retraining that simply add to their frustration and make valid therapeutic work more difficult. When assessing the child's reading situation, it is important to establish cause-effect relationships with care and with all the precision possible. For example, a poor reader may have a problem in visual acuity or phoria, but this in no way means that the vision problems are responsible for the reading disability.

Neurologic integration. Neurologic integration in children is difficult to define, and in this area, too, there has been a tendency to overdiagnose on flimsy evidence. We hear much today about minimal brain damage and soft neurologic signs; often, despite a positive diagnosis, the signs are so minimal as to be insignificant and so soft as to be mushy. Frequently tests that do not relate to the child's functioning in the life situation are given; their significance is, at best, questionable. This is especially true in relation to the diagnosis of so-called perceptual handicaps, a term so loose as to be often meaningless. If any child is given a sufficient number of tests, he will do poorly on some of them; all children vary in their specific competencies. The important thing is to be certain that the tests we use have meaning in terms of the child's actual real-life learning.

The question of neurologic readiness is often raised, and the concept of a developmental lag with spontaneous compensation is valid. The practical problem here, however, is the difficulty in determining whether a young child who reads poorly for his mental age will show spontaneous improvement with growth. At this point in our knowledge, it is usually wise to implement remedial programs for young children rather than to wait to see if spontaneous compensation will occur. In our clinics we see far too many adolescent boys who have had no remedial programming suffering from virtual illiteracy because someone waited for the child's growth to catch up.

Encephalopathy with brain damage may affect learning in nonspecific ways through interfering with impulse control and concentration. The hyperactive, impulse-ridden children, in whom the encephalopathy is expressed through motor channels and for whom special education is often indicated, are examples.

Symbolization skills. The capacity to deal with symbols is a specific language function that is essential to reading. This topic will be discussed later.

Emotional problems. When considering learning problems in children, one must differentiate the achievement of skills as measured on standard tests and the application of these skills in the classroom situation. Our studies at Hawthorne Center, Northville, Michigan, suggest that emotional problems tend to affect application more than achievement, except in the subgroup of neglected-deprived children. Many neurotic children, regardless of the severity of the neurosis, function relatively adequately on achievement tests, but they still may obtain failing grades because they cannot apply themselves to the tasks at hand. Anxiety, depression, displaced counteraggression, and similar emotional problems tend to affect learning in this way. There is a major clinical implication here: in general, psychotherapy may be expected to improve application of skills, but, when the skills themselves are impaired, remedial reading therapy is indicated, with or without psychotherapy.

At the present time at Hawthorne Center we are analyzing data on some 800 severely disturbed children for whom in-patient care has been indicated. We are attempting to correlate psychopathology with the academic learning situation. At this time one thing is clear—we can no longer rely on our too-customary clichés and overgeneralizations. It is no longer tenable for us simply to state that emotional problems lead to impaired academic learning. The situation is much more complex, and the ways in which specific disturbances affect both achievement of academic skills and their application must be defined as a prerequisite to remedial prescription.

Motivation. Motivation is closely related to the emotional freedom to learn. This constitutes a topic in itself, and in this discussion I would simply like to underscore the fact that in our junior high schools there are alarming numbers of potentially competent and productive children whose learning is impaired because of lack of involvement or motivation. This problem appears to be growing in severity and is, in large measure, culturally determined.

Opportunity. Despite intactness in every area thus far listed, far too many children in the United States are impaired in learning because they have not been offered sufficient opportunity at home, at school, or in the community. Belatedly, we are now giving attention to the special problems of our disadvantaged children; what we find is shocking and in some ways discouraging. Perhaps the saddest aspect of this problem is the fact that so often these children are held in double jeopardy—they are limited in academic skills because they have not been afforded opportunities for positive learning, and then they are blamed or scorned because they have failed to learn.

Unfortunately, objective criteria for these evaluations are still insufficient, but we are gradually improving diagnostic techniques. While we attempt to assess each of these factors in every child who comes to us with a learning problem, we do not wish to imply that we are always certain about the realities at hand. Often, more than one factor is involved, and there are numerous reciprocal influences among the factors. Opportunity, for example, affects motivation, and there is every reason to believe that this ultimately affects intellectual functioning. Hopefully, there is value in this type of process approach to a problem with practical challenges suggested at every level.

CLASSIFICATION OF READING RETARDATION

Reading retardation is defined as a significant discrepancy between the actual reading level and expected reading level for performance mental age. For practical purposes we considered as significant one year retardation in children up to 10 years of age, and two years retardation in children past 10 years of age. This is arbitrary but serves the purpose of defining terms. Dyslexia is viewed as one cause of reading retardation, among many other possible causes.

A classification of reading retardation based on etiology is suggested in the following outline:

1. Primary:
   a. Developmental dyslexia
2. Secondary:
   a. Other encephalopathy ⎰ Specific language impairment
   　　　　　　　　　　　⎱ Motor-concentration impairment

    b. Emotional disturbance

    c. Motivation or opportunity factors

    d. Deprivation or distortion in language experience

Basically, there are two groups of reading retardations: (1) those in which the reading retardation reflects a definitive neurologic dysfunction in the absence of history or signs of brain injury (referred to as primary reading retardation, or developmental dyslexia), and (2) those in which the reading retardation is not primary but is secondary, or reactive, to other pathology or problem.

The phrase "secondary to other encephalopathy" implies evidence of brain damage in the history and examination, with part of the total encephalopathic picture being a difficulty in dealing with symbols—a symptomatic specific language impairment. In other cases of encephalopathy, no specific language impairment exists, but concentration and impulse control are sufficiently affected to impair reading skills.

I have previously referred to the effects of emotional disturbance, motivation, and opportunity factors on academic learning, including reading.

A subject of major concern is the relatively low reading competence of many disadvantaged children. It is not unusual to find the mean reading level of disadvantaged children in the seventh grade to be lower than fifth grade, while their peers in privileged suburban communities may function at an eighth grade reading level. There is no evidence to suggest that this reflects a difference in original intellectual potential in the two groups, nor is it reasonable to postulate a specific neurologic dysfunction in the disadvantaged group. Many of these children have a limited exposure to language, especially abstract language. The question arises as to the process by which this experiential limitation has affected the reading process. The issues involved here are unclear. There is urgency in arriving at greater understanding as a prerequisite to implementation of appropriate remedial programming.

To review this important aspect of the topic, the following classifications are given as a summary of diagnostic groupings:

1. Capacity to learn to read is impaired without definite brain damage suggested in the history or on neurologic examination. The defect is in the ability to deal with letters and words as symbols, with resultant diminished ability to integrate the meaningfulness of written material. The problem appears to reflect a basic disturbed pattern of neurologic organization. Because this etiology is biologic or endogenous, these cases are diagnosed as *primary reading retardations (developmental dyslexia)*.

2. Capacity to learn to read is impaired by frank brain damage manifested by clear-cut neurologic deficits. The picture is similar to the early described adult dyslexic syndromes. Other definite aphasic difficulties are generally present. History usually reveals the cause of the brain injury, common agents being prenatal toxicity, birth trauma or anoxia, encephalitis, and head injury. These cases are diagnosed as *reading retardations secondary to brain injury*.

3. Capacity to learn to read is intact but is utilized insufficiently for the child to achieve a reading level appropriate to his mental age. The causative

factor is exogenous, the child having a normal reading potential that has been impaired by negativism, anxiety, depression, emotional blocking, psychosis, limited schooling opportunity, or other external influence. These cases are diagnosed as *reading retardations secondary to exogenous factors.*

The aforementioned classifications are clinically useful, and in many cases, but by no means always, we can be certain of the specific diagnosis. Mixed pictures are frequent. In my own work I am often obliged to diagnose "secondary reading retardation with a touch of the primary syndrome." Some workers have suggested diagnosing dyslexia by exclusion—the child has no visual problem, no hearing problem, no intellectual limitation, no other neurologic deficit, or no emotional problem, and he is well motivated and has adequate learning opportunities. This really would leave few children, if any. Other workers prefer to view reading competence on a continuum, suggesting that we have tended to diagnose the severe retardations as primary and the milder retardations as secondary. In an area as complex as language and reading, it is important to avoid being overcategoric and to recognize the reciprocal influences of many factors. Despite these cautions, the suggested classifications are helpful in both clinical and research work. I believe, or at least have the illusion, that competence in differential diagnosis increases with experience.

SYMPTOMS OF PRIMARY READING RETARDATION, OR DEVELOPMENTAL DYSLEXIA

I would like to define the syndrome of dyslexia in more detail. The clinical picture of dyslexia presents with surface symptoms, but can be dissected, as through concentric layers, to a core problem.

First, there is the presence of reading retardation as measured on standard achievement tests. The degree of impairment is usually greater in the primary dyslexic groups than among the secondary groups. Some of these children are virtually illiterate when first seen and range in age from 7 years up to 17 years. The degrees and quality of dysfunction can be seen in the examples of some dyslexic children's attempts at writing to dictation (Fig. 1-1). These five boys all have performance I.Q.'s in the average or superior range, and apart from the learning disability, none shows evidence of encephalopathy. Each has attempted to write to dictation, "The yellow pig saw the little baby."

In dyslexia, contrary to a commonly held impression, arithmetic skills are also impaired. Occasionally we see a child with a selective learning deficiency in which reading may be adequate but spelling very poor or a deficiency in which reading may be poor and arithmetic excellent. These cases of limited and specific disability are the exception. The dyslexic child's achievement test protocol usually indicates greatest impairment in spelling, somewhat less impairment in reading, and even less impairment in arithmetic. All three areas, however, are involved, and this is expected, in view of the fact that all three involve symbolization.

All school-aged children seen for psychiatric or psychologic study should have, as part of the examination, an adequate academic achievement screening. It might be well to include this in the pediatric evaluation and perhaps the

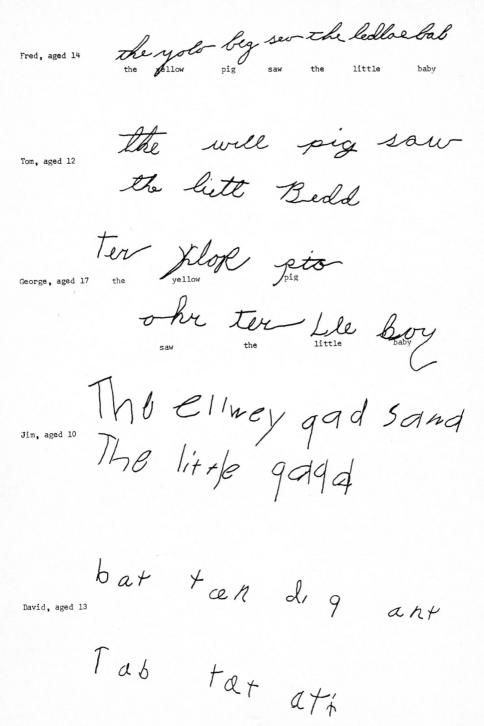

Fig. 1-1. Examples of handwritten responses by five dyslexic boys with performance I.Q.'s in the average or superior range.

ophthalmologic evaluation as well. In order for screening to be adequate, a standardized test must be used and administered, following standard procedures. With this in mind, we have developed at Hawthorne Center a new achievement screening test which we hope will be helpful in a wide variety of settings.

Second, there are defects in techniques for reading, the specifics of the reading process itself. With few exceptions, dyslexic children are deficient in both the visual and auditory functions required for adequate reading. In normal children, reading evolves as spontaneously as walking or talking. A combination of visual and auditory functions are utilized in varying ways and degrees in different children. Visual discrimination, visual memory, visual associations, auditory discrimination, auditory memory, and auditory associations are involved. By the end of first grade, normal children have attained a sight vocabulary, having memorized the visual configurations of various words and associated concepts to the configurations. At the same time, a beginning use of auditory clues is developing with letters and syllables being associated with their sounds, which are blended into whole words. For normal children the specific method of reading instruction used is probably of minimal significance. The child spontaneously tends to utilize both visual and auditory processes with the gradual evolution of intersensory transfer, visual to auditory and auditory to visual.

In dyslexic children the situation is very different. Usually, both visual and auditory techniques are impaired, and it is often particularly difficult for the child to master a sight vocabulary. In these cases the initial method of instruction may be vital, with the child tending to learn most positively when a determined and intensive attempt is made to teach phonetic analysis early.

When attempting to establish differential diagnosis in cases of reading retardation, detailed testing of reading and related skills is necessary, with qualitative analysis of the multiple visual and auditory processes involved. In large numbers of dyslexic children we have found few in which visual or auditory *discrimination* per se represents a major problem. Visual recognition and discrimination on a perceptual level tend to be intact, but the letter forms and combinations cannot be translated into meaningful wholes or concepts. Similarly, in the auditory sphere the difficulty is not in the differentiating of vowel or consonant sounds but in the translation of the sounds into their letter symbols. The difficulty, then, is not in recognition or discrimination but in symbolization in both visual and auditory fields. Critchley has wisely used the term "dyssymbolia" to describe the dysfunction. This represents an important practical point that is frequently overlooked, with inappropriate treatment efforts the result.

Another current trend that should be of concern is the confusion of motor handicaps with dyssymbolia. While there may be a tendency for some children with dyslexia to show minor motor difficulties also, perhaps because of more generalized encephalopathy, the motor problems are not relevant to the reading disability. Our understanding of neurology should be sufficient to avoid this confusion. Unfortunately, in the reading field today there is an alarming amount of pseudoneurology, both preached and practiced, and many children and their families are being victimized. Large or small muscle exercises may prove helpful in enhancing a child's motor coordination, although this is often questionable. Motor training cannot be expected to influence the child's capacity to deal with symbols and, therefore, to improve his reading. This issue is vital because many children and their parents have been given false hopes, and, then, when there has been no progress in reading, they have been held responsible for being unfaithful in carrying out a useless program. When a child has been deluded through inappropriate intervention, his frustration increases, and it becomes all the more difficult later to implement appropriate remedial reading therapy.

Third, there are other or broader language deficits that represent deeper disturbances. Reading is only one aspect of language function, and, as expected, children with dyssymbolia that affects reading also tend to show deficits in language comprehension or expression. In daily conversation the child may be able to compensate, but careful attention to the language pattern frequently reveals imprecise articulation, difficulties in specific name finding and immature syntax. The following examples are taken from transcripts of the language of dyslexic children. They tend to be extreme examples, but we look for similar, less severe disturbances in expressive language in all dyslexic children.

Question: Why is it better to build a house of brick than of wood?

Answer: Well, just in case a hurricane the house can break down, but you put brick on, it can just hit it but not break nothing down. (Aged 9 years)

Question: What must you do to make water boil?

Answer: You should put it under a fire. (Aged 10 years)

Question: How did he get hurt?

Answer: He sprang a thing, a arm when he felled out of that tree. (Aged 11 years)

Question: Is it nighttime or daytime now?

Answer: Daytime. It's, well, clouds are out and stuff. It's white the clouds, it's lightsen up, the clouds and stuff. (Aged 9 years)

Question: Is it morning or afternoon?

Answer: It's in the noontime. Noon. In the noon. (Aged 9 years)

Fourth, there is specific concept-symbolization deficiency in orientation that generally accompanies dyslexia. Because of general incompetence in the use of symbols, it is not surprising to find that many, although not all, dyslexic children have trouble translating orientational concepts into symbols. Concepts of height, distance, or time may be appreciated by the child, but he is uncertain about the units of measurement—he cannot express his concepts in symbolic terms. Thus, he knows which of two people is taller, but he cannot define their height in feet and inches. He knows clearly that he has a long vacation from school every year, but he is unable to name the season as summer or the months as July and August. Deficiencies in dealing with time are probably commonest and most severe. In an effort to explore this orientation-symbolization factor more thoroughly, we have developed the Hawthorne Concept-Symbolization test, now standardized, which we hope may be of use with young children as an early diagnostic and prognostic aid.

Fifth, coming to the core, there is a neurologic deficit, the specific nature of which is still unknown but which appears to represent, at least in part, a parieto-occipital dysfunction. This intriguing but still too mysterious basic etiology will be clarified in the future.

No discussion of reading problems in children should avoid mention of the inordinate suffering experienced by otherwise normal youngsters, cut off from communication channels that are increasingly vital for survival today. In earlier discussions on the topic the inevitable negative psychologic effects of the disability have been described.

"With limited resources to meet their specific needs, we are obliged all too often to limit our involvement with these children to documenting their successive psychologic reactions from initial anger to guilt feelings, depression, and ultimate resignation and compromise with their aspirations.

"Work in clinics throughout the United States has encouraged us to hope that early intervention by well-trained language therapists may permit many children with primary reading retardation to develop at least functional reading competence. Major needs are for early diagnosis and the provision of intensive remedial programs in the public schools. In addition, an adjusted curriculum throughout the school years, relying minimally on literacy, must be devised for some students. It is interesting, if disconcerting, to note how much further advanced our speech correction programs are in comparison with those for reading therapy. It may be that the speech correction workers have been more aggressive in presenting their reasonable demands and have in the past had more clear-cut programs to offer. But now, as reading diagnostic issues are becoming clarified and as specific remedial techniques are evolving, the time is ripe for implementation of large-scale special education reading services in our public schools. Such programs, financed by special reimbursements available in many states, must take their place alongside those already established for children with speech, visual, hearing, orthopedic, and other handicaps. In view of the fact that no responsibility of the public school is greater than to teach all children to read, the inclusion of remedial reading as a recognized branch of special education would seem as logical as it is essential."[*]

---

[*]Rabinovitch, R., and Ingram, W.: Neuropsychiatric considerations in reading retardation, Reading Teacher **15**:433-438, 1962.

Chapter 2

Development of cortical localization

Douglas Buchanan, M.D.

It is very difficult to establish any detailed neuroanatomy and neurophysiology relevant to dyslexia.

The earliest reference to the brain in known written history is in the Edwin Smith *Surgical Papyrus*. This is a copy made about 1700 B.C. by an Egyptian scribe. The original from which he copied may have been written by Imhotep, the architect-physician who flourished 5,000 years ago. In this incomplete copy is the first reference to the brain that is known in any human records. There are excellent descriptions of the brain, of the meninges, and of the cerebrospinal fluid and descriptions of cranial injuries and their effect on the body and on life. It is strange that the Bible has no clear description of the brain, although some historians have interpreted the silver cord and the golden bowl in Ecclesiastes as the brain and the spinal cord.

The next clear description of the brain is in the writings of Hippocrates (460–370 B.C.). He gave detailed descriptions of the effects of wounds of the head and of contrecoup injuries, and he knew that injuries to the brain had effect on the opposite side of the body.

Galen (A.D. 131-201) was a remarkable neurologist who knew the difference between motor and sensory nerves and knew the peripheral distribution of the segmental levels of the spinal cord. The story of Galen and Pausanias gives an example of his knowledge of neuroanatomy. Pausanias, the traveler, who wrote the first and still the best guidebook for Greece, appeared in Rome about A.D. 180. He complained of pain and numbness in the last three fingers of his left hand; various complicated drugs were applied to his fingers without success. Then, Galen was consulted. He was then the medical officer to the gladiators and was experienced in injuries. He put poultices on Pausanias' neck and not his hand, because the injury, he said, was at the level of the seventh cervical body. He also told Pausanias that he had injured his neck some three or four weeks before. Pausanias then remembered that he had fallen from his chariot when it had upset and that he had fallen on his back, striking his neck on a rock. This is the first record of an injury to a cervical intervertebral disk and the first record of knowledge of segmental levels in the spinal cord and of the difference in action of anterior and posterior spinal nerves.

This observation of Galen was forgotten for 1,800 years. Then, in 1943 Robert Semmes and Francis Murphy wrote their classic article in which they demonstrated that pain in the ulnar distribution in the left arm is not always evidence of heart disease but sometimes results from a displaced cervical disk.

After Galen, the next great figure in physiology was René Descartes (1596–1650). He regarded the human body as a machine that was directed and controlled by a rational soul situated in the pineal gland. His famous phrase, "I think, therefore I am," is still a part of philosophic thought, but his evidence that the pineal is the seat of the soul is less secure. Interest in the pineal has recently been revived, however, and the actions of that gland are now the subject of much modern investigation.

Thomas Willis (1621–1675) introduced the word "neurology" to the language and was the first neurologist. He described the vascular circle of the brain, which bears his name, although the plates were drawn by his friend, Christopher Wren (1631–1723). Willis believed that control of movement rested in the corpus striatum, but he also believed that sensation was controlled by regions of the cortex.

Robert Whytt (1714–1766) of Edinburgh, who is known for his accurate clinical descriptions of tuberculous meningitis, first described a reflex in 1751. This was the reaction of the pupil of the eye to light.

Despite the work of these physicians and despite the revival of anatomy by Andreas Vesalius (1514–1564), investigation of the action of the cerebral cortex was delayed until the middle of the nineteenth century.

The three persons who first regarded the cortex as the substrate of the mind were Emmanuel Swedenborg (1688–1772), Franz Joseph Gall (1758–1828), and Sir Charles Bell (1774–1842).

The idea that the animal body was built of cells, as was a plant, did not appear until Theodor Schwann (1810–1882) demonstrated this in 1839. This most fundamental contribution was given by Schwann in rather an offhand way in his monograph on the microscopic structure of animals and plants.

For centuries the brain was believed to be a solid organ of uniform structure. The first attempt to give cerebral localization of function an anatomic foundation was made by Franz Joseph Gall (1758–1828) and his pupil Johann Spurzheim (1776–1832). In the time of Gall, anatomy of the brain was mainly concerned with the white matter, because white matter did not decompose so rapidly and was easier to work with than the gray matter. The gray matter was believed to be part brain and part body, for it was believed to consist mainly of small secreting glands. The white matter was regarded as the functional center of the brain, the seat of thought and of emotion. Gall suggested that the brain was a very complex organ with many different parts and systems each with a specific function, and he believed the cortex to be the locus of thought and of the mind. The excellent anatomic work of Gall was, unfortunately, soon lost in the theatrical errors of phrenology.

During this same period Luigi Rolando (1773–1831) studied the effects of ablation of portions of the cerebrum and the cerebellum. He worked on the island of Sardinia with small animals, and he concluded that the cortex initiated voluntary motor activity and that the cerebellum controlled involuntary activity.

Marie Flourens (1794–1867) repeated Rolando's work and made an excellent contribution to the physiology of the cerebellum. His major error, however, was his belief that there was no specific motor area in the cortex and no division of the cortex into different functional units. This agreed with the opinion of most scholars, who believed that perception and the mind were too elaborate and specialized to have any vulgar anatomic substrate in the brain. Flourens was elected to the Académie des Sciences, an honor refused to Gall, because Flourens' error was accepted as truth and Gall's idea that thought was related to the cortex was regarded as wrong. Flourens continued to succeed, and in 1840 he was elected to the Académie Française, defeating Victor Hugo in the election. Flourens' error was still acceptable while Gall's anatomic reputation steadily diminished, but the proof of Gall's ideas about the functional differences in various parts of the cortex came soon after.

The cerebral cortex of the adult human brain has an area of about 2½ square feet. In this area there are blood vessels and special cells, neurons, and the glia. During the Middle Ages there were interesting calculations of the number of angels who could stand on the point of a needle. Somewhat better calculations suggest that the cortex contains about 14 billion neurons. The other cells are astrocytes, oligodendrocytes, and the cells of the microglia. The number of these cells is unknown but is many times that of the neurons. Some of the astrocytes are the servants of the body of the neuron, and the oligodendrocytes care for the myelin sheath covering the axon. These glial cells have a life of their own, as was first suggested by Ramón y Cajal (1852–1934). They can move from place to place and can reproduce themselves. The neuron sits like a Buddha in a cave, the protoplasm of the cell body constantly streaming. At irregular intervals the neuron belches, and chemical changes and electrical discharges flow down the axon.

In man, cell division of the neurons of the cerebral cortex is complete by the fifth fetal month, and at that early time in life the number and quality of these important cells is permanently determined. Any neurons that are destroyed by injury or by disease are not replaced by other neurons. Injured neurons are removed by the microglia, which engulf them and carry them to the nearest venous system. Their place is filled by astrocytes and astrocytic fibers. All treatment and all prognosis in neurology must recognize this fact. It may seem strange that the neuron, the most important cell in the body cannot be replaced, but, if replacement were possible, memory could not exist and language and learned actions would have to be relearned every few months. Since the glia retain the power of reproduction and the neurons do not, most neural tumors of the brain consist of abnormal glial cells and there are very few tumors of abnormal neurons.

Localization of function in the cortex started with the work of Jean Bouilland

(1796–1881) and his pupil, Pierre Paul Broca (1824–1880). Both men were intensely interested in speech, in reading, and in writing. Bouilland claimed that speech disorders always had the associated lesion in the frontal lobe. Paul Broca in 1861 demonstrated the brain of his famous patient, Tan, who had suffered for many years from aphémie, renamed aphasia by Armand Trousseau (1801–1867). There was a lesion in the left frontal lobe, in the third left frontal convolution; this soon became known as Broca's convolution.

It was not until some years later that Broca realized the significance of the left cerebral hemisphere in speech. The concept of unilateral cerebral dominance had been proposed by Marc Dax (c. 1770–1839) of Montpelier in 1836, but his writings were not published until 1877.

Forty years after Broca's demonstration, Pierre Marie (1853–1940) re-examined the brain of Tan and found parietotemporal lesions as well as the lesions in the frontal lobe. Despite these faults, Broca's reputation remains as the first to attempt functional localization in the cortex.

Carl Wernicke (1848–1905), when only 26 years old, published a small monograph on aphasia in which he described sensory or receptive aphasia and localized the related lesion in the posterior part of the first temporal convolution of the left hemisphere.

The first recognition of a structural organization within the cortex came in 1776, when Francisco Gennari (1750–c. 1795), as a medical student, noticed a white line running through the cortex in the occipital region. This was soon confirmed by Félix Vicq d'Azyr (1748–1794), but only later was it realized that this was the visual center.

Seventy years later, in 1840, Jules Baillarger (1806–1890), French psychiatrist, cut thin layers of the cortex, placed them between glass, and illuminated them from behind. Then he saw the cortex divided into six layers of alternate white and gray laminae.

Another 25 years passed before microscopic study of the cortex was started by Theodor Meynert (1833–1892) and expanded by Ramón y Cajal. At the beginning of the twentieth century general schemes and maps of the architecture of the cortex were evolved by Alfred Campbell (1868–1937) in 1905, by Korbinian Brodmann (1868–1918) in 1908, and by Constantin von Economo (1876–1931) in 1925. The most recent study of the cytoarchitectonics of the human isocortex was published in 1951 by Percival Bailey and Gerhard von Bonin.

The experimental approach to the neuroanatomy and neurophysiology of the cortex came soon after the development of electrical methods of stimulation. The famous team of Eduard Hitzig (1838–1907) and Gustav Fritsch (1838–1891) investigated the excitability of the dog's brain. They displayed the anatomic limits of the motor strip and finally disproved Flourens' belief that the cortex was not excitable.

David Ferrier (1843–1928) demonstrated with precision the cortical regions in the monkey that were excitable to electrical stimulation. He was a pupil of John Hughlings Jackson (1835–1911), and by experiment he demonstrated the truth of Jackson's belief that there were areas in the human cortex where movements of the limbs were represented. Jackson had concluded this from his skillful and thoughtful observations of the actions of patients with convulsions.

The first recorded electrical stimulation of the human brain was done by Roberts Bartholow on the twenty-sixth of January, 1874. The patient was Mary Rafferty, 30 years old, a native of Ireland, and a patient in the Good Samaritan Hospital of Cincinnati, Ohio. In both parietal regions of the skull there was erosion of the bone with exposure of the dura. Both galvanic and faradic stimulation were used, and Bartholow observed that no pain was produced by needling of the brain substance and that stimulation of the parietal regions produced movement of the arm and of the leg on the opposite side. The most detailed and accurate observations of the effects of stimulation of the human cortex were made by Harvey Cushing (1869–1939) in 1909 during operations with local anesthesia upon two patients who had suffered from convulsions.

The corresponding observations on the cortex were the early recording of the spontaneous electrical activity. This was first done by Richard Caton (1842–1926) in Liverpool in August, 1875, with the living rabbit brain, using a galvanometer as the indicator. He found that "feeble currents of varying direction pass through the multiplier when the electrodes are placed on two points of the external surface, or one electrode on the gray matter and one on the surface of the skull."

Hans Berger (1873–1941) of Jena in 1925 made the first recording, through the intact skull, of the spontaneous electrical activity of the brain in man. This was the original electroencephalogram.

Campbell described 20 cortical fields, Brodmann increased the number to 47, and von Economo, to 109. Brodmann's cortical map is still most widely used; the areas that may be related to visual perception in dyslexia are areas 17, 18, and 19. The region of the cortex called the angular gyrus is also frequently referred to in writings about dyslexia.

If identification of an area of the brain that was specifically related to reading was possible, it might then be possible to devise a test which would reveal a lesion in that region. Demonstration of such a lesion would help to diagnose dyslexia, although failure in identification would not necessarily exclude it. Unfortunately, such an anatomic locus has not been recognized nor the specific test devised.

The angular gyrus is a region of the cortex frequently described in anatomic writings about dyslexia. It surrounds the terminal portion of the superior sulcus of the temporal lobe. The relation of the superior sulcus to reading was first recognized by Joseph Dejerine (1849–1917). In 1892 he described an adult who, after an intracranial vascular accident, lost the ability to read but still could write. Postmortem examination of the brain revealed an infarct in the angular gyrus.

Another less specific reference comes from the work of Paul Flechsig (1847–1929) on the process of myelination of various regions of the brain. He demonstrated that, in the cortex of the angular gyrus, myelination comes later than in the neighboring regions. If myelination were unduly delayed, this might give an anatomic basis for developmental dyslexia. It might also explain why some children with dyslexia tend to improve as they grow older. This is a neat and attractive theory, but there has been, as yet, no demonstration of its truth.

Many animals, including man, have paired cerebral hemispheres joined by the corpus callosum and connecting commisures, so that there are two third frontal convolutions and an angular gyrus on both sides. The reason for the double brain and for the crossing of most of the pyramidal fibers is still uncertain, although the reversal of an image on the retina and the crossing of visual fibers in the optic chiasm are probably involved. To this double innervation there is added the complication of the dominance of one cerebral hemisphere over the other. Most people are right-handed, and most have the anatomic basis for speech in the left hemisphere. But it is by no means clear that this left hemisphere dominance is usually present in the physiology of reading. Knowledge of representation of intellectual functions in the cortex is still vague, contrast studies of the brain are crude, and electroencephalographic tracings are complicated and variable. Because of these difficulties there is as yet no objective test that can display an anatomic or physiologic lesion underlying dyslexia.

Chapter 3

Isolation of the specific dyslexic

Macdonald Critchley, M.D., F.R.C.P.

Most neurologists believe that a form of dyslexia exists which is organic, pure, specific, and constitutional in nature. This is not to say that other types of reading retardation do not exist, but the neurologic conception of dyslexia refers to the dyslexia that exists in its purest form, the primary reading retardation of Rabinovitch (Chapter 1).

Dyslexia is constitutional for two very good reasons. The first reason is the genetic determination. Observation has been documented since 1905, when Thomas first reported two or more cases of dyslexia in single families. Since then, almost every writer on the subject has substantiated this observation, particularly Hallgren of Sweden in his extensive monograph published in 1950.

The second reason is the unusual sex incidence. Specific developmental dyslexia, the pure type, occurs more often in boys than in girls. Although the difference is described as very great, there may be a fallacy because of socio-economic familial factors that tend to identify boys as more significant members of a family. When a boy fails to learn to read as he should, the parents per-haps take more vigorous measures than if a girl fails. Still, there can be no doubt that dyslexia is commoner in males than in females.

Hence, the neurologic position is that specific developmental dyslexia is a genetically determined constitutional disorder. This is extremely important, because it means that developmental dyslexia arises independently of environ-mental factors. The first putative adverse environmental factor would be, of course, perinatal trauma. But specific dyslexia has nothing to do with perinatal trauma nor with fetal infection, fetal damage, anoxia, or icterus neonatorum. Of course, a patient with genetically determined dyslexia may also have a history of perinatal trauma, but this is a coincidental element in the case.

Second, environmental factors that have also been implicated are language and race. It has been postulated that developmental dyslexia has its greatest incidence in English-speaking cultures and, therefore, has something to do with the spelling absurdities of the English language. Also, it has been alleged that the high incidence of developmental dyslexia in Scandinavian countries should be blamed on the illogicality of the Scandinavian spelling. But this, of course, is not the explanation. Very little is known about the precise geographic distribution of developmental dyslexia, but we do know that it occurs in Italy, where the language has an extremely logical spelling and pronunciation. It also occurs in Russia and in Romania, where the language is pronounced as it is spelled and spelled as it is pronounced.

Further than that we cannot go. It may be thought that race is a factor, in that race is a constitutional aspect. Possibly there is a racial factor in the incidence of developmental dyslexia, but, unfortunately, we know little about dyslexia occurring in Asiatic peoples in the Middle East or in African races. Indeed, I can remember only one isolated case of developmental dyslexia reported from Japan.

Surely one of the topics for future research is the tabulation of the distribution of dyslexia on a world-wide scale, with notation of whether it is evenly spread or patchy.

Analysis of the role of the laterality of the written language would be helped by comparing the incidence of dyslexia in those languages, like ours, in which the print runs from left to right with those that proceed from right to left, such as Arabic, Hebrew, Persian, and Hindi.

One case in my series was a bilingual boy. He was born in Syria and lived in Beirut; one parent is a Syrian Arab, and the other parent is English. The boy is dyslexic in both languages. I dictated a short sentence for the patient to write (Fig. 3-1), and as can be noted, the bottom line says, "The chemist could not

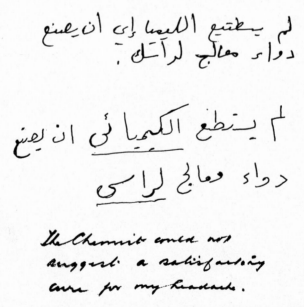

Fig. 3-1. Dyslexic writing of Arabic script (top) compared with perfect Arabic script (middle) and English equivalent (bottom).

suggest a satisfactory cure for my headache." The top line represents the boy's rendition of the sentence in Arabic. The middle two lines represent the same sentence written by an Arabic scholar, who at once pointed out the numerous mistakes and omissions in the boy's writing in Arabic. There are two instances of rotations, and there is another error where the boy, instead of writing a symbol which indicates Te, wrote one that stands for Ta. This is the one and only case in the world's literature, as far as I know, of developmental dyslexia in an Arab.

The third factor that is sometimes erroneously considered to be etiologic is polyglottism or bilingualism in the home. It is sometimes said that the incidence of dyslexia is higher in families where two languages are spoken interchangeably.

There is some substance in this statement but not a great deal. Recently, I saw a boy with developmental dyslexia, the son of a university lecturer who had gone from one part of the world to another, taking his family with him. The father's first appointment was in Johannesburg, South Africa, where the boy, attending school for the first time, learned Afrikaans and English. After 2 years the family moved to southern Ireland where, for nationalistic reasons, the lad learned Gaelic. Finally, the boy returned to London, and, at his present school, he is trying to learn, in addition to English, both French and Latin. He is dyslexic in all five languages.

Of course, such a circumstance is not the cause of specific developmental dyslexia. It represents merely a terrible added burden and a handicap. The boy who went from South Africa to Ireland and then to England illustrates another factor that is sometimes blamed for developmental dyslexia—changing schools often.

Only too often this changing of schools happens unavoidably, and I have seen many examples of dyslexia in youngsters of diplomats, service personnel, and missionaries, who because of necessity move from country to country in a most upsetting fashion. Again, this is not the explanation of specific dyslexia but merely a very aggravating factor.

Fourth, current educational or pedagogic techniques in the teaching of reading are, at times, blamed as an etiologic explanation. One question concerns the age at which a child first attempts to read. In England a child goes to school at 5 years of age. By that time he usually knows his letters, because his mother has taught him the alphabet. In the United States most children go to school at 6 years of age. In some countries the child enters school at 7 years of age and in others at 8 years of age. At various times remedialists have indicated that learning to read too early or too late is the explanation, but there is uncertainty as to which practice is deleterious. In any event, the age for learning to read is not the cause of developmental dyslexia.

As a fifth factor, I wish to mention two perceptual errors: visual impairment and defects in hearing. Although errors in refraction, muscle imbalance, or other peripheral visual defects have, at times, been claimed, particularly by nonmedical examiners, to be the cause of symbolic confusion or dyslexia, neither a true cause-and-effect relationship nor controlled treatment serves to support any such contention. The same problem arises regarding hearing defects.

I do not believe that any child with developmental dyslexia is dyslexic because he does not hear well. Of course, if he does not hear accurately, this constitutes a compounding handicap. A more subtle type of hearing defect for which otologists do not ordinarily look by audiometry or other methods exists; it may be termed "dysphonemia," a confusion on the part of the child between phonemes which are somewhat similar but which he fails to distinguish clearly, like "t" and "d" and "b" and "p." If a child happens to have difficulty in distinguishing between various comparable phonemes, his reading difficulty is thereby intensified, but it is not initiated by this defect.

These diverse factors, both environmental and physical, are aggravating and hinder the progress of a dyslexic child. They intensify the condition, but they do not produce it. The initial cause is a genetically determined constitutional disorder.

The final area of dispute I wish to mention is the belief, often expressed by pediatricians, that developmental dyslexia is actually the expression of minor brain damage, that it is but one facet of a complex that is organically determined and that it may include a mild spastic condition, some hyperkinetic disorder, or similar disturbances of that type.

We are all familiar with dyslexia occurring as a symptom in children with diplegia, spasticity, or double athetosis or in children after encephalitis, brain injury, or cerebrovascular disease. But such a dyslexia is symptomatic or secondary, and I propose the term "symptomatic dyslexia" just as one speaks of symptomatic epilepsy. This corresponds with Rabinovitch's secondary reading retardation.

As Rabinovitch has stated, at times it is far from easy to distinguish at the bedside or in the consulting room a case of primary developmental dyslexia from a case of secondary or symptomatic dyslexia; sometimes the two coincide in the same individual.

By definition, neurologists identify developmental dyslexia by eliminating all those children who are emotionally disturbed, who have perceptual defects, or who have low intelligence. Most neurologists would hesitate to make the diagnosis in a child whose I.Q. on the Wechsler Intelligence Scale for Children is less than 100.

If developmental dyslexia is constitutionally and genetically determined, there is no logical reason why, occasionally, developmental dyslexia should not happen to affect a child whose I.Q. is well below 100, or a child who is traumatized by birth injury or by disease in early childhood, or a child who is emotionally disturbed. These combinations of primary and secondary dyslexia are most difficult to diagnose and assess.

Chapter 4

Early prediction of reading disability

Katrina de Hirsch, F.C.S.T.
Jeannette Jefferson Jansky, M.S.

This report is based on an investigation supported by the Health Research Council of the City of New York and was conducted under the auspices of Columbia University in the department of and with the guidance of William S. Langford. The investigation is preliminary in nature.* A validation study on 500 New York City Public School children is underway.

Twenty years of experience with intelligent but educationally disabled children, whose learning drive was often severely damaged, has convinced us that a sizable number of these youngsters would not have required remedial help if their difficulties had been recognized before first grade entrance. In many instances early identification would have obviated the need for later remediation. Prediction of reading, writing, and spelling disorders—i.e., early identification of a specific pattern of dysfunctions—was the purpose of this investigation.

Prediction of reading success or failure has been the objective of a number of clinical and more formal studies. Among the statistical investigations, some researchers have used single variables, such as auditory discrimination,[19] visuomotor competence,[11] anxiety level,[4] or self-concept as measured in kindergarten or first grade,[21] to predict reading competence from 9 to 12 months later. A few investigators constructed a battery of predictive tests.[16] One of the earliest and best tests was constructed by Monroe.[14]

This investigation differs from others in three respects: (1) it explores a larger section of the child's perceptuomotor and linguistic organization than do other projects; (2) it predicts spelling and writing in addition to reading achievement; and (3) the interval between prediction and outcome is more than twice as long as in most other studies.

Of course, schools have assessed children's readiness for years,[1] relying basically on three types of evaluation: (1) reading-readiness tests; (2) determination

*The preliminary study was published under the title Predicting reading failure, New York, 1966, Harper & Row, Publishers.

of I.Q. (mostly of a group variety); and (3) informal "sizing up" of the child by the kindergarten teacher. All of these techniques are legitimate, but they all have certain disadvantages. Reading-readiness tests do not always reveal enough about a child's specific weaknesses and strengths to assist the teacher in the planning of educational strategies; moreover, most reading-readiness tests fail to predict writing and spelling achievement.

Reliance on intelligence tests has been challenged because (1) severe reading disabilities are known to occur on virtually all intellectual levels, (2) an I.Q. represents at best a global rather than a differentiated evaluation of a child's potential, and (3) an I.Q. does not necessarily take into account important perceptuomotor factors that are significant for reading success or failure. The developmentally oriented kindergarten teacher's assessment of a child, although often remarkably accurate,[9] cannot be easily duplicated. Such a teacher will often observe that a given child is immature, but she may be unable to state what went into her judgment.

Our attempts at prediction in the Pediatric Language Disorder Clinic at Columbia–Presbyterian Medical Center, New York, go back over 20 years. The predictions were largely informal, stemming from experience with preschool children referred for a variety of oral language deficits. An extraordinarily large proportion of these children developed reading, writing, and spelling difficulties several years later. The clinical impression of these youngsters was one of striking immaturity. Despite adequate or better intelligence, their performance on a variety of perceptuomotor and language tasks resembled that of chronologically younger subjects. Our original predictions were based primarily on a clinical evaluation of the child's developmental level and only secondarily on his performance on a battery of tests that we had assembled over the years. By and large, our predictions were successful,[10] but they raised a number of new questions. We were dealing with a clinical group of language-defective subjects, and we were by no means certain that our predictions would hold for an unselected sample of children. Furthermore, we did not know how far our predictions relied on clinical judgment and how far they relied on the children's objective scores on tests. In any case it became clear that whatever the basis of our clinical judgment, it could not be handed on to someone else.

Thus, we became convinced that we would have to use statistical tools. In order to shape an instrument for the schools that would enable them to identify what we term "academic high risk" children at early ages, we believed we would have to (1) use an instrument that was relatively untainted by subjective clinical judgment and (2) use, in addition to a clinical group, an instrument that would be representative of a school population.

A sample of fifty-three children from the general population and a sample of fifty-three prematurely born subjects were the populations studied. The children came from homes where English was the predominant language spoken; they did not present significant sensory deficits or psychopathology as judged clinically. Their I.Q.'s were in the average range, and their parents belonged to a segment of a lower middle-class population. Coefficients were computed measuring the correlation between a series of kindergarten tests and a number of background variables on the one hand and standardized reading, spelling, and writing tests administered at the end of the second grade on the other hand.

The investigation of the children from the general sample was designed to assist us in our practical goal: to shape a predictive instrument for use in schools. The study of the prematurely born youngsters, who can be assumed to have started life with neurophysiologic lags, would, we hoped, teach us something about the relationship between neurophysiologic immaturity and difficulties with the written and printed forms of language.

Thus, the heart of the investigation consisted of an attempt to determine which of thirty-seven perceptuomotor, linguistic, and reading-readiness tests administered at the kindergarten level would prove to be potential predictors of reading, writing, and spelling abilities 2½ years later. A further goal was to combine the best potential predictors to yield an instrument of widespread applicability.

We fully realized that a multiplicity of social, environmental, and psychologic factors enter significantly in the acquisition of reading skills, and we believed, as did Fabian,[6] that learning to read requires the developmental timing of both neurophysiologic and psychologic aspects of readiness.

Development proceeds from a state of relative globality and undifferentiation in the direction of increasing articulation and hierarchic organizations.[22] Our tests, some of them standardized, some adapted by us, and some fashioned by ourselves, reflected our theoretic position derived from Piaget,[17] Gesell,[8] and Werner,[22] who postulated evolving states in sensorimotor and linguistic development. Since development is a consistent and lawful process, we assumed that a kindergarten child's perceptuomotor and oral language status would forecast his performance on such highly integrated tasks as reading, writing, and spelling. The tests administered covered several broad aspects: behavior and motility patterning, large and fine motor coordination, figure-ground discrimination, visuomotor organization, auditory and visual perceptual competence, comprehension and use of oral language, and, more specifically, reading readiness.

Computation of a coefficient of association between the thirty-seven kindergarten tests and a number of background variables on the one hand and performance on standardized reading, spelling, and writing tests administered at the end of the second grade, on the other hand, provided a basis for ascertaining which early tasks might be associated strongly enough with subsequent achievement to have predictive value. Those tests for which the coefficient of association with second grade performance were statistically significant at the 0.05 level of confidence or less were considered potential predictors.

As can be seen from Table 4-1, nineteen of the kindergarten tests were significantly related to reading, twenty to spelling, and sixteen to writing. The fact that intelligence did not basically account for the correlations between any kindergarten tests (except letter naming) and second grade achievement was one of the most interesting findings. Intelligence quotient, when treated as a single predictor, was significantly related to achievement 2½ years later. However, I.Q. ranked only twelfth among predictive measures; eleven other tests were bet-

Table 4-1. Correlation among thirty-seven kindergarten tests, and reading, spelling, and writing achievement at end of second grade*

	ORP index	*Metropolitan spelling test*	*Writing test*
Behavioral patterning			
1. Hyperactivity, distractibility, and disinhibition index	0.46†	0.40†	0.48‡
Motility patterning			
2. Concomitant movements	0.03	0.04	0.05
Gross motor patterning			
3. Balance	0.09	0.14	−0.15
4. Hopping	0.22	0.18	0.18
5. Throwing	0.10	0.14	0.06
Fine motor patterning			
6. Pegboard speed index	0.17	0.23†	0.27†
7. Tying a knot	0.13	−0.16	0.38
8. Pencil use	0.34†	0.27	0.46‡
Body image			
9. Human figure drawing	0.23†	0.20†	0.11
Laterality			
10. Hand preference index	0.10	0.15	0.18
Visual-perceptual patterning			
11. Figure-ground organization	0.05	0.12	0.16
12. Visuomotor organization	0.44‡	0.45‡	0.33‡
Auditory-perceptual patterning			
13. Tapped patterns	0.30†	0.36†	0.23
14. Auditory memory span	0.28	0.20	0.29
15. Auditory discrimination	0.26†	0.31†	0.11
16. Word recognition	0.21	0.26†	0.16
17. Language comprehension	0.21	0.20	0.06
Expressive language			
18. Consonant articulation	0.12	0.03	0.01
19. Articulatory stability	0.16	0.24	−0.17
20. Word finding	0.20	0.26	0.18
21. Story organization	0.28†	0.27†	0.05
22. Number of words used	0.40‡	0.32†	0.27†
23. Sentence elaboration	0.18	0.23	0.16
24. Number of grammatical errors	0.09	0.07	0.01
25. Definitions	0.07	0.10	0.14
26. Categories	0.24†	0.36†	0.23†

*From de Hirsch, K., Jansky, J. J., and Langford, W. S.: Predicting reading failures, New York, 1966, Harper & Row, Publishers.
†$0.01 \leq P \leq 0.05$.
‡$P \leq 0.01$.

Table 4-1. Correlation among thirty-seven kindergarten tests, and reading, spelling, and writing achievement at end of second grade—cont'd

	ORP index	Metropolitan spelling test	Writing test
Reading readiness			
27. Name writing	0.43‡	0.32†	0.30†
28. Copying of letters	0.16	0.30†	0.35†
29. Letter naming	0.55‡	0.56‡	0.34†
30. Reversals test	0.36‡	0.34†	0.25‡
31. Word matching	0.35‡	0.37†	0.19†
32. Word rhyming	0.22†	0.15	0.13
33. Word recognition I (Pack)	0.40‡	0.39‡	0.38‡
34. Word recognition II (Table)	0.48‡	0.45‡	0.24†
35. Word reproduction	0.42‡	0.39‡	0.31‡
Style			
36. Ego strength	0.48†	0.39†	0.35†
37. Work attitude	0.43†	0.46‡	0.38†

ter predictors. Furthermore, the correlation between spelling and I.Q. was low, supporting our clinical experience that severe spelling disabilities are highly specific and cannot be easily compensated for by intelligence.

The fact that most tests predicted better for girls than for boys may have been due, in part, to the fact that as a group the girls were slightly older. However, even when age was taken into account, predictions were higher for girls, perhaps because the developmental course of girls is more consistent than that of boys.

The significantly poorer spelling of the Negro children as compared to the Caucasian children may possibly have been the result of inferior auditory discrimination of the Negro children. Whether the greater instability of their auditory-perceptual experiences is related to differences in dialect or, as Deutsch maintains,[5] to sociologic factors could not be answered on the basis of our data.

Contrary to expectations, no significant correlations were found between end-of-second-grade achievement and various measures of environmental stimulation. This was surprising, since it is well known that parental educational status, ordinal position in the family, and maternal employment are all important variables in terms of a child's language mastery.

Our expectations that certain kindergarten tests would be predictive of subsequent performance were based on our clinical experience and on reports of other researchers. As could be expected, only those activities that differentiated between the kindergarten children proved to be predictive. Gross motor skills such as throwing, hopping, and balancing were clearly so well established in the group as a whole that they did not differentiate between subjects, though, quite possibly, a year or two earlier these same gross motor activities would have differentiated between subjects and, thus, might have been predictive. To some extent this was true for our figure-ground discrimination task, which the overwhelming majority of our children found easy. A more demanding task of the same type might have better served predictive purposes.

Ill-defined lateralization at kindergarten age did not preclude adequate or better reading at the end of the second grade.

Certain results were of particular interest: For instance, a kindergarten child's ability to grasp the pencil was associated not only with end-of-second-grade writing but also with reading, indicating that symbolic determinants beyond motor determinants play a part in graphic activities.

A child's ability to draw a human figure does not primarily measure his motor skills; this is suggested by the fact that drawing ability as measured by this performance was not associated with end-of-second-grade writing but with reading and spelling. Birch and Belmont[2] believe that defects in body schema and praxis enter into reading failure, and it is thus possible that such deficits might be reflected in the immature and fragmented human figure drawings of preschool children.

Our clinical, 20-year experience with the Bender Gestalt test led us to expect that this task would be highly correlated with reading and spelling; this was indeed the case. Apart from reading-readiness tests, most of which are heavily dependent on previous training, the Bender Gestalt test ranked at the top of predictive tests.

Orton[15] was the first to emphasize the close relationship between oral and printed aspects of language in children. Since then the close association between the two aspects has received much attention in the literature, but little is actually known as to the precise nature and extent of this relationship.

Five oral language tasks proved to be predictive in our study—although one of them, imitation of a series of tapped-out patterns, actually tests ability to respond to a nonverbal auditory configuration. In view of the abysmally poor auditory discrimination of most of our children with severe spelling disabilities, it did not come as a surprise that auditory discrimination at kindergarten age proved to be predictive of both reading and spelling achievement 2½ years later. The number of words used by the child in telling the story of *The Three Bears* was by far the best predictor among expressive oral language tests. The number of words varied enormously, ranging from 54 to 594. While the richness of a child's verbal output is largely related to environmental stimulation and to the affect bond between the child and his parents, it also reflects— better than most other measures—the child's inherent linguistic endowment.

Most of the reading-readiness tests are predictive of subsequent performance. However, many of them—letter naming, for instance, which is a good predictive tool at kindergarten age—are heavily dependent on previous training.

If one looks at the constellation of potential predictors, one finds that they are not confined to one specific area of kindergarten functioning. Reading-readiness tests such as Word Matching are tasks that are very similar to those required for the reading process itself. Other predictors, however, such as the human figure drawing and the Bender Gestalt, assess competences that have no apparent or direct relation to reading. Both require ability to organize parts of a gestalt into a meaningful whole; in other words, they call for a high degree of integrative competence—that function of the organism which combines and relates discrete cues to make a unified response possible. The predictive efficacy of the tests thus depended not on the specific skills involved but on the degree to which they measured integrative ability. Weakness in integrative competence at kindergarten age augurs poorly for reading and spelling at the end of the second grade, because, according to Birch and Belmont,[3] by this time the child must be able to integrate information gained from both auditory and visual clues.

Positive correlations were found also between clinical assessment of the child's ego strength and work attitude at kindergarten age and all achievement measures at the end of the second grade. Difficulties with integration are assumed to account for defects in ego organization. It is a pity that our investigation could not explore the fascinating interaction between integrative lags on the physiologic level and those found on the level of ego organization.

Certain aspects of our study appear to clarify the concept of maturational lags and their relationship to reading and related disabilities. One of them, to be discussed in Chapter 6, refers to the performance of prematurely born children.

Another argument in favor of the maturational bias involved some statistical procedures. Gesell[8] maintains that maturation is largely a function of age; Piaget[17] believes that the development of organizational schemes is age linked.

We, therefore, classified all thirty-seven kindergarten tests according to the degree to which they discriminated between the oldest and the youngest kindergarten children. Those tests on which the oldest subjects did best and the youngest did less well were considered to be maturation sensitive. According to this criterion, twenty-five of the thirty-seven kindergarten tests administered were considered maturation sensitive. The expectation that these particular tests would be better predictors of performance than the nonmaturation sensitive tests, those that did *not* discriminate between the oldest and the youngest kindergarten children, was upheld by the findings. Of the maturation sensitive tests, 76 percent were significantly correlated with second grade scores as against 17 percent of the nonmaturation sensitive ones.

School admission procedures are, of course, based on chronologic age, and to the degree that chronologic age reflects the level of a child's maturation, it is, in fact, a fairly good predictor of subsequent achievement.

However, the focus in our study is on those intelligent children in whom chronologic age does *not* reflect maturational status; the children who suffer from maturational lags and who, therefore, present a high risk of academic failure. For these children chronologic age is misleading as a predictor.

There were eighteen children in our study who were 6½ years old or older at the time of first grade entrance. On the basis of chronologic age and I.Q. they should have done adequately. However, four of them failed in both reading and spelling at the end of second grade. Our predictive tests that assessed developmental level identified three of these four children at kindergarten age; data on the fourth child was incomplete.

The findings thus support our contention that there is, indeed, a close link between a child's maturational status at kindergarten age and his reading and spelling achievement several years later.

Since the administration of twenty separate tests would be far too cumbersome for use in schools, we decided to construct a Predictive Index (P.I.), consisting of those single predictors, which, in combination, would most effectively identify academic high risks. Since the intercorrelations between reading and spelling at the end of second grade were very high, we were able to use the same index for both. The original twenty kindergarten tests that had exhibited relatively high and significant correlations with achievement measures at the end of second grade and, thus, seemed promising, were then put together for trial indices. Over one hundred of them were tried out and compared in order to determine which combination would best single out those children in our sample who subsequently failed. The tests selected for the Predictive Index were: the child's ability to manipulate the pencil; his response to six of the Bender gestalten; his performance on twenty of the forty word pairs on the Wepman Auditory Discrimination test; the number of words he used in telling a story; his ability to produce generic names for three clusters of words representing concrete objects; his performance on a reversal test; his word matching ability (taken from Gates); and his recall and reproduction of two words taught at the beginning of the testing session. This battery identified, at kindergarten age, ten of eleven children—91 percent of the children who subsequently failed.

It is, of course, important to report on those cases in which the P.I. did *not* work. The P.I. entirely failed to pick out one boy whose performance at the kindergarten level had been acceptable. It selected, on the other hand, as prospective failures four children who did, in fact, make the grade. Two of the four were slow starters and failed all tests at the end of the first grade; the performance of one of the two was marginal at the end of the second grade. The third boy was a disturbed youngster and his original performance had been very spotty. He did, however, pass. The fourth youngster best exemplifies the pitfalls in this type of prediction. His initial performance was quite immature, but he made dramatic strides in the interim between kindergarten and second grade.

During the elementary school years a number of variables—poor teaching, illness, frequent change of schools, or major upheavals in the home—may be reflected in academic achievement and thus influence prediction. Limitation in time and funds did not permit us to take these important variables into account. It was, therefore, surprising that, despite these limitations, the Predictive Index effectively identified the overwhelming majority of failing children at kindergarten age.

Our tests should, however, do more than simply select the youngsters destined to do poorly; they should reveal in which particular area a child is lagging, what kind of help he needs, and what to do about it. Educational diagnosis is productive only if it can be translated into specific educational strategies. Comparing a kindergarten child's performance in the auditory and in the visual perceptual areas makes it possible to assess his specific strength and weakness and to determine which particular pathways facilitate learning. In our study, the majority of children did *not* show what we call erratic modality patterning. They did either well or poorly, both auditorily and visually, and their integrative competence or lack of it cut through all modalities. On the other hand, 19 percent of our children showed erratic modality patterning— striking deficits in the four visual-perceptual tests and superior competence on the four auditory-perceptual performances. Seven children belonged in this group; three others showed the opposite picture—excellent visual-perceptual ability and failure in the entire auditory-perceptual realm. The three children with superior *visual* competence did very well in reading despite their auditory lags, and they even made the grade in spelling. Reading is, after all, primarily a visual-perceptual task, and thus the usual procedures offered at school were entirely adequate. The seven youngsters with visual-perceptual deficits clearly needed phonics, and, in fact, the five youngsters who were heavily exposed to phonics did well, while the two who were not did poorly.

Teaching should not be method centered, but child centered. The youngster who does well in both auditory and visual perception will learn from any method offered him. The one who does poorly in both will need heavy reinforcement and the activation of as many pathways as possible. The poor visualizer needs phonics. To some brain-injured children who have severe integrational deficits, phonic teaching may present overwhelming difficulties, because they are unable to analyze and synthesize. Their failure to cope with phonics may lead to a castastrophic reaction—the disorganized response of the organism that is exposed to a task with which it is unable to cope. The point we want to make is this: teaching methods must be determined in terms of the individual child's inherent strength and weakness.

Fifteen percent of our children from lower middle-class homes showed a kind of performance at kindergarten age which clearly revealed that they would meet with total failure in second grade, an experience which would have seriously damaging effects on their self-image and might adversely affect their attitudes to learning in general.

Therefore, we suggest that the school system introduce transition classes between kindergarten and first grade for those children who, according to the Predictive Index are found to be immature.

The Predictive Index is, of course, only a formula, and it would be unfortunate if it were to draw the teacher's attention away from the child's actual behavior and performance. Rather than serving as a substitute for observation, the Predictive Index should assist the teacher in translating her often excellent but impressionistic judgment of the youngster's readiness into a more specific assessment of his perceptuomotor and linguistic status.

Stating that a child is not ready or is immature does not mean one can afford to sit back and let maturation take its course. This was done in the 1920's with unfortunate results. Schilder[18] stated that training plays a significant part even in those functions in which maturation of the central nervous system is of primary importance. The question is only what kind of training and above all, training at what level. A match between a child's developmental readiness and the type of teaching offered him is desirable. This need for a match must be met in what we call transition and the Swedes call maturity classes.[13]

The developmental timing of immature children is atypical. At kindergarten age immature children are unable to benefit from prereading programs. Repeating the kindergarten year would give them an additional year in which to mature and would, thus, have certain advantages. However, it would not provide the intensive and specific training they need. Promotion into first grade would not solve their problems either, since the pace is usually too fast for the child who is ready to learn but is, as yet, unable to cope with organized reading and writing instruction at the conventional age.

The transition class would aim at stabilizing the child's perceptuomotor world and would take him, in slow motion, through a program in which each step is carefully planned. Teaching methods in these small classes—unlike those in first grade, which provide fairly uniform training for all children—would be tailored to the child's individual needs.

Teachers in such a transition class would need special qualifications, since immature children require a greater degree of tolerance and empathy.

The transition class would, finally, provide an opportunity to translate into educational practice the insights gained from a careful study of the child's weakness and strength in the various modalities. Instruction would be geared differentially to children with auditory-perceptual deficits and to those with lags in visual perception. During certain times of the day, children with receptive and expressive language deficits would receive specific training in discrimination and listening, concept formation, vocabulary building, and verbal formulation. Others would receive assistance with visual discrimination and configurational techniques. A third group would work on directional and graphomotor patterning. In short, this class would be geared to fill in specific gaps in some areas and to utilize assets in others.

Marie van Hoosan[20] has called the interval between kindergarten and first grade the twilight zone of learning. It is this twilight period which would be served by the transition group.

A few children in such a class could be integrated into the regular first grade after a few weeks or months of intensive training. Most others would be ready to cope with first grade a year later. A small number of children suffering from severe and persisting lags might require continuing help for at least 2 or 3 years.

At present most schools do not provide remedial help until the end of the third grade. This is unfortunate; the development of perceptual and language functions probably follows a sequence analogous to that in organic morphologic development. According to McGraw,[12] there are specific critical times in the child's life when he is especially susceptible to certain kinds of stimulation. The basic perceptuomotor functions that underlie reading may be harder to train at the end of third grade than they are earlier. By the end of third grade, moreover, emotional problems and phobic responses may have so complicated the original problems that in some cases they may no longer be reversible.

The earliest possible identification of high risk children was the goal of our study. Identification is, however, only a first step toward reversing a situation that now results in an unjustifiable waste of educational opportunities. A second step is equally essential: academic high risk children must be provided at the earliest possible time with an educational approach that enables them to realize their potential and to become productive members of the community.

REFERENCES

1. Austin, M. C., and Morrison, C.: The first R: the Harvard report on reading in elementary schools, New York, 1963, The Macmillan Co.
2. Birch, H. G., and Belmont, L.: Lateral dominance, lateral awareness, and reading disability, Child Development 36(a):57-71, 1965.
3. Birch, H. G., and Belmont, L.: Auditory-visual integration, intelligence and reading ability in school children, Percept. Motor Skills 20:295-305, 1965.
4. Cohen, T. B.: Diagnostic and predictive methods with young children, Amer. J. Orthopsychiat. 33:330-331, 1963.
5. Deutsch, C.: Auditory discrimination and learning: social factors, Merrill-Palmer quarterly of Behavior and Development 10:249-263, 1964. Arden House Conference on Preschool Enrichment of Socially Disadvantaged Children.
6. Fabian, A. A.: Clinical and experimental studies of school children who are retarded in reading, Quart. J. Child Behav. 3:15-37, 1951.
7. Gesell, A.: The mental growth of the pre-school child, New York, 1930, The Macmillan Co.
8. Gesell, A.: The embryology of behavior—the beginning of the human mind, New York, 1945, Harper & Row, Publishers.
9. Henig, M. S.: Predictive value of a reading readiness test and of teachers' forecasts, Element. School J. 50:41-46, 1949.
10. de Hirsch, K.: Tests designed to discover potential reading difficulties at the six-year-old level, Amer. J. Orthopsychiat. 27:566-576, 1957.
11. Koppitz, E. M.: The Bender Gestalt test for young children, New York, 1964, Grune & Stratton, Inc.
12. McGraw, M. B.: The neuromuscular maturation of the human infant, New York, 1943, Columbia University Press.
13. Malmquist, E.: Organizing instruction to prevent reading disability. In Figurel, J. A., editor: Reading as an intellectual activity, Conference Proceedings of the International Reading Association 8:36-39, 1963.
14. Monroe, M.: Reading aptitude tests for the prediction of success and failure in beginning reading, Education 56:7-14, 1935.
15. Orton, S. T.: Reading, writing and speech problems in children, New York, 1937, W. W. Norton & Co., Inc.
16. Petty, M. C.: An experimental study of certain factors influencing reading readiness, J. Educ. Psychol. 30:215-230, 1939.
17. Piaget, J.: The origins of intelligence in children, New York, 1952, International Universities Press, Inc.
18. Schilder, P.: Contributions to developmental neuropsychiatry, New York, 1964, International Universities Press, Inc.
19. Thompson, B. B.: A longitudinal study of auditory discrimination, J. Educ. Res. 56:376-378, 1963.
20. van Hoosan, M.: Just enough English, Reading Teacher 18:507, 1965.
21. Wattenberg, W., and Clifford, C.: Relation of self-concepts to beginning achievement in reading, Child Development 35:461-467, 1964.
22. Werner, H.: The concept of development from a comparative and organismic point of view. In Harris, D. B., editor: The concept of development, Minneapolis, 1957, University of Minnesota Press.

Questions and answers: First session

MODERATOR: HERMANN M. BURIAN, M.D.

Dr. Burian: Dr. Buchanan, how and by whom was the term "dyslexia" first coined? What was the original expressed meaning of the term?

Dr. Buchanan: I will pass this question to Dr. Critchley, who has a copy of his own book on the table.

Dr. Burian: May I add that intelligence consists in knowing where to find things. It is impossible for any human being to know everything, but if he knows where to find it, he is intelligent. In his own book, for example.

Dr. Critchley: To quote my book, Kussmaul, in 1877, first spoke of "word blindness," but the word "dyslexia" was first suggested by Professor Berlin of Stuttgart in 1877 in his monograph, "Eine besondere Art der Wortblindheit (Dyslexia)."

Dr. Burian: Dr. Buchanan, is there any theoretic or other evidence that the genes carry a dyslexia chromosome?

Dr. Buchanan: No one has yet recognized a chromosome or a gene that is responsible for the presence of dyslexia. In this meeting some of us have been trained in neurology, ophthalmology, and other biologic fields, and others have been trained in education. Many try to find data acceptable to their own ideas and their own prejudices, and many challenge and reject conclusions that seem foreign to their early training. Many teachers believe that dyslexia is solely a problem in education, while those trained in biology believe that dyslexia springs from a biologic fault. Although a specific gene has not yet been recognized, the available evidence supports the biologic explanation.

Dr. Burian: Dr. Rabinovitch, what is the relative incidence of primary dyslexia as a main problem in relation to the total number of children with reading problems under the age of 10 years? What is the overall incidence of dyslexia in all its forms? What percent of children who have primary dyslexia have true psychiatric problems?

Dr. Rabinovitch: I do not think any of us know the absolute incidence. I am not greatly concerned about what we call these children. Sometimes we get so lost in semantics that we do not really define the process disturbances or meet the true needs.

As we explore what we all call primary reading retardation, or developmental dyslexia, certain subgroups emerge. Certainly the eight cases that Dr.

de Hirsch describes in Chapter 6 are not all alike, nor are ours. There is great variety. There is one subgroup that has mixed dominance or a cortical-dominant problem; perhaps 15 or 20 percent have this problem. On the other hand, there is another 80 or 85 percent who do not. This seems to apply in all the diagnostic correlations. So, when you ask the exact percentage of children having dyslexia among children with poor reading, it would depend on your frame of reference. The number of children at age 10 years who read 2 years or more below their chronologic age varies tremendously with the economic level of the community. It is very high in the inner cities. It is much lower in the suburbs and in privileged communities. This could even suggest nutritional factors or prenatal factors in the poorer families, but this does not explain the magnitude of difference. There are also qualitative differences between reading problems in the deprived child and the dyslexic child or a child with a neurologic handicap.

There are no good incidence studies. An educated guess would be that about 10 percent of children by the seventh grade have significant difficulties in reading and probably about one-fourth of those would qualify in everybody's book as being dyslexic. This would be 2 or 3 percent of the school level population. That may even be high.

There are, unfortunately, some people who consider all children with reading difficulties to have the same problem, and they would place incidence nearer 20 percent. My guess is that between 2 and 5 percent of children in our public schools have some degree of neurologic deficit that interferes with the reading-learning process.

Dr. Burian: I have another question for Dr. Rabinovitch. Can you indicate an age range beyond which the effects of education or cultural deprivation are irreversible?

Dr. Rabinovitch: I wish we could. This is a question that worries us tremendously. Dr. Bender has been interested in this for years. I hate to say this, but many of us who have been involved in the large city programs of attempting to rehabilitate or provide enrichment experiences for severely disadvantaged youngsters have not been happy with the results. Results of the attempts at enrichment are not all in.

Some say this proves that the poverty program is politically unsound, and that it is nothing more or less than sadistic. We must do more and not less for children whom we have neglected. What to do, however, is a real problem. Among the language-deprived children, sometimes the level of exposure and cultural endowment is so limited that the English language tends to be laconic. A middle-class mother may say to a child, "It's time for school. You'd better get ready. You'll be late. It's happened three times in the last week." In a very disadvantaged family, where the mother is burdened, she may say, "Git!" This is the language exposure that some dyslexic children have.

We must do more for much longer periods to give a compensatory educational experience to disadvantaged children. It is not fair to give them a Headstart Program followed by something in the first grade and then to cut back even though they may need continuing special help for 7 years. These children must have help as long as they need it, or they are lost. We have asked our teachers sometimes to say, "We'll give you 6 months to catch up." However, you do not take Dilantin away from an epileptic child after 6 months because he is not cured, or you do not take glasses away from the hyperopic youngster who has not fully outgrown such a refractive error. If we program help as long as they need it, our results will be better.

Another point is that prevention is better than treatment; just as in the psychopathic child who has been denied gratification early, you can only add so much, but you can prevent. The answer for the disadvantaged child's language, reading, and learning problems is a decent life for him and his family from the beginning.

Dr. Burian: Clearly, we have here different approaches predicated on different aspects of the problem. The approach that Dr. Critchley takes is of a distinct neurologic problem with eugenic implications. In consequence, four questions to Dr. Critchley essentially boil down to this question: What evidence is there for the existence of genetically determined dyslexia? What makes you feel that primary dyslexia is not caused by anoxia or slight brain trauma? How does one isolate pure genetically determined dyslexia?

Dr. Critchley: The evidence is based upon many years of clinical experience and literally hundreds of case records in the literature, some of them intimately studied generation by generation, showing the genetic factor to be extremely important.

From my point of view, in the past 6 years I have been seeing, I suppose, four to six new cases of dyslexia a week, and it is the exception for me to find a family without one or more similarly afflicted persons.

Then, too, there is the evidence of many recorded cases of dyslexia in twins. Morrie and Halgren had forty-five twins, twelve of whom were monozygotic, or identical, and thirty-three of whom were dizygotic, or nonidentical. Of the twelve monozygotic twins with dyslexia, there was 100 percent concordance; of the dizygotic twins, one of whom had dyslexia, there was a 33 percent concordance.

Dyslexia is said to follow an autosomal, monohybrid, dominant pattern of inheritance.

I am often asked, "why is this not caused by some common environmental factor?" The evidence going back generation by generation is overwhelmingly against such mechanism.

Last, someone asked how I am sure that developmental dyslexia is not caused by anoxia or minor brain injury. There is no evidence in the cases which I have documented of anoxia as based on perinatal histories, obstetric data, or on the most intimate neurologic examination. Furthermore, even if there were positive findings in some cases, this would still not explain the demonstrated genetic incidence.

Dr. Burian: The next set of questions deals with testing. What specific testing materials are available for office testing and evaluation of the dyslexic child? What should be the minimal diagnostic evaluation? What tests or plans do you employ to determine the differential diagnosis of dyslexia? Who makes the final diagnosis?

Dr. Critchley: The diagnosis is, perhaps, best arrived at by teamwork in which obstetric, pediatric, neurologic, ophthalmic, audiometric, psychologic, and perhaps psychiatric and electroencephalographic evidence is gathered and assessed.

Who makes the final diagnosis depends on the city or academic center. In London, it is usually a team that arrives at the final diagnosis, but the tentative dyslexic patient is usually regarded as a neurologic problem in diagnosis.

In regard to tests, please remember, I am a neurologist, not an educationalist or a psychologist, so I do not employ pure psychologic or educational tests. My chief reliance is on conventional (routine) neurologic examination supplemented by more subtle data.

I know of no specific and indispensable testing material for office use, except perhaps a percussion hammer, paper, and pencil.

Dr. Burian: Dr. Critchley, please define perceptual difficulty. How do you test for it?

Dr. Critchley: I do not remember using the term "perceptual difficulty," but if I did, I would have had in mind a failure or difficulty on the part of the child in interpreting symbols presented either through visual or auditory channels. How do I test for it? That would take me about an hour to discuss.

Dr. Burian: Time is too short now; but here is another question. Have you ever seen a dyslexic child with a paradoxic reaction to phenobarbital? I have employed such a test in late diagnosis.

Dr. Critchley: No, I have not, but, of course, I am very familiar with phenobarbital aggravating behavior disturbances in young epileptic patients.

Dr. Burian: Are difficulties in impulse control characteristic of children with developmental dyslexia?

Dr. Critchley: I am not quite sure what the term "impulse control" means, unless it refers to hyperkinetic children. This is generally not apparent by the time they come to me. I see these children at an older age than Mrs. de Hirsch does, and many of them are adolescents, or young adults. By this time, very few show pathologic hyperactivity.

Dr. Rabinovitch: Someone mentioned perception. This has been a real "show stopper" in recent years. Parents and governmental agencies are now talking about handicapped children, and all sorts of lay societies are developing for the perceptually handicapped. Why should not people just want to have a society for children with reading problems? I wonder why we have to pick up fancy names, especially when their meaning is unclear?

Perception may mean everything from peripheral organ senses to deepest central gnosis, but we are really dealing with agnosia. We are not significantly dealing with peripheral problems. A child with obvious nystagmus or a major near-point vision deficit or poor amplitude of fusion has a problem that can be corrected by the ophthalmologists. This is not the symbolization problem we are talking about. Neglected eye problems or peripheral problems of sight lead to interference in viewing problems and certainly must be ruled out.

There has been a great tendency in recent years for less than highly critical people to talk about perception as being sort of a peripheral thing and being relevant to the major reading or specific dyslexic problem. This has created additional difficulties, because many of these children and even their parents are being exposed to eye exercises; there is both time and economic exploitation in certain areas on the part of some eye practitioners who have entered this field. I think this is very serious.

Another important point is that when Mrs. de Hirsch and others talk about possible clumsiness in these children, it does not mean that these children should get on the floor and creep as a solution to their reading problems. There have been tremendous problems and confusion here.

If there is a motor problem in a child, if a child trips on a carpet, it is not going to make him dyslexic. There may be, in children with severe reading problems, minor motor problems, or even major motor problems, but there is no evidence of causal relationship from the motor defect to the interpretive defect. This has been another problem and obstacle to understanding in the United States.

We must ask whether we can expect, along neurologic pathways, a direct transfer of skills from large muscle activities to the symbolization process. By what magic would you expect a dyslexic child who is taught to bang harder and faster, directly to learn to use symbols effectively? I will turn the question over to Dr. Critchley and Dr. Buchanan.

Dr. Critchley: Well, it sounds to me like absolute nonsense.

Dr. Buchanan: Although I entirely agree, as Dr. Critchley knows, with everything that he has said, let us return to the question of genetic determination of dyslexia. If some members of a family in the same generation or in succeeding generations suffer from dyslexia, it is a reasonable assumption that this is an inherited genetic fault. However, there is evidence that broad beliefs in biology may change. For example, some progressive destructions of the brain that have been universally considered to be primary degenerations have recently been demonstrated to be the result of viral infection. So, if dyslexia were produced by a viral invasion of the brain, different members of a family might be exposed to the same virus and might react in a similar way; then the genetic explanation, although plausible, would be false. Each conclusion must be considered on its own merits. At present, although there is as yet no chemical or other objective proof that dyslexia is genetically determined, this can be regarded as the most reasonable explanation.

In description of some defects in action of the brain and spinal cord, expressions have come into fashion because, although they are so vague as to be useless, they have the false appearance of being scientific. One of these is cerebral palsy, which may refer to any degree of intellectual defect or weakness or stiffness of the body and the limbs. Another such diagnosis, unhappily quite commonly used, is brain damage. This may mean mild and temporary confusion or massive destruction of any region of the brain from trauma or disease. The present most fashionable variations of this diagnosis are minimal brain damage and perceptual handicap. The first, strictly interpreted, could refer to the loss of only one of the fourteen billion neurons in the cerebral hemispheres. The second may mean any degree of defect in vision or in hearing, of cutaneous sensitivity, or of understanding. All such expressions should be avoided, because it is only in *Through the Looking Glass* that it is possible to say, "When I use a word, it means just what I choose it to mean—neither more nor less."

Chapter 5

Correlated disturbances: Etiologic, associated, and secondary

Part 1: Minor neurologic defects in developmental dyslexia

Macdonald Critchley, M.D., F.R.C.P.

When a dyslexic patient presents himself for neurologic examination, ordinarily there is no gross abnormality to be detected. In fact, it would be exceptional to find traces of spasticity, increased reflexes, or pyramidal or extrapyramidal deficits. Furthermore, the average dyslexic shows no conspicuous abnormality in growth or physical habitus. With more subtle neurologic testing, it is also quite exceptional for me to find any defect in constitutional tasks in the dyslexic patients sent to me.

Neither do they show what is sometimes called finger agnosia, despite Harriman's reports. In Denmark, the idea was put forward that developmental dyslexia is actually a type of congenital Gerstmann's syndrome. Today, the status of the so-called Gerstmann syndrome has come under serious suspicion, and many neurologists are dubious as to whether this syndrome exists at all. One other important negative finding in my experience is the absence of difficulty in picture interpretation. This constitutes one of my routine tests: I show these children a series of representational pictures that are not entirely obvious or straightforward. A subtle incongruity is present in each picture, and one is surprised and gratified to find how well the dyslexics fare on this rather difficult test of picture interpretation.

Fig. 5-1 is one of the pictures I always show my patients. It is not a fake picture but an actual photograph of a street in Portsmouth, England. The traffic keeps to the left, and there is an intersection; and the man who painted SOLW must surely have been dyslexic himself. I have shown this illustration to every

Fig. 5-1. Traffic control sign on a street in Portsmouth, England, apparently painted by a dyslexic workman.

dyslexic patient whom I have examined, and not one has detected the spelling error. Many say, "Well, it's a road crossing," or "I don't know what those letters mean," or "Oh, that's SLOW." A few say that it indicates stop.

It is often stated that if one makes an extended or deeper probing of neurologic function, particularly of neuropsychologic activities, certain subtle defects, which would elude a superficial examination, become apparent. This is certainly true in many cases. Among these subtle defects, which are sometimes called soft neurologic signs, I would place a lack of firm cerebral dominance, whether left-sided or right-sided. In other words, if a patient is put through a battery of tests for cerebral dominance, one often finds a mixed picture.

Reliable tests for handedness, eyedness, and footedness are sadly needed. A sure test for these three activities does not exist. Many tests are necessary, and one probably comes out with a sort of formula at the end; a child may rate, eventually, as 80 percent left-brain dominant and 20 percent right-brain dominant. Dyslexic patients often prove to be something like 65 percent versus 35 percent.

Tests of handedness are often invalidated because many of them are culturally determined. Among the Chinese, one may find a left-handed patient still using the right hand for chopsticks, because there is a taboo against using the left hand for feeding. This is true not only in China but also in India and, indeed, throughout the Orient.

Certain motor skills may be artificially imposed upon the left-handed or the right-handed person. Thus, the sinistral person may have been taught or forced to use his right hand in a specific skill. As a result, it becomes difficult to determine with confidence the true handedness of an individual.

An anatomic test of handedness would be very helpful. It has been suggested that the pattern of the veins on the dorsum of the hands or in beds of the fingernails may be more elaborate on the dominant hand. An ingenious anatomic test, which may conceivably correlate with handedness, is the position of the scalp hair whorl. The whorl is usually said to overlie the dominant hemisphere, but confirmation of this statement is needed. I always make a note of the position of the hair whorl, but sometimes it is quite difficult to determine the position of the whorl. This observation should always be noted.

In children with dyslexia, cross laterality is common, i.e., predominant right-handedness and right-footedness combined with left-eyedness or some similar discrepancy.

Another soft neurologic sign that most dyslexic children show at some time (although they may outgrow it) is a confusion regarding spatial dimensions. This is shown particularly in the visual sphere. For example, one may learn from a child's parents that the child was late in learning to tell the time. When the child draws a clock or a bicycle, the various items of the clock or bicycle may be uncoordinate and disintegrated. Sometimes the figures are not arranged around the entire inner rim of the circumference but are clustered within one-half of the rim, very much as one sees in the case of a patient with a parietal lesion.

Many of these children have difficulty in drawing an arrow pointing in a given direction. Others have trouble in correctly placing the points of a compass (north, south, east, and west). Usually, the vertical directions are not confused as much as the lateral dimensions (east and west, right and left). The child, under an extended, increasingly difficult battery of tests, demonstrates a difficulty in indicating right and left. He may succeed in saying, "This is my right ear; this is my left." But when the child is told to, "Put your left hand on your right ear," this crossover test proves rather difficult. When one asks a dyslexic child, "Which is my right hand?" and then crosses the arms and asks, "Which is my right hand now?" difficulties may become apparent. Difficulty in laterality may extend to inanimate objects. For example, quite a difficult task is presented to many dyslexic children if one picks up the child's shoe, turns it upside down, and asks, "Which is this, left or right?" Or, one may show them a glove and ask, "Is this a right or a left?" Lastly, one may confront the child with a doll and ask, "Which is the doll's right hand? Which is the left?" Then, turning the doll around, "Which is the left leg? Which is the right leg?" With the doll upside down one may ask, "Which now is the right, and which is the left?" When the doll has been turned upside down, back, and front, very few dyslexic children can score 100 percent.

The literature often reports clumsiness or lack of manual dexterity in dyslexic children. Clumsiness is an inadequate and imperfect term, without any meaning to a neurologist. There are so many different types and causes of gaucherie. Parents sometimes assert that their child is a little awkward in hand movements and digital manipulations. But, when you put these children to the test, the majority of them score well. The hobbies and pastimes of these children often include modeling and assembling bricks, Lego sets, and Meccano sets—taking

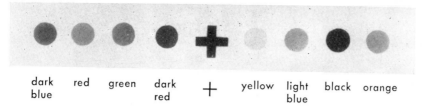

| dark
blue | red | green | dark
red | + | yellow | light
blue | black | orange |

Fig. 5-2. Variously colored dots to be named following visual fixation on central cross in a test for preferred lateralization.

them apart and putting them back again—these pastimes are particularly well performed.

As a rule, dyslexic children are neither awkward nor gawkish on their feet. Some, indeed, are extremely adroit, if one may use that word with regard to feet. The little girls with dyslexia are sometimes very adept as ballet dancers. The boys are usually quite good at football and cricket, and a surprising number excel at swimming, horse riding, and cycling. The factor of clumsiness has been exaggerated, I believe.

Extending the battery of neurologic tests a little further, one commonly finds mild electroencephalographic dysrhythmias, often asymmetrically distributed.

Abnormal eye movements during the act of reading are common, although they are difficult to detect in the clinic. Special mechanical or electrophysiologic methods of estimating or recording the ocular movements are needed. Although the majority of children with dyslexia show abnormal eye movements, we must not make the mistake of regarding abnormal eye movements as the explanation for the dyslexia.

One of my routine tests of dyslexic patients entails the use of Ishihara's pseudo-isochromatic color plates. I have been rather surprised to stumble upon many minor color defects, often unknown both to parents and the child.

Another important test that needs elaboration is the preferred direction of lateral gaze. There is a connection between the dominant eye, the temporal field of vision, and the preferred direction of lateral gaze. A crude test for this may be performed out-of-doors by telling a child to look at a row of trees, a group of people, or a herd of cows in the distance and then to enumerate them. It is interesting to observe whether the child proceeds from left to right or from right to left. A reliable test for use in the consulting room would prove invaluable. I have devised a card with a horizontal row of colored dots to either side of a central black cross (Fig. 5-2). I tell the child to look at the cross; then I say, "You see a number of colored balls, don't you? Tell me the names of any of the colors." The average child with left cerebral dominance shifts his gaze from the center to the extreme left and then proceeds from left to right, saying, "Blue, red, green, dark red, yellow, light blue, black, orange." Occasionally a subject with right cerebral dominance does the opposite and shifts his gaze from right to left. One also finds many other unexpected patterns of deviation. Random scattering can also occur at times.

Part 2: Neuropsychiatric disturbances

Lauretta Bender, M.D.

It is generally recognized that emotional and behavioral problems are associated in children with dyslexias and reading retardation, but it is controversial as to which are primary and secondary or which are cause and effect.

Orton,[22] in his classic 1937 paper, described emotional reactions and behavior patterns secondary to stress, to feelings of inferiority, and to frustrations engendered by reading disability. With Orton's characteristic thoroughness, he described the patterns of emotional blocking, instability, neuroticism, and rebellious acting out. These patterns depend, in part, upon the basic emotional make-up of the child and the social environmental factors that are acting at the time.

Hallgren[17] of Sweden described a wide variety of behavior disorders secondary to dyslexia in Swedish boys who were referred to his clinics as behavioral problems. In a control group of dyslexic children showing behavior compatible with the normal population, he found no appreciable increase in neuropsychiatric disorders. Hallgren believed that the dyslexias were definitely the cause of the social problems. This again points up the much greater incidence of dyslexia in males as compared to females and the question of sex-linked genetics. The occurrence of several cases of dyslexia in one family constitutes some genetic evidence, but not all siblings in each generation are dyslexic, and, therefore, children in a family in which psychogenic factors might be considered causal are not disturbed by them unless the genotype is also present. Two other points are that boys numerically exceed girls in most problems which arise from developmental disorders, maturational disorders, or genetic disorders and that the number of women with emotional problems exceed men after adolescence.

Critchley,[11, 12] from his work in England, has emphasized that the dyslexic individual is not fundamentally neurotic or lazy until he finds himself an alien within the community.

The majority of neuropsychiatrists who have studied dyslexic children believe that reading disabilities in growing children are essentially congenital dyslexias or word blindness, and, consequently, the emotional and behavioral problems are secondary.

Although this concept of primary dyslexia is well accepted by many educators, psychiatrists, and child psychologists regarding the majority of retarded readers, other investigators, such as Rabinovitch,[23] point out that another group of reading retardations are secondary to other factors, especially various environmental factors.

It is important to differentiate general academic retardation from general cultural deprivation, each with the association of specific reading retardation. These two differentials must be kept clearly in mind. There are proportionately more retardations in reading as compared to arithmetic and other specific areas of learning, a fact that shows the effects of general cultural deprivation and impoverishment.

However, considering the fact that there may be a group of children who are secondarily involved in reading retardation, Blanchard,[7] a psychoanalyst, accepted Gates'[15] figure of 20 percent of retarded readers as reacting to a primary personality maladjustment. Blanchard's classic psychoanalytic studies were begun in the 1920's, contemporary with Orton's work. Blanchard postulated that sometimes unconscious, emotional parent-child relationships are carried over into the teacher-pupil relationship and result in general or specific academic failure. It is not clear, however, why the specificity of a failure, such as reading, should occur.

Psychoanalyses of other individual cases have demonstrated several specific mechanisms in the ego development of dyslexic children. Buxbaum,[9] for example, found that a partial symbiotic relationship with an infantile mother prevented one child from functioning independently, while in another boy, a success neurosis caused by an oedipal conflict with an overpowerful and successful father, inhibited learning in the son.

Jarvis[19] described a scoptophilic reaction to fantasies of the primal scene and to anxiety problems in reaction to phallic or castrating mothers. Rosen[24] accepted Orton's concept of congenital disorder of the dominant hemisphere in strephosymbolia, and he also accepted Schilder's[25] concept of an agnostic deficiency in integration of the visual structure of the word and its sound caused by developmental dysfunction in the cortical apparatus. As a result of psychoanalyzing a severely dyslexic but gifted mathematician, Rosen offered the interpretation that his patient had identified the two ego-apparatus functions, i.e., visual and auditory percepts, with his parents, who were in sharp conflict during the child's early developmental period. Consequently, the synthetic process between vision and audition did not occur, thus causing failure in learning to read, write, and spell.

Rosen explained that "the genetic origin of the disability may be due to precocious maturation of certain ego sectors involved in visual and auditory perception, so that they become involved in the oedipal conflict at a crucial stage in development."[24] The word "genetic" may be used here in psychoanalytic meaning. Interestingly, psychoanalysis did not cure the man's reading disability, but he continued as a very gifted mathematician.

There can be no objection to such explanations as long as they represent specific mechanisms in individual cases. However, Blau, in his monograph,[8] is not so restrictive. He states, "Language disturbance is secondary and only one of the many symptoms of the personality disorder, which is a negativistic type of emotional disturbance." He assigns it more often to boys because boys are more often negativistic. He did not clearly establish why this was true.

Also, Fabian,[14] in a study of retarded readers in the public schools of New York, concluded that, "Reading retardation is a symptom of an underlying individual, and very often, familial psychopathology. The learning disability is one of many symptoms which these ego-disabled, emotionally retarded, infantile, dependent children—especially boys—show."

There seems to be one concept in common among all students of dyslexia, i.e., the concept of immaturity in whatever function is being studied. Controversies occur in explaining these immaturities, their origin, and their relationships to the specific problem—reading and language development.

Rabinovitch,[23] when defining the difference between primary and secondary causes of reading retardation, noted that differentiation is complicated by neuroses stemming from distorted parent-child relationships in both groups studied. Also, the features specific to primary reading disabilities proved to be more widespread than he at first thought.

My own convictions are that the congenital immaturities and maturational problems vary in degree in different children. In children less grossly impaired, reading retardation results when the child, less able to compensate, is beset by exogenous factors. In other words, a child with potential reading disability may compensate and never manifest a clinical problem in the absence of exogenous strains.

There are, indeed, cases of reading retardation due to purely exogenous influences; e.g., the many Puerto Rican children in New York City. On theoretic considerations, we may assume that inborn defects producing maturational lags in various cerebral functions constitute the basic pathology. Therefore, neuropsychiatric disturbances facilitated by developmental defects in our recently evolved, highest human cerebral areas for language are a major concern.

My own concept of maturational lag evolved during studies with the visual motor gestalten[1] over the last 30 years. It is based on neurologic, intellectual, and personality functions maturing from undifferentiated or primitive stages. Maturation lag signifies slow differentiation in an established pattern. It does not specify that the deficit be local, structural, specific, or fixed. There is no obligatory limitation in potential; indeed, subsequently accelerated maturation often occurs.

Maturation is a lifelong process which runs through a specific course that is not fixed but is constantly changing in pattern as emphasized by Katrina de Hirsch.[13]

Implicit in the concept of maturation lag is the concept of plasticity as the embryologists Hamilton, Boyd, and Mossman use the term: "An area fundamental to the study of differentiation is the concept of determination; that is, the fixation of a definite time in development of the fates of different parts of the embryo. Before the developmental fate of a part of an embryo has been fully fixed, and while it is still in the pleuri-potential or plastic state, it is said to be undetermined."[18]

We postulate that this undetermined pleuri-potential, plastic state is specifically characteristic of those human brain functions which are the latest in continuing evolutionary development, namely, the language areas. In all areas of functioning in a child with learning disabilities such as dyslexia, the characteristic primitive plasticity and maturational lags may be demonstrated.

The neurologic aspects of dyslexia have been recently summarized by Whitsell.[27] He emphasizes heredity with a variety of soft neurologic signs, pointing to parieto-occipital dysfunction and cerebral ambilaterality. He also identifies a secondary dyslexia in children with minimal cerebral dysfunction resulting from identifiable perinatal disturbances. Overlapping, of course, may occur among these subgroups.

The concept of soft neurologic signs is derived from the work of Paul Schilder and myself.[25] The term applies specifically to neurologic deviations that occur in childhood developmental disorders, maturational lags, childhood schizophrenia, and the developmental dyslexias. It does *not* refer to a mild or borderline neurologic sign.

The maturation pattern of motility lags in these children is evident on careful testing of the postural reflex attitude and the tonic reflex attitude. Neck reflex dominance or whirling motility on the longitudinal axis normally becomes submerged when the child is between 5 and 7 years of age but may continue somewhat in dyslexic children. Gesell[16] has shown relationships between these attitudes in the fetal infant and subsequent action patterns. He suggested that these attitudes are very early manifestations of cortical dominance.

The postural reflex position, which reveals increased tone and, therefore, a higher position in the dominant hand constitutes a biologic test for dominance. In the configuration of the scalp hair whorl, mentioned by Critchley, I have looked for the scalp whorls as clockwise or counterclockwise. Perhaps left-handed persons have whorls that are counterclockwise. Orton discussed this about 30 years ago and believed the clockwise or counterclockwise pattern to be more significant than the lateralization of the whorl to the right or left side of the scalp.

Silver and Hagin[26] have reported that a discrepancy between the hand used for writing and the dominant hand as determined by the hand position test is diagnostic of dyslexia in the children studied by them. They also noted other soft neurologic signs, such as defects in right-left orientation, and visuomotor immaturities.

Cohn,[10] a neurologist, observed soft neurologic signs, time and space disorders, and right-left disorientation, and related them to slow maturation rates. He also showed behavioral distortions, which he interpreted on the basis of immaturities.

There has been some recent, important, sophisticated psychologic research by Birch and Belmont[6] that points out immaturities in development, relating to the integration of auditory and visual stimuli and to the maturation of right-left orientation in the body schema.

The visual motor gestalt function lends itself readily to study for plasticity through the Visual Motor Gestalt Test.[1, 5] It represents a scale of maturation of the visual motor gestalt function and reveals many immature characteristics in the child with learning disabilities.

De Hirsch, after her years of predicting, diagnosing, and correcting dyslexia in the young child, emphasizes especially the problems of maturation lags particularly in perceptual motor language and behavioral areas.[13] Anxiety is seen as an inherent factor in dysmaturation, further disorganizing the more vulnerable child, but often assisting the more capable.

The body image is the most complete gestalt experience involving the integration of all perceptual experiences impinging on the organism. It passes through maturational stages which in the child may be followed through the human figure drawing.

I would like to summarize the neuropsychiatric aspects of children with dyslexia. Neurologic patterns remain immature and poorly differentiated, and the longitudinal course shows lags in maturation. Global primitiveness and plasticity in all the perceptual experiences with immature perceptual motor gestalten involve the child's own self-awareness, body image, identification, time, and space orientation and object and interpersonal relationships. There is a specific deficit in symbol formation involving auditory, visual, and kinesthetic images and their interrelationships; there is also wide variation in the relative severity of the deficit in each of these perceptual and conceptual areas. Specific problems related to right-left disorientation and to clockwise versus counter-clockwise movement tendencies in both perceptual and motor activities occur.

Personality immaturity and infantilism are associated with inhibitions, withdrawal, regressions, unorganized "wild" behavior, and dependency. A deficiency in goal directedness is a conspicuous feature. Neurotic reactions or symptoms are influenced by inherent personality characteristics, life experiences, and the immediate situation. Anxiety and bewilderment drive the child to some type of solution which may lead to any type of emotional or behavioral disorder as a secondary characteristic.

Neuropsychiatric disturbances in children with dyslexia are as directly related to the congenital immaturities or maturational lags as the reading disability itself. The neuropsychiatric disturbances are characterized by plasticity in patterning of the undifferentiated, pleuri-potential global state, which is manifest in neurologic, perceptuomotor, language function, self-image, and personality areas. This has been documented by research from many areas. Many other types of reactive emotional and behavioral disorders may be expected in addition.

There also must be a solid understanding of the differential diagnosis between specific reading disabilities and other maturational lags, or of childhood schizophrenia, or minimal brain damage as a result of perinatal trauma; there is a chance that it is all four. There is no guarantee that a child has only one problem. Most children who come for help have problems in family experiences, life experiences, sociocultural setting (no one is perfectly oriented in his sociocultural setting), educational exposure, and teacher relations. It is also likely that there has been some minimal brain damage.

The incidence of dyslexia can be put in some sort of figures, perhaps 10 percent of the preschool population. Childhood schizophrenia also has a specific incidence, but we are even less sure of this. If 10 percent of children are dyslexic, then perhaps 10 percent of the schizophrenic children are dyslexic, perhaps 10 percent of the mentally defective children are dyslexic, and possibly 10 percent of most other children who have any problems are also dyslexic. We should expect combinations of dysfunctions and should less frequently expect a single dysfunction, such as dyslexia, in a child.

REFERENCES

1. Bender, L.: A visual motor gestalt test and its clinical use, New York, 1938, American Orthopsychiatric Association.
2. Bender, L.: Childhood schizophrenia, Amer. J. Orthopsychiat. **17**:40-56, 1947.
3. Bender, L.: Problems in conceptualization and communication in children with developmental alexia. In Hoch, P. H., and Zubin, J., editors: Psychopathology of communication, New York, 1958, Grune & Stratton, Inc.
4. Bender, L.: Psychiatric aspects in symposium on the concept of congenital aphasia from the standpoint of dynamic differential diagnosis, Washington, D. C., 1959, American Speech and Hearing Association.
5. Bender, L.: The visual motor gestalt function in six and seven year old normal and schizophrenic children. In Zubin, J., and Jervis, G. A., editors: Psychopathology of mental development, New York, 1967, American Psychopathological Association.
6. Birch, H. G., and Belmont, L.: Auditory-visual integration in normal and retarded readers, Amer. J. Orthopsychiat. **34**:852-861, 1964.
7. Blanchard, P.: Psychoanalytic contributions to the problems of reading disabilities, Psychoanal. Study Child. **2**:163-187, 1947.
8. Blau, A.: The master hand: a study of the origin and meaning of right and left sidedness and its relation to personality and language, New York, 1946, American Orthopsychiatric Association.
9. Buxbaum, E.: The parent's role in the etiology of learning disability, Psychoanal. Study Child. **19**:421-447, 1964.
10. Cohn, R.: Delayed acquisition of reading and writing abilities in children, Arch. Neurol. **4**:153-164, 1961.
11. Critchley, M.: Inborn reading disorders of central origin, Trans. Ophthal. Soc. **81**:459-480, 1961.
12. Critchley, M.: Developmental dyslexia, London, 1964, Wm. Heinemann Medical Books.
13. de Hirsch, K., Jansky, J. J., and Langford, W. S.: Predicting reading failure, New York, 1966, Harper & Row, Publishers.
14. Fabian, A. A.: Clinical and experimental studies of school children who are retarded in reading, Quart. J. Child Behav. **3**:15-37, 1951.
15. Gates, A.: The role of personality maladjustments in reading disabilities, J. Genet. Psychol. **59**:77-83, 1941.
16. Gesell, A.: The embryology of behavior—the beginning of the human mind, New York, 1945, Harper & Row, Publishers.
17. Hallgren, B.: Specific dyslexia (congenital word blindness), a clinical and genetic study, Acta Psychiat. et Neurol. **65** (suppl.), 1950. Copenhagen, Denmark.
18. Hamilton, W. J., Boyd, J. D., and Mossman, H. W.: Human embryology, Baltimore, 1962, Williams & Wilkins Co.
19. Jarvis, V.: Clinical observation on the visual problems of reading disabilities, Psychoanal. Study Child. **13**:451-470, 1958.
20. Koppitz, E. M.: The Bender Gestalt test in young children, New York, 1964, Grune & Stratton, Inc.
21. Mountcastle, V. B., editor: Interhemispheric relations and cerebral dominance, Baltimore, 1962, Johns Hopkins Press.
22. Orton, S. T.: Reading, writing and speech problems in children, New York, 1937, W. W. Norton & Co., Inc.
23. Rabinovitch, R. D., Drew, A. L., DeJong, R. N., Ingram, W., and Withey, L.: A research approach to reading retardation, Proc. Assoc. Research Nerv. & Ment. Dis. **34**: 363-396, 1956.

24. Rosen, V. H.: Strephosymbolia: An intrasystemic disturbance of the synthetic function of the ego, Psychoanal. Study Child. **10**:83-99, 1955.
25. Bender, L., editor: Contributions to developmental neuropsychiatry, by Paul Schilder, New York, 1964, International Universities Press, Inc.
26. Silver, A. A., and Hagin, R.: Specific reading disabilities—a delineation of the syndrome and relationship to cerebral dominance, Comp. Psychiat. **1**:126-134, 1960.
27. Whitsell, L. J.: Neurological aspects of reading disorders. In Flower, R. M., Gofman, H. F., and Lawson, L. I., editors: Reading disorders, Philadelphia, 1965, F. A. Davis Co.

Part 3: Ophthalmic disturbances

John V. V. Nicholls, M.D.

I shall discuss herein the manner in which ocular disturbances may affect reading ability, and I shall attempt to delineate the role of the ophthalmologist.

As an ophthalmologist, working in a university environment in a field which has fascinated me for nearly 20 years, I have examined and assisted in the handling of over 300 dyslexic children, a great number of whom I have been able to follow to this time.

An ophthalmologist is often the first to be consulted by the parents of a dyslexic child. The first thought appears to be that reading is done through the eyes, so let us see an eye physician. The ophthalmologist soon realizes that dyslexia is a complex problem—complex in etiology, complex in the analysis of cause in a particular case, and complex in treatment. *Only infrequently is dyslexia primarily an ocular problem.* Solution usually requires the coordinated efforts of people of several disciplines—family physician, neurologist, psychiatrist, pediatrician, otologist, ophthalmologist, psychologist, and educationalist—all of whom play important and correlated roles in the investigation, solution, and management of dyslexia. Treatment, in the final analysis, centers about education, assisted, of course, by the aforementioned disciplines.

When thinking of pure dyslexia, I am aware of my 20-year experience at the Low Vision Aid Clinic of the Royal Victoria Hospital, Montreal. Here we see children with very great visual deficiencies who have learned to read with facility. We must start from the base, therefore, that visual defects generally are only an added or associated difficulty. Of course, there are notable exceptions, which serve to keep the physician on guard; they do not alter the rule.

To an ophthalmologist, it is easiest to think of dyslexic patients as falling into one of the following three groups:

Congenital, or developmental, dyslexia. Congenital, or developmental, dyslexia is a specific, sometimes designated as primary, reading disability occurring in the presence of average or above-average intelligence, predominantly in males; it is apparently the result of neurologic dysfunction in the parietotemporal lobe of the dominant cerebral hemisphere, possibly genetic in origin.

The slow reader. Retardation in the slow reader is secondary to low intelligence, faulty vision or hearing, underlying emotional disturbances, or other detectable defects.

The mixed type. The mixed type of dyslexia is a combination of the previous groups; it forms the largest group.

Accurate diagnostic and etiologic categorization of a child is frequently difficult, reached only after much study by several people of different disciplines and the evaluation or elimination of one possible factor after another.

When considering the role of ocular disturbances in reading difficulties, one should start from the concept that reading is the recognition of visual symbols in terms of their auditory or phonetic equivalents, which, when interpreted through processes involving memory and association, lead to meaning. In this mechanism the ocular apparatus may be involved in the following two ways:

1. The child may find it impossible to obtain a clear, unitary visual image or to maintain such an image for a significant period of time.
2. The child may have to exert such an effort to obtain and maintain a clear unitary image that fatigue occurs, thus discouraging reading.

The first group of disorders to be considered here are refractive errors. The eye, which is basically a camera, may be affected by the three following types of refractive error:

1. Hyperopia, or farsightedness
2. Myopia, or nearsightedness
3. Astigmatism (In astigmatism the ocular curvatures, or refracting surfaces, are asymmetric [as in a football rather than a basketball] so that the image formed is out of focus, or blurred, in one axis.)

These disturbances occur in a wide range of severity and in many combinations. No eye is optically perfect or absolutely free from all irregularities. A small amount of refractive error can be found in every eye. Considerable experience and careful evaluation of symptoms in relation to physical measurements are required to determine the significance of the aberration found. A particular refractive error may be significant under certain circumstances but insignificant under other circumstances. The age of the patient, his visual requirements, his ocular health, and his general health, both physical and emotional, must be considered when making a decision.

Such a decision is a job for the medically trained eye physician—the ophthalmologist. In the absence of binocular coordination problems, there is no defense for prescribing lens corrections for small refractive errors or for prescribing bifocals.

Many investigators have studied the effect of refractive errors on reading ability. It is not surprising that there have been conflicting reports. Blake and Dearborn,[4] Farris,[9] and Taylor[15] all have noted a positive correlation. Eames[8] found hyperopia (farsightedness) of one diopter or more in 43 percent of children having reading difficulties, as against 12 percent in the control group. The correlation was not high in any of these studies because factors other than simple refractive error are operative. Eames also found, as one would expect, that astigmatism may cause fatigue and, therefore, interfere with perseverance in learning. Also as expected, Farris found that myopia is no handicap in reading.

Disturbances in ocular coordination or motility may also cause fatigue or asthenopia, but such disturbances are a relatively infrequent cause. The inability to keep one eye in alignment with the other eye is an obvious potential problem. A child with intermittent misalignment (heterotropia) when reading tends to lose his place because the reading matter may seem to jump or actually may be seen double. He will make regressions, and he will have difficulty progressing from line to line. Such poor progression in ocular fixations is common in congenital dyslexia even if no ocular motility problem is present. Thus, both central and peripheral components must be assessed for significance.

Absolute perfection (orthophoria) in ocular alignment is never found. Very commonly if the eyes are dissociated by covering one, the covered eye will wander or deviate. Binocular alignment is obtained and maintained through effort that originates in the desire to bring the center of sight of each eye to bear simultaneously upon the observed subject. If one eye deviates from the other, there will be diplopia, or double vision. The assessment of significance in any tendency for the eyes to deviate (heterophoria) depends upon the state of the innate muscle balance found and the particular clinical technique used to measure it, as opposed to the evaluation of the child's ability to maintain ocular alignment, i.e., his distaste for diplopia or his desire for binocular fusion. This assessment must take into consideration not only the ocular status of the child but also his general health, both physical and emotional, and his cerebral function. This, again, requires a fully qualified eye physician—the ophthalmologist.

Children very quickly evolve compensatory mechanisms for ocular motility problems that they find difficult to control. They may learn to suppress the image formed by one eye, usually the nondominant eye. This can be, and often is, learned in a few days. With the establishment of suppression, or amblyopia of disuse, the child no longer need attempt to control ocular alignment, and visual symptoms such as diplopia, headache, and ocular fatigue, which may have been intermittent or constant, disappear.

Many studies have attempted to relate motility disturbances to reading difficulties. Again, because of the complexity of the ocular assessment and multiple associated factors, there have been conflicting reports. Park[14] found esophoria or exophoria of more than 4 diopters significantly more often in poor readers. On the other hand, Eames[8] could not confirm this. More recently, Gruber[12] could find no significant correlation.

Eames,[8] Park,[14] and, more recently, Benton[1] and Frankling[11] have found convergence insufficiency significantly more frequently in children with reading difficulties, but this correlation is not high. Theoretically, convergence insufficiency in the presence of unstable binocular control (fusion) could lead to jumbling of reading matter, place losing, regressions, and difficulty in line changing. These latter dysfunctions accompany congenital dyslexia anyway, even in patients in whom there is excellent convergence and binocularity. An understanding and objective appraisal of measuring techniques are essential to assess possible ocular contributions in any particular dyslexic patient. One must also remember that convergence is the least stable of all coordinated ocular movements and is easily disturbed by poor health or emotional upsets.

Generally ocular motility problems (heterotropia and heterophoria) are not causative factors in the actual reading defects. Suppression of one eye is a very easy way out for a child, particularly in the preschool years. However, the effort required to control and maintain binocular alignment may be so great as to cause fatigue and discourage reading.

Dunlap[7] recently emphasized the role of heterophoria in slow readers as distinguished from specific dyslexic patients. Under certain conditions he believes even small misalignments in the absence of suppression may be significantly encumbering. Small vertical deviations, which always are difficult for the patient to control, were frequent in his selected series. He advocated surgical repositioning of the involved muscles. I cannot agree with a surgical approach to small horizontal deviations, and small vertical deviations can usually be adequately managed with prisms.

Another problem for ophthalmologists, neurologists, and remedialists is cerebral dominance—homolateral or crossed. Cerebral efficiency and muscular action appear to be facilitated when the hand, the eye, and the foot are dominant on the same side. The role of crossed, or mixed, dominance in dyslexia is difficult to assess and is controversial. Orton[13] in 1937 and, more recently, Berner and Berner,[3] Fink,[10] Crider,[5] Delacato,[6] and Benton, McCann, and Larsen[2] have stressed its importance. Some studies elicited an extremely high correlation. Within my experience during almost 30 years of practice, a large proportion of which has been with children, I have records of many youngsters having crossed dominance who are average or above-average readers. In my opinion the correlation between crossed dominance and all reading difficulties taken collectively is not high. However, in certain subtypes crossed dominance may be a causative factor in the child who is unable to keep place and makes regressions, and most certainly it would appear to be a significant factor in persistent reversals and mirror writing. My plea is to assess each patient in terms of the specific pathogenesis and the correlated disturbances.

REFERENCES

1. Benton, C. D., Jr.: Ophthalmological approach to the problem of retarded readers among elementary school children, J. Florida Med. Assoc. 47:1123, 1961.
2. Benton, C. D., McCann, J. W., and Larsen, M.: Dyslexia and dominance, J. Pediat. Ophthal. 2:55, 1965.
3. Berner, G. E., and Berner, D. E.: Relation of ocular dominance, handedness, and controlling eye in binocular vision, Arch. Ophthal. 50:603, 1953.
4. Blake, M. B., and Dearborn, W. F.: The improvement of reading habits, J. Higher Educ. 6:83, 1935.
5. Crider, B.: The importance of the dominant eye, J. Psychol. 16:145, 1943.
6. Delacato, C. H.: The treatment and prevention of reading problems, Springfield, Ill., 1959, Charles C Thomas, Publisher.
7. Dunlap, E. A.: Role of strabismus in reading problems, Trans. Pennsyl. Acad. Ophthal. Otolar. 18:9, 1965.
8. Eames, T. H.: Comparison of eye conditions among 1000 reading failures, 500 ophthalmic patients and 150 unselected children, Amer. J. Ophthal. 31:713, 1948.
9. Farris, L. P.: Visual defects as factors influencing achievement in reading, J. Exp. Educ. 5:58, 1936.
10. Fink, W. H.: The dominant eye: its clinical significance, Arch. Ophthal. 19:555, 1938.
11. Frankling, S. R.: A study of reading difficulties in Toronto school children, Canad. Med. Assoc. J. 85:237, 1961.
12. Gruber, E.: Reading ability, binocular coordination and the ophthalmograph, Arch. Ophthal. 67:280, 1962.
13. Orton, S. T.: Reading, writing and speech problems in children, New York, 1937, W. W. Norton & Co., Inc.
14. Park, G. E.: Reading difficulty from the ophthalmic point of view, Amer. J. Ophthal. 31:28, 1948.
15. Taylor, E. A.: Controlled reading, Chicago, 1937, University of Chicago Press.

Part 4: Audiologic correlates

Philip E. Rosenberg, Ph.D.

In many animals, hearing contributes relatively little to life. In the large birds, for example, vision is of primary importance to preserving life. Vision is used to obtain food, to escape predators, and to find a mate. Hearing is relegated to secondary importance. In most small mammals, however, hearing is of great importance. Many small animals depend upon their hearing for food, for reproduction, and for their very existence. Still other creatures use hearing in other than a signal and warning sense. For example, the bat achieves superb locomotion and guidance through a highly developed and exquisitely sensitive auditory organ. Man falls somewhere in between and yet beyond in his use of hearing. Man uses his hearing not only for signal, warning, and awareness of his environment but also for the hallmark of his humaness—language.

It is difficult to speak of reading without putting it in a broader context of the general language function. In the normal developmental schedule, reading is one of the last language arts to be learned. The acquisition of receptive and inner language skills followed by expressive language in the form of speech normally occurs during the first 2 years of life. By the age of 5 years, the normal child's language facility is remarkably advanced and, in fact, largely crystallized. But the normal child is not the concern of this conference. Rather, it is the child with specific language disability which is frequently but a part of a broader, more pervasive language disorder.

A disturbing trend in the early diagnosis of language disorders has appeared in recent years. This trend concerns the concept of disorders that are not peripheral in origin; and terms such as "aphasia," "congenital aphasia," "neurologic scramble," "central auditory imperception," "central dysacousis," "neurologic deafness," and "central deafness" are widely used. Although such entities exist, the proliferation of these diagnoses is absurdly out of proportion to the possibility of their occurrence in the general population. The inability of the young child to develop language skills according to a developmental schedule often results in a diagnosis of mental retardation, emotional disturbance, autism, or brain damage. This is not necessarily so.

We have seen in the Audiology Department of Temple University Medical Center a large number of children between the ages of 1 and 5 years who exhibit language deficiency of greater or lesser degree. Occasionally we see an almost total lack of language development; more frequently we see language deficiency or retardation in one or more areas. We find that the majority of these children, many of whom have been diagnosed as aphasic, autistic, or retarded, have a peripheral hearing deficit that is causing the language problem. Other factors may coexist to confound the problem, but more frequently they do not.

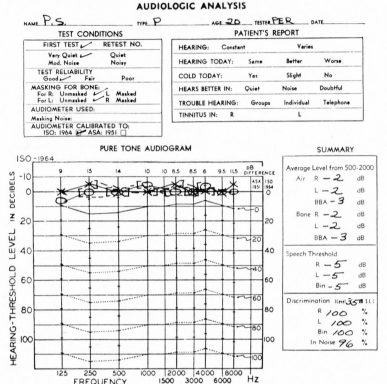

Department of Otorhinology - Section of Audiology

TEMPLE UNIVERSITY MEDICAL CENTER

Philadelphia, Pennsylvania 19140

AUDIOLOGIC ANALYSIS

Fig. 5-3. Normal audiogram.

Audiologists study hearing in several ways. First, we are interested in auditory thresholds for pure tones. Although people rarely listen to a single frequency, their responses to these sounds provide helpful quantitation about the auditory system in general. Fig. 5-3 shows a normal audiogram. Thresholds are obtained from 125 cycles per second through 8,000 cycles per second. Although human beings are able to hear well below 125 and substantially above 8,000 cycles per second, this is not of particular interest. The overtones of the piccolo or the subharmonics of diapason organ pipes contribute little to human communication, although they add to aesthetic fulfillment. On the right side of Fig. 5-3 you see tests of meaningful material in which speech is the stimulus. These tests concern threshold sensitivity and the ability to discriminate among speech sounds and words when they are made loud enough to hear. A child with hearing such as this would certainly have no auditory defect contributing to a language problem. Fig. 5-4 shows the audiogram of a deaf child. Only a fragment of hearing limited to high intensity levels remains; this child is unquestionably deaf. He will not develop speech without intensive special education and guidance. His

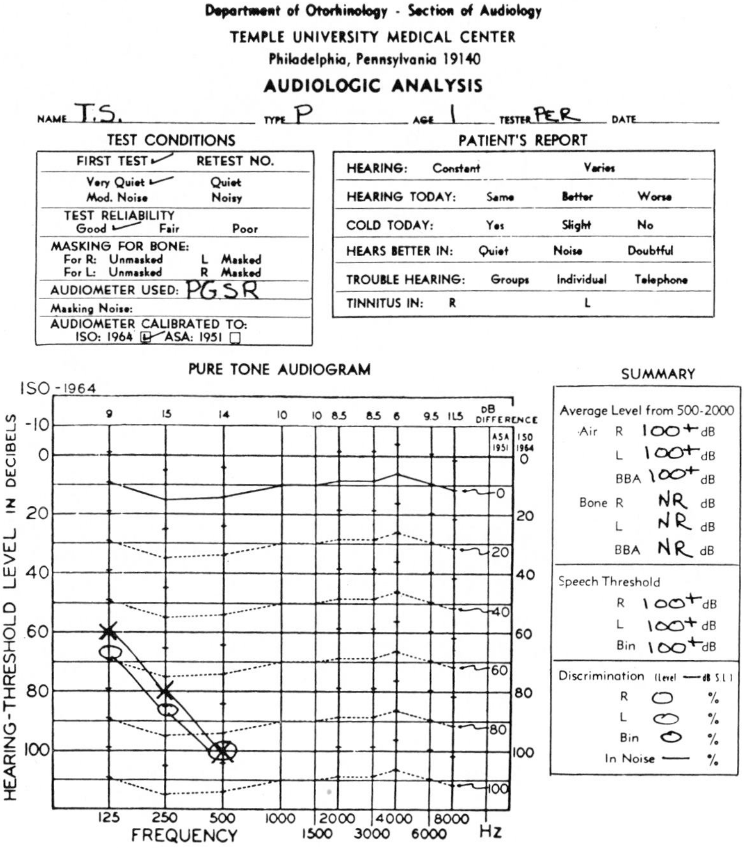

Fig. 5-4. Audiogram of a deaf child.

language skills will suffer because of retardation in the development of receptive, inner, and expressive function. All children, however, do not fall into these two categories. There is a type of child who develops speech on schedule, although the speech is frequently defective. His language behavior is often barely adequate, and his reading facility is frequently poor. This is the child with a relatively simple but easily missed type of hearing problem. Fig. 5-5 shows the audiogram of such a child. Note that hearing in the low frequencies is entirely normal. If you recall that the fundamental frequency of laryngeal vibration is approximately 100 cycles per second in the male and 200 cycles per second in the female, you can see that this child would hear at normal levels; i.e., if somebody spoke to him, even softly, he would be aware of the acoustic signal. When this child was an infant, if somebody made a slight noise while he was sleeping, he would awake. If somebody spoke softly behind his back, he would turn. However, in a real sense he does not hear. He hears speech as a loud signal. He hears vowel sounds clearly and distinctly and hears some consonant sounds only fairly well. He does not hear most of the consonant sounds. He frequently has articulatory

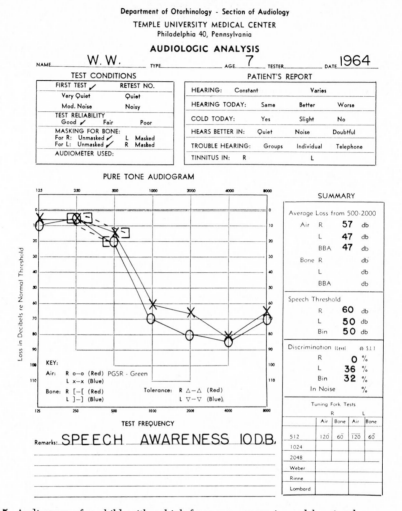

Fig. 5-5. Audiogram of a child with a high-frequency, sensorineural hearing loss.

errors in speech that reflect the way he hears others talk. Fig. 5-6 is a similar audiogram of a bright child, diagnosed as aphasic, who had been attending a special school for aphasic children. His progress was poor until auditory testing revealed the hearing deficit. He was fitted with a hearing aid suitable to his defect, and his subsequent development of language, including reading, was meteoric.

Despite remarkable improvements in medical and surgical amelioration of deafness over the past 20 years, the problems that have been discussed in this section cannot be treated by these means. Most medical and surgical procedures that have been widely publicized are used to treat conductive hearing impairments. These are impairments caused by external or middle-ear malformation or disease, and they occur with relative infrequency in children. Furthermore, the

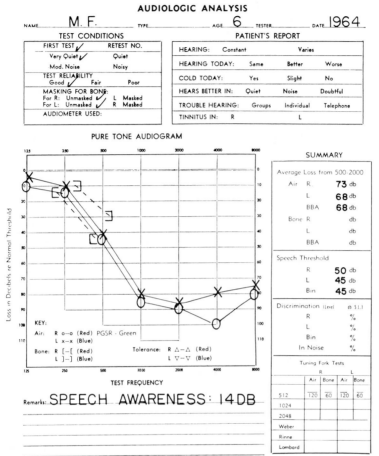

Department of Otorhinology - Section of Audiology

TEMPLE UNIVERSITY MEDICAL CENTER
Philadelphia 40, Pennsylvania

AUDIOLOGIC ANALYSIS

NAME __M. F.__ TYPE ___ AGE __6__ TESTER ___ DATE __1964__

Fig. 5-6. Audiogram of a bright child with high-frequency hearing loss, misdiagnosed as aphasic.

type of hearing loss they cause is more typical of the stereotype of auditory deficiency, since the child will respond to sound only if it is loud and then he responds consistently. Children who develop language problems, however, have hearing losses that are purely sensorineural. The pathology is in the hair cells of the organ of Corti, in the spiral ganglion, or in the eighth cranial nerve. On rare occasions the brain stem or the auditory radiations of the temporal lobe may also be involved. For these problems, unfortunately, there is neither medical nor surgical treatment. There are many causes for the high-frequency, sensorineural hearing loss that affects all areas of language development. Rh incompatibility with resultant erythroblastosis fetalis, maternal rubella, birth anoxia, and hereditary factors can all cause this type of impairment.

The physiology of hearing is charmingly described by Aldous Huxley in *Point Counter Point*. Huxley describes Lord Edward's hearing as follows:

> Pongileoni's blowing and the scraping of the anonymous fiddlers had shaken the air in the great hall, had set the glass of the windows looking on to it vibrating; and this in turn had shaken the air in Lord Edward's apartment on the further side. The shaking air rattled Lord Edward's membrana tympani; the interlocked malleus, incus, and stirrup bones were set in motion so as to agitate the membrane of the oval window and raise an infinitesimal storm in the fluid of the labyrinth. The hairy endings of the auditory nerve shuddered like weeds in a rough sea; a vast number of obscure miracles were performed in the brain, and Lord Edward ecstatically whispered "Bach!"

When these obscure miracles do not take place or take place imperfectly, the signal, whether it be music, noise, or speech, is either absent or distorted. The children I see with high-frequency, sensorineural hearing impairments hear music with adequate loudness and undisturbed rhythm. The melodic line, however, is practically destroyed. The rich overtone structure of the music is largely absent. The understanding of speech is even more severely affected. Vowel sounds may be heard normally, while high-frequency consonant sounds are not heard. This often renders speech totally unintelligible.

The early development of children with such auditory discrimination losses in terms of response to sound and the acquisition of language follows a fairly regular pattern. In the early months of life, sometimes until the age of 1½ or 2 years, these children respond consistently to auditory stimulation just as other children. They attempt to localize sound, they turn to it, and they smile at noises. Soon, however, their responses become inconsistent because sound carries less meaning than it does to other children. Sometimes they respond to soft sounds. At other times even a loud sound will not elicit a response. They begin to fall far behind in language structure. Although speech develops (slower than usual), it tends to contain many articulatory disorders. When the child is 5, 6, or 7 years old, his inner language structure is not sufficient to afford normal learning of reading, and he begins to encounter academic difficulties. Because of the language deficit and apparent inconsistency of the auditory response, the physician or the teacher frequently suspects brain damage. Indeed, the symptoms presented by the child are not unlike those of the brain-damaged child. A diagnosis of aphasia or minimal brain dysfunction is then applied. The specialized teaching techniques used with brain-injured children do not succeed with this child, and he falls further and further behind.

If a child's hearing is examined thoroughly and competently by a skilled examiner, the auditory defect can be detected and described by the age of 1 or 1½ years. Proper remedial efforts may then be undertaken. With the advance in modern electronic science, hearing aids that emphasize the specific defects and permit no amplification in ranges where hearing is good can be obtained. This type of hearing aid improves the child's understanding of speech dramatically while not influencing his already good hearing acuity. The use of a hearing aid by itself may often overcome the language deficit. More frequently, however, it is necessary to enroll the child in a special program of language training and auditory rehabilitation. This combination of special amplification and special education yields dramatic improvement in language skills. If the loss is detected early enough and if rehabilitative measures are employed when the child is 2 or 2½ years of age, it is probable that by the age of 5 or 6 years the child will be able to enter a normal classroom with language skills commensurate to his age. Reading then presents no greater challenge to him than to the child with normal auditory function. Many techniques for diagnosis and rehabilitation are available today. If children with the peripheral deficit were diagnosed and treated properly, a small segment of the apparently dyslexic population would disappear. The possibility of this rather specific hearing loss should be considered when a deficiency is observed in any of the language areas. Delayed speech, faulty articulation, apparent receptive or expressive language difficulties, or dyslexia should suggest the possibility of a peripheral hearing impairment, which may be resolved through the use of amplification and special teaching techniques.

Language should be thought of in a broad context. John Milton may have been speaking of language when, in "Il Pensoroso," he spoke "of forests and enchantments drear, where more is meant than meets the ear."

Chapter 6

Kindergarten protocols of high achievers, slow starters, and failing readers*

Katrina de Hirsch, F.C.S.T.

Jeannette Jefferson Jansky, M.S.

This chapter describes the kindergarten functioning of three groups of children whom we identified at the end of the second grade on the basis of their achievement scores in reading and spelling. The groups were as follows:

1. The children whose reading and spelling scores were very high—the high achievers.
2. The children who presented difficulties in learning to read at the end of the first grade but who managed to pass achievement tests by the end of the second grade—the slow starters.
3. The children who entirely failed all tests at the end of the second grade—the failing readers.

How did these three groups of children function at kindergarten age, i.e., before they were exposed to formal education? To answer this question we went back not only to the children's performance on the thirty-seven original kindergarten tests (Chapter 4) but also to the notes and observations we collected for the profiles written about each kindergarten child, in which we attempted to catch their characteristic style of approach. Our main interests were, of course, the failing children, and we hoped that a description of their kindergarten functioning would help teachers in the identification of such high risk youngsters.

CHARACTERISTICS OF THE FAILING READERS

Eight children showed massive reading and spelling difficulties at the end of the second grade. All of them scored zero on the Gray Oral Reading test

*As was Chapter 4, this presentation is based on a study supported by the Health Research of the City of New York Contract U-1270 and carried out under the auspices of Columbia University in the department of and under the guidance of William S. Langford. The investigation is preliminary in nature, and a validation study is underway.

administered at the end of the first grade. Five of them failed to score a year later; the remaining three children rated 9 months below the norm. Thus, 2 years in the elementary grades made little or no impression on these youngsters as far as reading and spelling were concerned.

The failing reading group consisted of three Negro children and five Caucasian children. In all but one case, one or both parents had, at least, attended high school. Seven of the eight children were enrolled in kindergarten; at the end of the second grade they attended eight different schools—three parochial schools and five public schools. Intelligence quotients in the group ranged from 94 to 116.

Six of the eight failing children were boys. The preponderance of boys among children with difficulties in reading and related language skills has been interpreted in view of the theoretical position of the various researchers. Kagan[15] maintains that boys do not find activities in the primary grades congruent with their masculine role. We were considerably impressed, on the other hand, with Tanner's findings[24] that around the age of 6 years boys lag 12 months behind girls in skeletal age; in other words, there appear to be physiologic reasons for boys' inferior academic performance. Bentzen[5] believes that learning problems in boys may be the response of the immature organism to the demands of a society that fails to make appropriate provision for the biologic age differential between boys and girls. Bryant[6] speaks of the boys' lesser capacity to mature smoothly.

Five of the failing readers were unusually small in stature. In the absence of information as to parental stature, it would be hazardous to generalize from this observation. However, Olson[18] believes that biophysical and educational age are related and that reading is tied to the entire developmental process. Simon[22] reports that her failing subjects tended to be "immature" on a battery of anthropomorphic indices. Karlin[16] found a small but statistically significant correlation between carpal development and reading ability in first grade. Ilg and Ames[14] draw attention to the relationship between teething schedule and school achievement.

Clinically, it was evident from the start that the failing readers were unable to respond to the testing in a purposeful and organized way. Five of them were markedly hyperactive, distractible, impulsive, and disinhibited. They needed many opportunities to move around the room, and they became resentful when required to sit still. Three of the children presented the opposite picture in terms of activity level. They were hypoactive, had difficulties maintaining a sitting posture, and tended to slump.

While the throwing of the failing readers was slightly hypotonic, their gross motor performance was not, on the whole, particularly deviating. Their finer motor control, on the other hand, was quite poor. They were slow in inserting pegs into a board, and most had severe difficulties with graphomotor tasks and could hardly hold a pencil. One was reminded of Orton's observation[19] as to psychomotor lags in children suffering from difficulties with the spoken and printed aspects of language.

Contrary to expectations, ambilateral responses at kindergarten age were no more frequent among the failing readers than among the slow starters and the high achievers. Differences were, however, found in body image. While the failing readers' human figure drawings were not bizarre, they were fragmented, lacked cohesiveness, and were strikingly crude and undifferentiated.

The auditory, perceptual, and oral language tools of the failing readers were decidedly inferior as compared to those of the remaining subjects. Their auditory discrimination, for instance, seemed to be extraordinarily diffuse. In fact, several of the children insisted that words like pen and pin sounded exactly alike. At young ages the reception of these children was clearly diffuse and undifferentiated. Their recognition vocabulary was limited; they often showed gross gaps in language comprehension; in fact, a number of them were entirely unable to listen. Their way of coming to terms with the environment was through action. They had trouble understanding not only time and space concepts but also concepts like same and different, which handicapped them on reading-readiness tests. They had equally striking difficulties with the expressive aspects of language. Only two children presented severe articulatory defects, but the stories of five others were primitive, lacking in cohesiveness, and poorly integrated. Word-finding difficulties were a frequent occurrence. For instance, when shown the picture of a stove, the child might say, "That kitchen thing." In short, our failing readers showed numerous and severe oral language deficits at kindergarten age.

The failing readers were equally immature in the visual area. Leton[17] maintains that certain deficiencies in oculomotor functions are related to delayed maturation rather than to peripheral visual defects. Gesell,[13] in his book on vision in 1949, stressed the fact that vision in children cannot be discussed as a separate function; it is part of the child's total growth. Visual functions mature between the ages of 5 and 7 years or even later, and I am fairly sure that at kindergarten age our failing children were as immature visually as they were auditorily. Their immaturity clearly involved the total organism, not the peripheral visual apparatus alone. Reading is essentially a perceptual function, involving central processes; thus, one wonders as to the helpfulness of visual exercises for older children who are slow in learning to read. At any rate, our failing readers did poorly in visuomotor tasks. They had difficulties copying the Bender gestalten; their designs flowed into each other, testifying to the plastic and fluid character of their visuomotor experiences. Moreover, most of their copies were strikingly crude and undifferentiated and showed evidence of perceptual fragmentation. Practically all of the poor readers failed, at kindergarten age, to respond to the critical features of letters and words when asked to match them on reading-readiness tests. They failed to take in the overall gestalt of the word or its intricate internal design. Moreover, the word configurations did not seem to stick; they seemed to float and were as unstable as—for these children—were their auditory experiences. When the children were required to select from a number of words one which had been exposed earlier, they behaved as if the printed signs represented a series of meaningless designs, all looking more or less alike and lacking distinctive physiognomic features.

Bender,[1] whose insight into the complexity and pathology of growth processes is basic to our own investigation of clinical phenomena, has shown that development moves from the unstable and diffuse in the young child to the more stable and more sharply defined in the older child. The failing readers seemed to have progressed but little, and in this sense they resembled a chronologically younger group.

While all eight children appeared to be physiologically immature, five of them were specifically described in the protocols as infantile. Whining, difficulties with separation from the mother, and an excessive need for candy were subsumed under this term. Two of the five youngsters had to be taken on the examiner's lap to complete the testing. In terms of Anna Freud's[12] developmental lines, these children were relatively unseparated from their mothers; their dependency needs still were considerable. A child's readiness to meet new events is seen by Anna Freud as the direct outcome of the developmental process. An essential part of this progress from play to work is the transition from the pleasure to the reality principle. Our failing readers had not made this transition. Even those three youngsters who did not strike us as particularly dependent, who separated easily from their mothers, and who enjoyed the testing sessions (the attention they received and the play in which they were allowed to indulge) were quite unable to maintain the tension required for tasks that did not provide immediate gratification. To quote Anna Freud,[12] these children, like chronologically younger subjects, ". . . could not carry out preconceived plans with a minimum of regard for immediate pleasure yield, intervening frustration and maximum regard for the pleasure of the ultimate outcome." These particular three youngsters had plenty of energy, but they were unable to mobilize this energy in the service of the tasks. This inability appeared to be only one aspect of a pervasive organismic immaturity that could be observed in both the physiologic and psychologic segments of functioning. The failing readers' physiologic immaturity and their delayed psychic maturation appeared to be different aspects of the same developmental lag.

PROBLEMS OF PREMATURITY

Another group of children in our project consisted of prematurely born youngsters—children, in other words, who had started out life with neurophysiologic lags and who showed similar and, in some instances, striking developmental delays. The premature youngsters' objective performance on thirty-six out of thirty-seven kindergarten tests was weaker than that of their full-term peers and, in many instances, resembled that of the failing readers. These premature children showed signs of catching up in the early elementary school years, but even when I.Q. differences were taken into account, their performance on the Bender Gestalt and on end-of-second-grade reading tests was significantly inferior to that of the children born at term.

Clinically, many of our premature children acted very much like our failing readers. They seemed relatively diffuse and had trouble mobilizing energy in the service of the tasks. Many seemed very infantile. Their central nervous system patterning appeared to be primitive, and they presented subtle deficits in motor, perceptual, and visuomotor organization, difficulties which receded but which were still apparent in the early elementary grades.

CHARACTERISTICS OF THE SLOW STARTERS

Our group of slow starters consisted of four boys and four girls. Like the failing readers group, they scored zero on the Gray Oral Reading test at the end of the first grade. Unlike the failing readers group, they caught up at the end of their second year in the elementary grades. Thus, in reading at least, their difficulties were transient, and with continued growth and instruction they learned to cope.

The slow starters' kindergarten protocols did not reveal hyperactivity or disinhibition. At kindergarten age they had apparently achieved a measure of behavioral control. Their human figure drawings were less crude than those of the failing readers, their auditory discrimination less diffuse, and their stories less improverished and fragmented. They had far less trouble with the organization of the visual field. The slow starters, in short, did fairly well on less complex activities, but they began to fail when they moved on to activities that called for more highly integrated performances, such as the Bender Gestalt, story organization, and most reading-readiness tasks, all of which are fairly abstract tasks. At the kindergarten level the slow starters' perceptuomotor experiences were better organized and their central nervous system patterning less primitive than that of the failing readers, but on tests requiring more differentiated responses, their difficulties became apparent.

Up to a point, these difficulties persisted. While all eight slow starters managed to pass reading tests at the end of the second grade, the spelling achievement of one-half of the group remained inferior; a measure of perceptual instability continued to be a feature of their performance.

CHARACTERISTICS OF THE HIGH ACHIEVERS

The high achievers' test scores constituted the top 15 percent of the sample, both in reading and spelling. Their reading at the end of the second grade ranged from 1 to 2 years above the norm. The group consisted of two boys and six girls. When they entered the first grade they were older—6 years, 5 months or above—than were the two other groups, thus confirming Ilg and Ames'[14] contention of generally higher achievement among overaged pupils rather than among underaged pupils. (Exceptions have been discussed in Chapter 4.) The high achievers were specifically described in the protocols as mature and physically well developed. They were self-contained and able to organize themselves and their environment without apparent effort. The tests themselves exerted considerable pull on these children—their enjoyment of mastery for its own sake pointed to a measure of ego autonomy. Their kindergarten functioning was uniformly excellent; there were isolated drops in performance, but these were offset by top scores in all areas. The high achievers displayed advanced linguistic ability; the most complex sentence structures were found in the stories of children in this group. Their high order performance on the reading-readiness tasks, which require a high degree of integrative competence, was most impressive.

DISCUSSION OF FINDINGS

Fig. 6-1 shows the number of children in each of the three groups—failing readers, slow starters, and high achievers—who failed representative kindergarten tests. This clearly shows that the failing readers' kindergarten performance was strikingly inferior compared to that of the other two groups. The kindergarten functioning of the three groups as they ranged from failing to passing to superior shows a progression from primitive responses to differentiated responses among the superior achievers. French[11] states that some children have great difficulties stabilizing at high levels of perceptual organization. The failing readers were such children. Their kindergarten performance was less stable and more primitive than that of the other two groups.

However, it was not failure on any *single* task that distinguished the failing readers from other subjects in the study but rather the severity and the accumulation of deficits. As early as 1935, Castner[8] spoke of a *cluster* of traits that characterizes the kindergarten functioning of youngsters who were liable to have trouble with reading later on. Diagnosis of reading disability does not depend on any single pathognomonic sign but depends on an appraisal of the whole configuration of dysfunctions. We believe that these dysfunctions—as

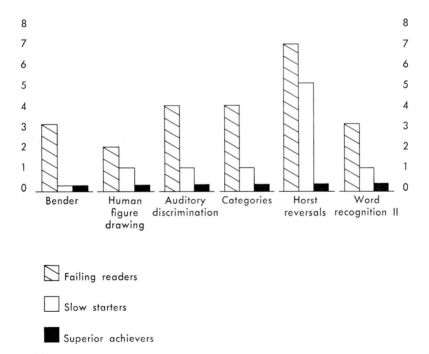

Fig. 6-1. Number of children in each of three groups, failing readers, slow starters, and high achievers, who failed on representative kindergarten tests. (From de Hirsch, K., Jansky, J. J., and Langford, W. S., Predicting reading failures, New York, 1966, Harper & Row, Publishers.)

long as they are not related to encephalopathy—indicate severe maturational lags, a concept we share with Bender,[2] Silver and Hagin,[20] Critchley,[10] and others. We are inclined to think—as does Zangwill[25]—that a tendency to immature patterning may rest on a genetic basis.

In the slow starters these lags were at least partially overcome with ongoing development. However, clinical experience shows that in some children severe lags may persist into later ages.

COMPARISON WITH OLDER DYSLEXICS

The practical limitations of our study did not permit us to follow the failing children beyond the second grade. As an alternate procedure, we inspected the records of older subjects—boys between 11 and 15 years of age who had been referred to us in 1964 for severe reading, writing, and spelling disabilities. We excluded those subjects who had been diagnosed by the referring psychiatrist or psychologist as primarily emotionally disturbed and those whose history gave rise to a suspicion of brain injury. These older boys—16 of them—came from middle-class or upper middle-class homes, all of them attended private schools, and their I.Q.'s ranged from 115 to 142.

Compared to our young failing readers, these subjects, being older, were no longer markedly hyperactive. However, they exhibited a relatively large number of associated movements on the finger-thumb touching test, a feature that normally disappears at earlier ages. Many of these older boys had failed to establish a functional superiority of one hand over the other. While such failure is common in young children, it is much rarer in the age range between 11 and 15 years. Identical phenomena have, of course, entirely different meanings at different ages. Associated movements, ambiguous lateralization and deficits in left-right awareness are normal in young subjects, but at older ages they reflect, as does the reading disability itself, immaturity of central nervous system organization. It is of interest in this context that Subirana[23] found more mature electroencephalograms in strongly right-handed than in ambidextrous children.

The perceptuomotor lags in our older boys were more subtle than those found in our failing readers at kindergarten age. Benton[4] maintains that these lags disappear entirely in older subjects. However, Silver and Hagin,[20] who followed severely retarded readers into young adulthood, reported persisting perceptuomotor deficits, and Bryant[7] found that most of his older reading disability patients continued to present some motor dysfunctions. Our own clinical experience confirms it. The particular group of intelligent older boys discussed here resembled our failing readers in a number of ways, although on a higher level. The older children's human figure drawings were less primitive, but they were, nevertheless, remarkably crude; their Bender Gestalt tests showed persisting difficulties with synthesis and spatial orientation. Particularly striking among the older boys was diffuse auditory discrimination. Word-finding difficulties and trouble with formulation of thought content was present in every case, and the oral and written verbal output of all of the sixteen boys was disorganized. None of them was able to tell a complex story coherently and clearly.

Most of them had graphomotor difficulties, and some held the pencil in an atavistic fashion. Their handwriting was jerky, messy, and tended to break down in longer compositions. The frequent association between writing and spelling difficulties has been stressed by Orton[19] and his pupils. One-half of the children in the older group became adequate readers; their intelligent use of contextual clues enabled them to compensate for their early perceptual deficits. Typically, they did fairly well on comprehension tests in which context helped them to figure out the correct answers to the multiple-choice questions on the test. However, most of them scored more than a year lower on the vocabulary section of the same test—in isolated words their perceptual difficulties came again to the fore. Bizarre spelling was an outstanding feature in the older group. The older boys found it impossible to "maintain a linguistic gestalt." Words for them looked different at different times and in different contexts. Their recall of the printed configurations remained unstable. Pervasive instability, which, according to Bender,[3] is the characteristic dysfunction in maturational lags, interfered with the reproduction of the printed configurations as it is required for spelling.

Reviewing the kindergarten protocols of our high achievers, we found a conspicuous absence of such instability. It was evident in the performance of our slow starters but less pervasive and less severe than in the children who failed all reading and spelling tests 2½ years later.

SUMMATION

When working with underprivileged children, one is struck with the instability, the diffuseness, and the primitivity of their auditory and visual perceptual experiences, even at relatively high age levels. Not only are these children deprived of affect and cultural stimulation but also a great many of them impress one as remarkably immature neurophysiologically. Of interest in this context is a recent report from Herbert Birch of the Albert Einstein group, New York, which comments on the relationship between protein deficiencies, on the one hand, and neurophysiologic immaturity and integrational difficulties, on the other hand.

Whatever the cause of such lags in neurophysiologic maturation—environmental, genetic, or other—these lags are bound to interfere with activities as complex as reading, writing, and spelling, which require a high degree of integrational competence. In some children this immaturity is transient; in others it is so severe that it seems rooted in the very biologic matrix of the child and constitutes a type of cerebral dysfunction.

Children who fail in elementary grades display a characteristic configuration of dysfunction at early ages; this configuration can and should be identified at the kindergarten level.

REFERENCES

1. Bender, L.: Problems in conceptualization and communication in children with developmental alexia. In Hoch, P., and Zubin, J., editors: Psychopathology of communication, New York, 1958, Grune & Stratton, Inc.
2. Bender, L.: Mental illness in childhood and heredity, Eugenics Quart. **10**:1-11, 1963.

3. Bender, L.: Plasticity in developmental neurology and psychiatry. In Hoch, P., and Zubin, J., editors: Schizophrenia, New York, 1966, Grune & Stratton, Inc.
4. Benton, A. L.: Dyslexia in relation to form perception and directional sense. In Money, J., editor: Reading disability, progress and research needs in dyslexia, Baltimore, 1962, Johns Hopkins Press.
5. Bentzen, F.: Sex ratios in learning and behavior, Amer. J. Orthopsychiat. 33:92-98, 1963.
6. Bryant, N. D.: Reading disability: part of a syndrome of neurological dysfunctioning. In Figurel, J. A., editor: Challenge and experiment in reading, Conference Proceedings of the International Reading Association 7:139-143, 1962.
7. Bryant, N. D.: Some conclusions concerning impaired motor development among reading disability cases, Bull. Orton Soc. 14:16-17, 1964.
8. Castner, B. M.: Prediction of reading disability prior to first grade entrance, Amer. J. Orthopsychiat. 5:375-387, 1935.
9. Cravioto, J., De Licardie, E. R., and Birch, H. G.: Nutrition, growth and neurointegrative development: an experimental and ecologic study, Pediatrics (suppl.) 38:319-372, 1966.
10. Critchley, M.: Developmental dyslexia, London, 1964, Wm. Heinemann Medical Books.
11. French, E. L.: Psychological factors in cases of reading difficulties, New York, 1953, Twenty-seventh Annual Conference of the Secondary Education Board.
12. Freud, A.: Normality and pathology in childhood, New York, 1965, International Universities Press, Inc.
13. Gesell, A., Ilg, F. L., and Bullis, G. E.: Vision: its development in infant and child, New York, 1949, Hoeber Medical Division (Harper & Row, Publishers).
14. Ilg, F., and Ames, L.: School readiness, New York, 1964, Harper & Row, Publishers.
15. Kagan, J.: The child's sex role classification of school objects, Child Development 35:151-156, 1964.
16. Karlin, R.: Physical growth and success in undertaking beginning reading, J. Educ. Res. 51:191-201, 1957.
17. Leton, D. A.: Visual-motor capacities and ocular efficiency in reading, Percept. Motor Skills 15:407-432, 1962.
18. Olson, W. C.: Child development, Boston, 1959, D. C. Heath & Co.
19. Orton, S. T.: Reading, writing and speech problems in children, New York, 1937, W. W. Norton & Co., Inc.
20. Silver, A. A., and Hagin, R.: Specific reading disability. Delineation of the syndrome and relationship to cerebral dominance, Comp. Psychiat. 1:126-134, 1960.
21. Silver, A. A., and Hagin, R.: Specific reading disability. Follow-up studies, Amer. J. Orthopsychiat. 34:95-102, 1964.
22. Simon, M. D.: Body configuration and school readiness, Child Development 30:493-512, 1959.
23. Subirana, A.: The problem of cerebral dominance: the relationship between handedness and language function, Logos 4:67-85, 1961.
24. Tanner, J. M.: Education and physical growth, London, 1961, University of London Press.
25. Zangwill, O. L.: Dyslexia in relation to cerebral dominance. In Money, J., editor: Reading disability, progress and research needs in dyslexia, Baltimore, 1962, Johns Hopkins Press.

Chapter 7

Word blindness: Neuro-ophthalmologic implications

Robert J. Kirschner, M.D.

When the ophthalmologist is called upon to evaluate a problem in dyslexia, there is a conventional tendency to study only the usual parameters of refractive abnormality and fusional status. We also must be aware of those cases of specific or developmental dyslexia in which a neurologic defect in the parietal areas of the cerebral cortex is presumed.

Since the report of Morgan, a vast literature, which attempts to draw analogy between congenital word blindness and the adult parietal patient, has developed.

Hinshelwood[8] proposed a detailed theory implicating the zone of parieto-occipital transition as the probable locus for many reading disorders. Critchley[2] has stated that such an association is strictly inferential because of a lack of autopsy material, but he has noted minor neurologic deficits in the developmental dyslexic patient that best fit the hypothesis of a parietospatial dysgnosia.

Mild forms of parietal dysfunction have been observed in the clumsy-child syndrome. Gubbay et al.,[6] in a study of twenty-one children presenting with severe clumsiness, noted a high incidence of agnosia and constructional apraxia, occurring with electroencephalographic abnormalities. Although developmental dyslexia may not arise from a single anatomic site as argued by Gallagher,[4] the cases of Drew,[3] Critchley, Gubbay, and others speak strongly for the existence of a congenital Gerstmann's syndrome.

Hermann[7] also states, "It is highly probable that congenital word blindness is dependent on the same disturbance of directional function which is responsible for the symptoms of Gerstmann's syndrome."

In 1924, Gerstmann[5] studied a 52-year-old woman recovering from a cerebrovascular accident and described right homonymous hemianopia, agraphia, acalculia, and finger agnosia. He ascribed the lesion to the region of the left angular gyrus. Later investigative work has confirmed the anatomic site of this so-called syndrome and reiterated the findings of laterospatial disorientation and defective word recognition.

Associated signs in the form of abnormal optokinetic nystagmus, defective depth perception, metamorphopsia, and color vision abnormalities have also been reported.

> **Case report.** A 46-year-old, right-handed female mathematician was seen in ophthalmologic consultation at the request of her neurologist. For several months prior to admission, she had noted increasing difficulty in the performance of simple calculations. She could no longer read business correspondence or recognize the characters on a telephone dial. The patient had previously undergone a laparotomy for ovarian carcinoma. Upon questioning, the patient was unable to name her own fingers or those of the examiner. There was no true right-left disorientation, but she claimed that, "People had large heads on small bodies." There was also a complete right homonymous hemianopia and an abnormal optokinetic response when the drum was rotated into the left field of gaze. Autopsy was obtained at her death. Pathologic examination showed a large solitary metastatic lesion deep in the left parieto-occipital region.

Several authors have called attention to impaired optokinetic nystagmus in such cases. Barany[1] believed that the slow phase of optokinetic nystagmus may originate in the angular gyrus or its underlying white matter. Smith and Cogan[10] have stressed the high incidence of primary parietal involvement when a positive optokinetic sign is present.

In a study of adults with proved minor hemisphere damage, Kinsbourne and Warrington[9] have demonstrated a high incidence of optokinetic abnormality. Their cases showed mainly paralexic difficulties as contrasted to the more profound abnormalities of perception when the dominant hemisphere is involved.

Since the ophthalmologist is often an early consultant in both pediatric and adult reading problems, he should be cognizant of the often subtle, soft parietal signs. Rarely, there may be a history of bizarre visual or sensory experiences, occasionally ending in a true motor seizure.

In children, parietal afflictions of long duration have been reported to cause atrophy or underdevelopment of the limbs on the involved side, as a result of spatial neglect and disuse.

From the neuro-ophthalmologic standpoint, careful visual-field examination and optokinetic testing can be performed by a variety of methods and are necessary for the complete evaluation of suspected visual agnosia in all age groups.

REFERENCES

1. Barany, R., Zur klinik und theorie des eisenbahnnystagmus, Acta Otolaryng. 3:260, 1921.
2. Critchley, M.: The parietal lobes, London, 1953, Edward Arnold and Co.
3. Drew, A.: Neurological appraisal of familial congenital word blindness, Brain **79**:440, 1956.
4. Gallagher, J. R.: Specific language disability (dyslexia), Clin. Proc. Child. Hospital, Wash. **16**:3, 1960.
5. Gerstmann, J.: Fingeragnosie eine umschriebene Storung der Orientierung am eigenen Korper, Wien. klin. Wchnschr. **37**:1010, 1924.
6. Gubbay, S. S., Ellis, E., Walton, J. N., and Court, S. D. M.: Clumsy children—a study of apraxic and agnosic defects in 21 children, Brain **88**:295, 1965.
7. Hermann, K.: Reading disability, Springfield, Ill., 1959, Charles C Thomas, Publisher.

8. Hinshelwood, J.: Congenital word blindness, London, 1917, H. K. Lewis & Co., Ltd.
9. Kinsbourne, M., and Warrington, E.: A variety of reading disability associated with right hemisphere lesions, J. Neurol. Neurosurg. Psychiat. **25:**339, 1962.
10. Smith, J. L., and Cogan, D. G.: Optokinetic nystagmus: a test for parietal lobe lesions; a study of 31 anatomically verified cases, Amer. J. Ophthal. **48:**187, 1959.

Questions and answers: Second session

Dr. Arthur Keeney: Mrs. de Hirsch, could you tell us what percentage of children in a school population might benefit from transitional classes?

Mrs. de Hirsch: All I can say is that in our sample, 20 percent of children were not ready for ordinary reading instruction. Ilg and Ames have found in their evaluation, which is not a predictive one, that in an upper middle-class population around Yale University, mostly professors' children, 40 percent of children were underaged at first grade entrance. I think that is putting it very strongly.

In any case, one probably can say safely that from 15 to 20 percent of children would do better if they were exposed to formal education somewhat later.

Dr. Arthur Keeney: Dr. Critchley, would you comment on dyslexia in relation to abnormal extinction phenomena, either visual, auditory, or tactile? Do dyslexics show abnormal extinction phenomena?

Dr. Critchley: What are extinction phenomena? Is this what we usually term "visual inattention"?

Dr. Arthur Keeney: Extinction phenomena, I presume, refers to the obscuration of one stimulus during simultaneous presentation of similar stimuli on each side of the body.

Dr. Critchley: Yes, I think what you mean by extinction is what we call inattention. Tactile or visual inattention occurs when, with bilateral simultaneous stimuli, only one stimulus is perceived. Inattention does not come into the dyslexia problem, as far as I know, in the visual or tactile sphere.

Dr. Arthur Keeney: I have another question, Dr. Critchley. If both eyes are normal, how can one eye be dominant when each eye supplies both halves of the brain?

Dr. Critchley: Because the eyes are used deliberately in an active function of looking; vision is not a passive process of reception. There are many circumstances in which one eye leads or does the work of two eyes, as, for example, when looking down a microscope or when aiming a gun.

Dr. Arthur Keeney: The next question is not addressed to a specific member of the panel, but probably Dr. Bender and Mrs. de Hirsch would like to comment. Are there any techniques that may speed up the maturation process?

Dr. Bender: I think Mrs. de Hirsch's statement that we have to deal with the child and not with techniques is a good answer to this question. I do not know of any techniques for speeding up maturation short of just time and living. One of the problem-producing features of our present culture is that we are in too big a hurry and want achievement from our children too fast. The idea that Mrs. de Hirsch suggests of an intermediate or transitional class would give more time to the child with the maturational problem. Time is the important factor.

Dr. Arthur Keeney: Would you amplify that, Mrs. de Hirsch?

Mrs. de Hirsch: Yes, I think one of the great gifts we can give a child is time. A child needs enrichment, stimulation, and care. All of these take time, as does, also, the development of interpersonal relationships. There is a type of child sometimes seen in first grade classes who is entirely disoriented in time and space. He does not know how he got there. He does not know why he is there. He has no idea what he is supposed to do, although he is quite bright. He has come to terms with the world so far only by action, not by way of verbalization. If you orient the child in time and space, if you orient him in terms of relationship, if you give him stimulation, and if you give him a chance to listen, I think you will do a good deal for him.

Dr. Arthur Keeney: Dr. Critchley has a comment to make on this topic.

Dr. Critchley: There may be another answer to this, in fact. For all we know to the contrary, lack of maturation or delayed maturation of the brain, constitutional and genetically determined though it be, may well be a metabolic dyscrasia.

Dr. Arthur Keeney: There have been some general questions concerning endocrinopathy in regard to dyslexia. Do you have a comment, Dr. Critchley?

Dr. Critchley: I know nothing about any endocrinopathic background to dyslexia. Neither do I know anything about any metabolic dyscrasia, but surely this is one way in which research will proceed in the future. We shall be looking for a genetically determined and transmitted metabolic dyscrasia, which *might* be reversible. In other words, there might be a chemical answer to this question of speeding up maturation.

Dr. Arthur Keeney: Dr. Bender, do you have a comment?

Dr. Bender: A great deal has been done on this in the United States, at least. An argument has been raised that dyslexic boys who are lagging in maturation in all the ways that have been described often have undescended testicles; therefore, treatment with male sex hormones has been tried. Also, thyroid has been tried on a similarly vague theory.

In the end, this has come to nothing except the poor boys have had some additional problems added onto their original difficulties.

Dr. Critchley: Rather than undescended testicles, I have in mind something more subtle, like an inborn error of acid metabolism.

Dr. Arthur Keeney: Next, a neuro-ophthalmic question. Are abnormal eye movements in dyslexia in the form of choreiform movements or of too many fixations, or do they become regressive movements?

Dr. Nicholls: This is a confusing area for the ophthalmologist. The frequent fixations and reversals that are so characteristic of the child with uncomplicated, or pure, congenital dyslexia, are very closely simulated by the child with an oculomotor problem. The ophthalmologist finds it difficult in many cases to determine the significance of his findings. For example, he may be tempted to interpret a measurable convergence insufficiency in the presence of unstable fusion as a truly significant factor in a particular case. On this basis the child may be given orthoptic exercises, and the fusion amplitudes may, thus, be brought to the accepted normal values; but then it is found that the child still has his problem—he still makes rapid short fixations, reversals, and repeatedly loses his place when reading. I do not know how to evaluate the significance of motor imbalance in any particular case except by trial and error. One merely eliminates the imbalances one finds and believes are significant.

Dr. Arthur Keeney: Dr. Critchley?

Dr. Critchley: This question really raises the problem of the nature of the eye movements during the act of reading. There have been some interesting pieces of work done on this, the latest from Paris. Undoubtedly, the eye movements, as recorded, are very abnormal indeed, with an excess number of fixations and also regressions. There is a great similarity between the ocular movements of a person when he is searching to identify the written word and the fingers of a blind man when he is reading Braille. Thus, if you record the finger movements of a blind man as he reads Braille, you find that the finger sweeps along until it comes to a difficult word. Then it halts, goes back a little, makes small circular movements over the Braille symbol, and carries on. Precisely the same pattern is to be found in the eye movements of a dyslexic child when he is trying to read. Technically, this is rather a difficult matter to demonstrate.

Dr. Arthur Keeney: Dr. Critchley, in the United States a photographic instrument, the ophthalmograph, has been used for several decades to make permanent records of eye movements while reading. It has fallen somewhat by the wayside. The instrument gives a photographic tracing of the corneal reflex from both eyes while the patient reads test material. Is this a valuable instrument in the diagnosis of ocular movement?

Dr. Critchley: This recording technique is also used by Dr. Yarbus in Russia. Professor Luria in Moscow has reported these tracings in cases of so-called visual agnosia. Here, the ophthalmogram reveals wide-range, sweeping ocular movements over the object under scrutiny, with or without an eventual hesitating identification of that object.

Dr. Arthur Keeney: Do you regard this as a practical instrument for diagnostic use in ophthalmic movement variation?

Dr. Critchley: Yes, even though it is not a perfect instrument. Some recording techniques are too crude, and some are far too delicate. We are still looking for the ideal method of recording eye movements.

Dr. Arthur Keeney: Dr. Bender, in the case of hyperkinetic children, is this activity a primary determinant of dyslexia, or is the hyperkinetic pattern secondary to other factors?

Dr. Bender: My concept of the hyperkinetic child is that the problem is not primarily hyperkinesis. This is a restless, seeking child because his structured environment is not getting through to his perceptive level. He is handicapped by his dyslexia or his immaturities and general lack of organization so that he is not getting enough gratification and satisfaction out of perceptual experiences. Therefore, he is restless and overactive, seeking to make some sense out of the stimuli which are produced in the world.

Additionally, there may be in these immature children and in children who have a degree of brain damage some impulse disorder which is usually increased reactivity. This generally is less important. The major problem is the child who is not getting enough gratification from his experience with stimuli from the world and does not understand them well enough.

Dr. Arthur Keeney: Dr. Critchley, do you think dyslexic children have comparable problems in reading musical scores?

Dr. Critchley: Occasionally, but not often. Nowadays, fewer children seem to be taught to read music. I have one excellent example in a patient who is a musician and a dyslexic, aged about 18 years. She is a pupil at the London School of Music, specializing in the cello. She plays beautifully and earns very high marks indeed, except in sight reading, which she cannot do. However, I do not believe there is any rule about this. I have known some dyslexics who can read music and others who cannot.

Dr. Arthur Keeney: Dr. Critchley, do you believe that dyslexia should be diagnosed before the age of 7 years? Can a definitive diagnosis be reached at this early age and yet be classified as developmental dyslexia?

Dr. Critchley: I am rather skeptical about the ability to do so.

Dr. Arthur Keeney: Mrs. de Hirsch, at what age should laterality be established or identifiable?

Mrs. de Hirsch: I do not think there is enough information about it. Everybody knows that young children are largely ambidextrous and that as they mature most of them develop a functional dominance of one side over the other.

Lateralization has both genetic and maturational aspects. There are many children, 7 or 8 years of age, who are still undetermined, and I do not think it means as much as if a child has ambiguous lateralization at 11 years. At the later age, it might mean encephalopathy; it might also mean an immaturity of central nervous system organization.

Dr. Arthur Keeney: My next question may produce some controversy from members of the panel. Can hand or eye dominance be changed? Dr. Critchley, would you comment?

Dr. Critchley: Yes, I think possibly both can be changed; certainly there is a natural trend for an ambidexter to become more right-handed.

Dr. Arthur Keeney: Is this a desirable therapeutic procedure in the course of handling dyslexic aberrant dominance?

Dr. Critchley: No.

Dr. Arthur Keeney: Is there any further comment from the panel in regard to the feasibility of changing ocular dominance?

Dr. Bender: Yes, I would raise a question as to whether you can change the dominance. I think you can train a child to use one hand or one eye or to acquire skill in this fashion, but the actual dominance is not changed. It will only appear changed, but the dominance itself, at a cerebral level, will probably not change. It is very questionable whether anything is accomplished by this in cases of dyslexia. Whether a child is more comfortable to be clearly right-handed rather than left-handed or mixed is a different matter. This is influenced by the cultural pattern. I question that it would have any effect upon the dyslexia itself.

Dr. Arthur Keeney: Would you describe a typical adult who has survived developmental dyslexia, Dr. Critchley? What are the findings in adult life by which you may recognize the developmental dyslexic?

Dr. Critchley: This is a most important question, and it emphasizes the need for longitudinal studies of dyslexics. We have many short-term follow-up studies of predyslexics and dyslexics, but what happens to the dyslexics in their 20's, 30's, and 40's is something we do not know enough about.

I have seen quite a number of adult dyslexics. Few are holding down a worthwhile profession or job because they simply cannot cope with the paperwork.

On the other hand, they can sometimes carry out forms of employment by dint of resort to memory. I can recall a dyslexic man about 30 years old who is a dental mechanic; he came to consult me, having driven his car from the north of England to London. I asked him how he managed to find his way and whether he could read the signposts. He said, "Not one of them." Despite this, he reached London without making any mistakes. Although he could scarcely read or write a word, he could remember, so his employer told me, the dental formulae of every one of the dental surgeon's patients.

In Honolulu recently, I saw an adult dyslexic engineer who employed twenty-seven subordinates, and he could not read or write. These are, however, rather fortunate and exceptional individuals. If one were to examine such adults from a neurologic and neuropsychologic point of view, I doubt very much if any abnormality or any of those soft neurologic signs we have heard about would be demonstrable.

Dr. Arthur Keeney: Mrs. de Hirsch?

Mrs. de Hirsch: I would like to draw your attention to a new study by Margaret Rawson. She has followed a group of dyslexic boys from age 11 or 12 years into their early 30's. These children, with help, moved ahead quite consistently throughout the years, and, interestingly, the vocational adjustment of these boys is surprisingly good.

I have had occasion to meet a number of engineers, and it seemed to me the number of successful engineers who are dyslexic is surprisingly large. It is true that most of them have learned to read, but most are left with severe spelling disabilities.

I do not think that one can generally say that dyslexic children do not achieve later. We need more studies. This study by Rawson is the only one, as far as I know, which has given some evidence of this.

Dr. Nicholls: I have been able to follow quite a number of these children over about 20 years, and it is my impression that there are degrees of intensity of dyslexia. About two-thirds to three-fourths of the children who have passed through my hands are now living successful lives, and many have gone through universities.

I might just mention my son, who had dyslexia. He is now 25 years old and a year or two ago earned an M.A. He received four A's and one B in his last year at university. His reading speed is around 350 words a minute. He is now, for amusement, writing poetry.

Dr. Arthur Keeney: Dr. Critchley, please sir?

Dr. Critchley: One of the determinants in the matter is whether the adult dyslexic had special tuition or not. There has been a very good follow-up study by Hermann at the Word Blind Institute in Copenhagen, in which he recorded the jobs the ex-pupils of the Institute were holding down.

Perhaps I should correct myself for painting a rather gloomy picture of the adult dyslexic. I quite agree that a certain number of dyslexics surmount the problem themselves eventually, provided they are not misdiagnosed to begin with and the correct diagnosis is made early, provided they are of high intelligence, and provided they possess a strong determination to cope with an unpleasant and boring task. In that case I think you reach a stage whereby you can call the patient an "ex-dyslexic." He will be able to read. Perhaps he will not read for pleasure's sake very much or perhaps he will not tackle textbooks of philosophy or psychology, but still he will be able to manage thrillers and westerns. His major disability will commonly be atrocious spelling, by which I mean not the spelling of an ignorant person but spelling which is bizarre in the extreme.

Dr. Arthur Keeney: Dr. Critchley, can you identify these people by their handwriting?

Dr. Critchley: Yes, I rather think I can. From a person's spontaneous efforts at writing, I think I could determine whether that person is or was dyslexic.

Dr. Arthur Keeney: Is this throughout life, sir?

Dr. Critchley: Well, I have not followed them to the grave, but the specific defects go on for a very long time.

Dr. Arthur Keeney: Mrs. de Hirsch?

Mrs. de Hirsch: The residual disability of the dyslexic was described by Orton many years ago in terms of spelling and writing disabilities. As you look at the writings of dyslexics, you sometimes know the way in which they talk. Their speech is as jerky and as arrhythmic as their handwriting. The cluttered speech of some of these boys *sounds* the way their papers *look*, and if you look at many of them, you get a very good clinical feel for this.

Dr. Arthur Keeney: Dr. Kirschner, statistics have been produced to suggest that myopic patients are the reverse of dyslexics and are better readers than are their emmetropic friends. Is there any evidence to support this, and if so, what are the underlying principles?

Dr. Kirschner: I am familiar with the reports of myopes having a reading advantage. I can see the arguments for it—the fact that the myope does not have to exert ocular accommodation in his near world and that he has an easily seen, enlarged view of this near world. They do tend to ignore the fuzzy distant world, and their near orientation is aided. I, personally, have not been convinced of any true reading advantages in these circumstances. I would enjoy a comment by Dr. Nicholls.

Dr. Nicholls: I have seen no correlation at all. Myopes do not seem to learn to read more easily or less easily. But if they are not given proper spectacles, they may not be attracted to outdoor sports and, therefore, may have more time for reading.

Dr. Arthur Kenney: Dr. Critchley, would you comment on what may be the actual or theoretic neurology of ocular dominance?

Dr. Critchley: I wish I could. This is a fundamental biologic problem which extends back through the entire evolution. It almost seems as though cerebral dominance is a human prerequisite, either wholly or mainly so. And it is difficult even for the anthropologist to know why this should be.

There is some linkage in homo sapiens between ocular dominance, cerebral dominance, and the acquisition of that distinguishing human endowment, namely language. It appears as though language and cerebral dominance are correlated somehow with one another. Just what this tie-up is and why it should be is extraordinarily difficult to say.

To diverge briefly, a perplexing question about the origin of speech in homo sapiens is to estimate at what stage in prehistory speech or language, as we know it today, first made its appearance. Did Neanderthal man speak? Did Pleistocene man speak? We will probably never know, of course, but the question does bear fundamental relation with other cerebral developments. One clue may be adventitious or may even be fallacious; I refer to the endocranial markings within the skulls of prehistoric men. There comes a time when early man shows an asymmetry of the two hemispheres as evidenced by such endocranial impressions. It is tempting to suggest that it was at this point that speech began.

Dr. Arthur Keeney: Thank you, Dr. Critchley. Dr. Bender, would you comment on the characteristics of the Bender Gestalt reproductions of dyslexic children?

Dr. Bender: The Bender Visual Motor Gestalt test is a series of designs presenting multiple kinds of form organization with dots, circles, squares, diamonds, et cetera, in various relations and combinations. In the child with a primary genetic dyslexia, his maturational lag is responsible for more primitive reproduction of the gestalt stimuli when asked to draw them. Diamond relationships are reduced to squares, squares simplified to circles, and circles to crude loops. There will be much more movement evident, described as rotation by some people.

Dr. Arthur Keeney: Dr. Nicholls, can eye or oculomotor exercises benefit a child with reading difficulty? I notice the word "dyslexia" is not used, but "reading difficulty" is the term in the question.

Dr. Nicholls: Eye exercises, in my opinion, do not directly affect the action of the muscles that move the eyes and keep them in alignment. They act indirectly, having an effect through motivation, that is, by increasing the desire of the child to use the two eyes together as a unit. These are called fusional exercises.

I do not believe that eye exercises have any effect upon the capacity to compensate for refractive errors, such as myopia or diplopia. I do not think they are of value in a purely motor impairment; their effect is solely through increasing the desire for binocular single vision by improving the sensorial awareness.

Dr. Arthur Keeney: Dr. Rosenberg, is there a significant correlation of vocal disability, or poor tune-perception ability, with developmental dyslexia?

Dr. Rosenberg: I think not. We have investigated so-called tone deafness in regard to a number of different developmental as well as auditory parameters and have found no correlation. I do not really know what tone deafness is. It is probably a higher function of cerebration, rather than either end-organ sensation or initial perception.

Dr. Arthur Keeney: Dr. Critchley, do you believe there is any correlation between the side of hair whorl and cerebral dominance?

Dr. Critchley: With respect both to Dr. Bender and others, I do not think we have really heard the end of the hair-whorl story. Dr. Bender told me something today which I did not know. She said it all depends on whether the whorl goes clockwise or counterclockwise. I have been taking a poll of the sidedness, rather than this point. If you make it a routine practice to look at the heads of all your children, you will see an odd variety of hair-whorl patterns. There is even a phenomenon of two hair-whorls, one on the left side and one on the right. There is also one that is absolutely centrally situated. In other persons, too, there is no whorl at all but a transverse slit which goes from left to right. So I think this is a little problem of cultural anthropology that we should go into in rather more detail.

Dr. Arthur Keeney: Dr. Bender, could the proficiency of the dyslexic in mechanical tasks or in sports be compensatory? He can succeed in these realms with less effort, even though he has been described as clumsy. Therefore, he does better here than in academic activities.

Dr. Bender: If any dyslexic boys have mechanical proficiency, they are fortunate. It is certainly not a universal compensation. As a matter of fact, Dr. Schilder and I wrote a paper describing some boys we had known who did quite superior artwork by which they could communicate as a compensation for their dyslexia.

Other people, including Dr. Silver and Dr. Critchley, have pointed out that dyslexics do very poor artwork. It is a question of a dyslexic finding a compensatory area in which he can function and that will vary from individual to individual because of genetic, environmental, and various other factors.

This resembles the old saw that mentally defective persons are all capable with their hands. We know very well that mentally defective people are likely to be generally defective and even worse with their hands than they are verbally.

Every individual who has a disability seeks a compensation, or at least he should aim at this. It may be achieved in individual cases by mechanical skills, but it is far from universal. As a matter of fact, the incidence of reduced dexterity by left-handedness and clumsiness often make the dyslexic person particularly incapable of carrying on compensatory activities requiring finely coordinated manipulatory activities.

Dr. Arthur Keeney: Can you suggest a few screening questions for quickly determining the presence of dyslexia at the age of 6 years and the age of 12 years?

Dr. Critchley: No.

Dr. Arthur Keeney: Mrs. de Hirsch, in your proposed transitional classes, what learning steps would you include for these people?

Mrs. de Hirsch: It would be better to answer that in terms of each child's individual needs. Some children need oral language stimulation. They have no way of expressing thought. They have no way of listening to or interpreting what other people say. Other children need help with motor activities. All need help in organizing themselves and their environment. Most children need assistance with body image and laterality. Practically all children must learn to discriminate among spoken sounds in all kinds of configurations.

It has been shown by Russian researchers that manual manipulation of objects helps in their discrimination, so in teaching these children letters, they may be aided by fingering wooden letters. There are many techniques, but they have to be tailored to the particular child.

Chapter 8

Origin and function of the Interdisciplinary Committee on Reading Problems

Archie A. Silver, M.D.

The origin and function of the Interdisciplinary Committee on Reading Problems will be discussed in this chapter. This committee originated in frustrations: frustration primarily in the gap between our knowledge and the practical application of such knowledge within the school systems; frustration of teachers and school administrators with the lack of direction and information from medical and psychologic practitioners and researchers; frustration of foundations and government funding agencies in obtaining interdisciplinary counsel for broad-based research; and frustration of parents in their efforts to help their children. The Interdisciplinary Committee on Reading Problems was formed in an attempt to bridge these accumulated gaps.

The committee consists of, at present, a small core of professional people from all related disciplines. Medicine is represented by pediatricians, neurologists, ophthalmologists, and psychiatrists; psychology, by clinical, experimental, and educational psychologists; education, by school administrators, remedial education specialists, and teachers of teachers. Other representatives come from the areas of linguistics, sociology, and statistics and from funding agencies.

This group of about fifty people was called together in 1966 by the Center of Applied Linguistics to function in the following five areas:

1. To collect, organize, and disseminate our existing knowledge (This is a clearing-house function, designed to serve at various levels of both professional and lay information.)
2. To assist and support local school systems in setting up and staffing diagnostic and treatment programs (This function implies the creation of demonstration projects and interdisciplinary model programs.)
3. To establish criteria for the teaching of special methods in schools of education and in the training of remedial experts
4. To offer existing organizations a central group for government and funding-agency contact and for authoritative press release

5. To describe and encourage basic projects needed for our further understanding of the cause, prevention, and treatment of language disorders

Each of these functions is, of course, a major undertaking. Even so simple
a problem as answering requests for information is a full-time job. Only 6 months
after this committee was mentioned in the national press more than 1,000 letters
from all parts of the United States were received from parents, school supervisors, teachers, pediatricians, mental health clinics, psychiatrists, psychologists,
and neurologists. Some letters offered support, but all wanted information concerning diagnosis, treatment, and available training facilities. We have attempted
to answer every request, but we do not have full or authoritative information
on, for example, training facilities throughout the United States. Even on a
professional level, at the first committee meeting in September, 1966, the mere
problem of definition of dyslexia or reading disability evoked protracted discussion.

This initial meeting, however, was highly valuable in the formation of an ongoing organization with interdisciplinary task units to inventory *critically* the
present state of our knowledge concerning dyslexia.

The inventory critique is divided into the following five task units:

1. Definition, etiology, and diagnosis
2. Incidence and implication (Sociologic, psychologic, and national contribution to the problems of mental health and delinquency)
3. Treatment and prevention (An evaluation of current remedial techniques,
   experimental methods, motor patterning, and pharmacologic and psychotherapeutic approaches)
4. Administrative procedure in education (Current administrative practices
   in detection, treatment, and teacher training; legislative programs, present
   and planned)
5. Research (Current and projected areas of investigation, new methods, the
   definition and procedures used, the actual findings relative to conclusions,
   and the areas of research needs, particularly those lending themselves to
   broad-based interdisciplinary attacks)

A compendium of knowledge in these areas should delineate the current state
of the art and provide guidelines for the future. Hopefully, within 1 or 2 years
a summary of findings in each of these areas will be available.

Organizationally, each task unit is composed of members of the interdisciplinary committee who will call upon appropriate experts and organizations
in approaching their specific assignments. In turn, the entire committee is available for consultation with other concerned organizations including those of
teachers, remedial experts, parents, legislators, and school administrators. Liaison
is underway with international groups such as the Canadian Commission on
Emotional and Learning Disorders and the Word Blind Association in England.

The 250-page transcript of the initial September, 1966, meeting is being
reduced and will be available in January, 1967.

The contributions of Alfred Hayes, Director of Education and Research for
the Center of Applied Linguistics, and his assistant, Jim Broz, must be acknowledged. They have brought together diverse opinions from all disciplines and

all parts of the United States and, in a sense, have created the unified committee. This is a working committee, not a membership committee, representing the thinking of all disciplines.

The ultimate goal of the committee is to have each child in the United States, by the time he reaches junior high school, possess language skills appropriate to his intelligence.

Chapter 9

The problem of delayed recognition
and its correction

William M. Cruickshank, Ph.D.

Delayed recognition is almost standard procedure with respect to children currently discussed. It is the rule and not the exception. We tend to approach this issue in an ostrichlike manner until forced into recognition either by behavior-management problems or by severity of resultant learning failures. Several distinct factors contribute to delayed recognition.

First, there is confusion in defining dyslexia. If the child diagnosed as dyslexic in Philadelphia moved to Bucks County, 10 miles north, he would be called a child with a language disorder. In Montgomery County, Maryland, a few miles south, he would be called a child with special or specific reading problems. In Michigan, he would be called a child with perceptual disturbances. In California, he would be called either a child with educational handicaps or a neurologically handicapped child. In Florida and New York State, he would be called a brain-injured child. In Colorado, the child would be classified as having minimal brain dysfunction.

Since 1955, forty-three different terms, generally referring to the dyslexic child, have appeared in the literature. Fortunately, although the name for the disorder may change, the child remains the same. This confusion in terminology makes it difficult for educators and those people legally responsible for implementation of programs to meet the needs of these youngsters either in terms of direct service or, as Dr. Silver mentioned, in training of teachers and others.

A large, current study has recommended that we refer to these children as having minimal cerebral dysfunction, which is like saying a woman is slightly pregnant. It is not a matter of minimal dysfunction. Any neurologic disorder is something more than minimal, and dysfunction is a dysfunction of something, not a noun by itself. Therefore, the term "minimal cerebral dysfunction" does not critically serve the needs.

Second, the problem of delayed recognition is due, in part, to the infancy of efforts. Thirty years ago only a handful of professional people were aware of dyslexia not only in the United States but also in other countries. These people were, essentially, in the fields of neurology, psychology, and education. Today, most of us still come to the problem with a paucity of professional training; professional training does not exist in more than a very few centers in the United States. We hear that this is a pediatric problem, but there are few pediatricians who have sufficient understanding of neurologic and educational problems to handle the matter completely. We hear that this is a neurologic problem, but the number of neurologists who understand the matter functionally is too small to serve the population's needs. We hear that this is an ophthalmologic problem, but the number of ophthalmologists who understand the neuro-ophthalmologic substructure sufficiently to contribute to educational programs is very small. We hear that this is a psycho-educational problem, but the number of teachers or psychologists who have sufficient background in neurology, ophthalmology, pediatric psychiatry, and other disciplines that must be brought into focus is practically negligible. Recently the superintendent of schools in a large county system needed 100 teachers formally trained in dyslexia; there have not been 100 teachers prepared to approach this need in the United States in the last 5 years. The problem, then, of delayed recognition is part of the problem of an immature profession.

Third, the problem of delayed recognition is complicated by the fact that an interdisciplinary attack is mandated. However, we have had, at best, multidisciplinary efforts, not interdisciplinary attacks; the two concepts are quite different. If we are honest, the involved disciplines have no history of close or continuous endeavor. We are all pressured and too busy within the perimeters of our own professions to take the time needed to learn and work effectively with adjacent fields. Thus, children suffer. When we can make this effort, children profit.

During the last 10 years I have worked with three or four truly interdisciplinary teams and have learned that in order to be effective we must give people who are sophisticated in their own professions a period of practice at being interdisciplinary. Most interdisciplinary teams fail because we have not administratively built into them an opportunity for practice; this cannot be accomplished in much less than 18 months. When we can achieve close and continued cooperation so that educators learn not to be afraid of physicians and physicians learn not to be afraid of educators, then the problems of semantics can be reduced, all professional statures can rise, and children can profit. This calls for a breadth of professional growth and for changes in the nature of professional education over the coming decades. I believe we will have a broader sharing of understanding and of information than we have now and from this will evolve the true interdisciplinary concept essential in working with the problem of human behavior.

Fourth, the problem of delayed recognition is complicated by the fact that in the research area there are too few down-to-earth, solid programs in any of the professional fields. Thus, all professional consultation is hesitant, and most children are not discovered until the second or third grade when they have already failed to learn to read. Thus, dyslexia is one symptom of broader basic pathology. It is only one of many problems in 7 or 8 years of failure experiences, based, probably, on a neurologic defect that had its inception at a prenatal or very early postnatal level.

In my experience about 90 percent of severe dyslexia problems are neuro-logically based or present characteristics that are identical with those children who have positive neurologic findings. We have two studies which are now complete and which will probably indicate that this problem also involves the senses of smell and taste and the inability of the child to adjust to sensory stimuli or to changes of relative humidity and temperature. We have the totality of a problem that comes to a focus in some children in terms of dyslexia.

On the positive side, I am concerned with the early diagnosis of dyslexia because educators and parents immediately want to direct such problems to the remedial reading specialist. This is not a matter of remediation; this is a matter of complex analysis, first involving diagnostic steps.

Correction of dyslexia involves several steps. First, it involves early diagnosis. Early diagnosis may now be more difficult than formerly. One of the first positive signs is inability of the child to accept a nipple or a bottle when feeding is started. This may be the first clue, and I believe it should be high on the pedia-trician's list of actions to note. To what extent cannot this child suck or swallow, or to what extent does he drool? These findings are symptomatic of possible neurologic disorders affecting fine motor movement and may ultimately be seen not only in this very specific kind of reaction but also in visuomotor activity or in eye-hand coordination.

Early diagnosis involves evaluation of these children by sensorimotor, psycho-motor, and educational assessment. From the diagnostic steps must come con-ceptualization and implementation of a modus operandi for each child based on the individual characteristics of his psychopathology. Psychopathology may be related to ophthalmologic function, auditory function, or four or five other sensorimotor areas.

Hyperactivity, hyperkinesis, and distractibility are outstanding characteristics in these children, less on a motor basis than on a sensory basis. These youngsters are unable to refrain from reacting to extraneous stimuli in the environ-ment and, therefore, cannot attend to those things which the educator places before them as bases of learning. These children have attention spans of ap-proximately 90 seconds to 2 or 3 minutes, and only during this period of time can positive education take place. If a teacher has a 20-minute reading lesson and the children have only a 2-minute attention span, the last 18 minutes of the lesson become a disciplinary hassle. The failure experience is accentuated, and such children do not tolerate failure experiences. They have had failure experi-ences ever since they began to nurse at the age of 2 days.

Second, a corollary characteristic in the correction of dyslexia is motor dis-inhibition, which accompanies sensory hyperactivity. The youngsters are unable to refrain from stimuli that elicit a motor response, and, therefore, these youngsters show motor immaturity, both gross and fine, which requires highly specialized handling. These are youngsters that the psychologists and psychiatrists identify as characterized by perseveration, or prolonged reaction to a stimulus and the interference of this stimulus with subsequent activities. These youngsters, from an ophthalmologic point of view, sometimes appear to have figure-ground pathology. In reality, this often is not a visual problem but a matter of stimuli attractivity. These youngsters are unable to inspect specific figures carefully because of extraneous stimuli in the environment. Look at a book and start reading with the first word on the first paragraph, or more difficult, the first word of the first line of the second paragraph. Every other word on the page constitutes many stimuli, and if a child is hyperactive to extraneous stimuli or unable to react thoroughly because of a short attention span, he may never see the indicated word. Although he may know the word, he does not read, and the teacher looks upon him as a child with a reading problem. He has a reading problem, but it is the end result of a more basic issue that the teacher has not attacked.

Third, these youngsters are characterized by the psychopathology of dissociation, an inability to conceptualize objects as a unity. Macdonald Critchley, in his early volume, *The Parietal Lobes* (1953), discusses this uniquely and remarkably. The inability to conceptualize objects as a unity because of a tendency to segment or divide results is a psychopathic and distorted self-concept of body image. If, diagnostically, the educator has a carefully worked out description of the status and psychopathologic characteristics of the child, then he should be able to develop a technique that will complement and exploit the psychopathology to the benefit of the child.

Five major techniques for teaching dyslexic children are discussed in the following paragraphs:

First, it is necessary to reduce the stimuli for dyslexic children. For children who are overly reactive to stimuli, whether visual, auditory, or otherwise, an environment that is as stimulus free as possible must be provided. This is not a figment of imagination. There are dozens of good educational programs in the United States employing minimal stimulus environments quite contrary to the environments to which most children are exposed. These are not classrooms filled with all kinds of motivational material; the best classroom in the city of Philadelphia for normal children is the worst classroom for dyslexic children. There is too much stimulus in the typical classroom environment for a distractible child; it is impossible for him to attend to that which the teacher indicates.

Second, it is necessary to reduce space around dyslexic children; they become more insecure as the space increases. Stimuli should be reduced and contained within an amount of space over which the youngster psychologically believes he has command. We sometimes find it necessary to reduce the amount of space to a point where the children can touch three walls of their environment. Because of this I have been labeled "the cubicle man." I have no hesitation in recommending a small 3- or 4-foot-square cubicle, appropriately set and lighted.

Third, there must be a corrective view of concept and structure in the total educational concept. Dyslexic youngsters have an extraordinary experience with failure, are disorganized, and rarely have had experiences that would help them develop an integrated self-concept. An educational program must be established on a living theory, involving conditioning with heavy psychoanalytic support. We must go back to a level, sufficiently primitive, in which there was some success experience from which to start conditioning. When moving back to a primitive level, there is more than creeping and crawling; we must build on this in a structured manner—a motor program and psychotherapeutic program that, over a few years, will bring these youngsters to a recognition of achievement. It is gratifying to watch the psychologic and psychiatric aspects of therapy as children experience success, as opposed to 7 or 8 years of previous failure. At this point, life becomes much better for parents, for educators, and for the child.

Fourth, there is the necessity of constructing and implementing an entire new concept of teaching material. Most of what we now have to work with is wrong for the kind of children we are addressing; it fails to consider the psychopathologic manifestations of the children. These children are hyperactive to stimuli, and any reading books currently on the market present, on a given page, about 400 words, four pictures, or four colors. A new arithmetic book, to actual count, presented over 200 stimuli per page.

With two pages of paper containing 200 different stimuli per page in front of a highly distractible child, how is this child going to add a two-digit arithmetic problem embedded in the center of that page? It cannot be done. It is not being done, and these children are being called failures because the materials are inappropriate for their needs.

Fortunately, some educators are beginning to move into this area, and shortly we will have more teaching materials that are specific to the nature of the learning problem these children present.

To exploit the hyperactivity of a dyslexic, consider the word "dog" written in the same size letters, with the same intensity of black ink, and with the same spacing and give this to a hyperactive child. There is not enough stimulus value in those three similarly presented letters to attract the child's attention long enough for an intellectual reaction. Is there any reason why we could not have a red D, a purple O, and a green G? D O G in different sizes and shapes, increasing the stimulus value in terms of color, shape, and size and giving the youngster visual stimuli, would attract him long enough for the teacher to get intellectual conditioning under way.

Fifth, there are motor training and visuomotor training, which are important in developing fine and gross motor achievement skills such as handwriting. Motor training is also necessary to help the youngster develop a concept of organization of his own body. Many dyslexic children with whom I work do not know their right leg from their left leg. When they lie on gym mats and are asked to raise their left leg, two legs, one leg and two arms, or the whole body go into action. They have poor concepts of body parts. They are disoriented to themselves, and motor training is included as a part of the program to bring the child to a higher level of lateralization.

In summary, I have covered a large number of concepts, and I apologize for some brevity. On the other hand, dyslexia is a broader issue than a single sensory entity. It is a broader issue not only in diagnosis but also in remediation, and until the educators are trained in the broadest sense and until they have behind them the responsible moving forces of the community, affected children will have protracted and inefficient care. Until the teachers are backed up by competent diagnostic reports from the ophthalmologist in terms of daily visual capabilities and competent reports from the audiologist, the psychologist, the pediatrician, and the neurologist, all in understandable language, we will not serve these children. People in the professions must join together and become more intimately involved in working together for longer periods if we are going to serve these children who are in every school system and, probably, in every classroom in the United States.

Chapter 10

Vision, perception, and related facts in dyslexia

Herman Krieger Goldberg, M.D.

The failure of some children to keep up in reading with other children of the same age and intelligence has been subject to much romance and conjecture. Inability to interpret written material has been blamed on a number of factors. These fundamental factors as known today in the etiology of dyslexia are as follows:

1. Heredity (There is need to tabulate the patterns of inheritance and the distinct elements that manifest themselves as phenotypic evidences, which are still largely unknown. Although I accept Critchley's extensive genetic evidence, his evidence would be more secure if it could be corroborated by animal studies or human chromosomal data.)
2. Brain damage (Brain damage is important in the nonhereditary dyslexic.)
3. Psychiatric disturbances (There are distractive factors that may be superimposed on almost any case or, rarely, may come before the dyslexia as a primary problem.)
4. Education (Educational factors include variations in school systems, frequent migrations of a family, changing the child from one school to another, and the unfortunately frequent use of inexperienced teachers in the first grade.)
5. Anxiety (Anxiety is the role of emotional stress in the inhibition of learning.)
6. Visual and auditory dysfunctions (Visual and auditory dysfunctions may underlie the reception of symbols and create sensory obstacles.)

There are three basic groups of students in our primary educational system: (1) the developmental reader, (2) the corrective reader, and (3) the remedial reader. Although the remedial reader is discussed in this book, it is important to recognize the developmental reader and corrective reader as two significant parts of the school population. Different methods of reading therapy are indicated for each group; no one program should be applied to the needs of all three groups.

Sixty percent of children are classified in the developmental reader group. They learn independently of techniques and read well by any means. They read commensurately with their intelligence level. If these children have an I.Q. of 150, they will read at the 150 level; if the I.Q. is 80, they will read at the 80 level. These children perform in harmonious patterns.

The corrective reader is the child who is falling behind because of some difficulty at home or in the classroom, such as not understanding his teacher or perhaps some mild emotional disturbance as is associated with sibling rivalry. This child can be brought to grade level in his reading, which is usually one or two grades below grade level. The normal classroom techniques are adequate for his recovery.

The remedial reader creates a different problem. This is the child, predominantly male, described as left-handed with poor dominance and poor laterality. He demonstrates a persistence of the normal childhood tendency to reverse letters and symbols, such as "p" for "q" and "d" for "b." He also has a tendency to reverse words, such as "stop" for "tops" and "was" for "saw." He

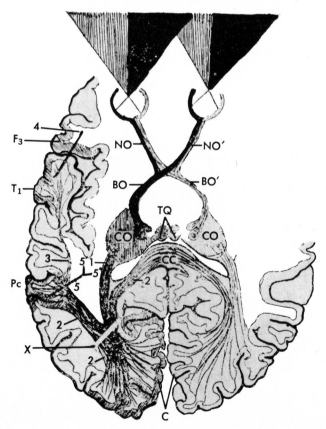

Fig. 10-1. Scars of vascular accidents in left (dominant) lobe of brain of patient who had acquired dyslexia. (From Dejerine, J.: Mémoires de la Société de Biologie 4:61, 1892.)

may show a tendency to read from right to left (in rare cases there is actual mirror writing). He may fail to see differences in the form of words, such as "on" and "no" or "pub" and "bud." He is usually of normal or superior intelligence and frequently does better than average in arithmetic. Emotional problems are usually of subsequent origin. Less than 15 percent of American children fall into this group. Rabinovitch[28] cited an incidence of from 2 to 5 percent, and this may be a low figure. The varying severities of this defect lead to different incidence figures. The inclusion of slow bloomers, or children with delayed maturation, in some series increases these figures.

Dyslexia, as a congenital form of reading difficulty, has similarities to the acquired form of reading difficulty called alexia. The anatomic basis of alexia was first shown by Dejerine[13] in 1892 when he demonstrated the postmortem specimen of a patient with alexia. This patient had two vascular accidents. After the first vascular accident, the patient could see a printed paper, but he could not understand its contents. Words had no meaning for him, and he demonstrated many of the characteristics of patients who suffer from dyslexia. This patient died of a second vascular accident. Fig. 10-1 shows two separate vascular accidents in the posterior parts of the brain. One was healed and scarred and obviously was the area that caused the alexia. The more recent vascular accident caused his death.

Schiffman[32] has made a significant contribution in his studies of about 10,000 children. He found that when diagnosis of dyslexia is made within the first two grades of school nearly 82 percent of dyslexic children can be brought back to normal grade classwork. When diagnosis is not made until the third grade, salvage drops to 46 percent. By the fourth grade, it is down to 42 percent. If these children are not diagnosed before the fifth, sixth, or seventh grades, regardless of the teacher or technique used, only 10 or 15 percent can be brought to a normal grade level. In Baltimore we usually do not diagnose dyslexic children until they are in the fourth, fifth, or sixth grades, and our correction rate is correspondingly poor. Early diagnosis is important to therapeutic success.

Katrina de Hirsch and J. Jansky[12] have made a major contribution in the early identification of children with potential reading disability, but further research with the collaboration of the educator must continue, lest this work be forgotten as was a similar effort by Castner[7] in 1935.

Twenty-five therapeutic techniques are used in Maryland. This multiplicity of techniques indicates that no one method of learning is applicable to all students.

Every teacher, in some way, uses visual, auditory, kinesthetic, and tactile stimuli (frequently abbreviated as VAKT) as a means to learning. A very helpful typewriter has been used by Mary Goodwin of Cooperstown, N. Y. This is a computerized instrument that responds verbally as the student presses a key. If the child pushes the "A" key, there is a verbal reinforcement by a voice that says "A." The same is true in the use of words. The word "boy" is typed, and then the instrument sounds this word in voice. Goodwin has used this instrument with a number of catatonic schizophrenic children and also with completely disorganized nonreaders. Many of her schizoid individuals who had been hospitalized in mental institutions are now attending grade school. Some of her disabled readers are now progressing almost at grade level. The presumptive explanation is that the typewriter employs VAKT: it gives a visual, then a kinesthetic, and finally an auditory stimulus. More importantly, the machine works in a neutral atmosphere, completely devoid of teacher or parent aggression.

Attempts have been made to assist the developmental readers whose I.Q.'s are below 70 to lead normal and self-directed lives. Project Headstart has contributed in this field. In certain children, however, it must be realized that there is a degree of futility in attempting to impart information and skills beyond the capacity to learn. This fact is widely recognized, and I suspect the motivation of those who attempt to teach children information they cannot learn. Instead of attempting to teach beyond a child's grasp, simplification should be made in the program to achieve satisfaction rather than frustration.

The developmental and corrective readers should be treated quite separately. Some teachers and parents still believe that the remedial reader can achieve with more determined effort. Often the terms "lazy" and "stupid" have been directed at the child.

I want to reemphasize the caution expressed by Cruickshank. Remedial instruction is often subject to rapidly changing methods, which present many types of therapy, too often with inadequate thought given to the primary cause of the disturbance. Reading specialists repeatedly point out the confusion within their field. Roy Kress acknowledges this confusion in pointing out that the terms "emotional block," "anxious parents," and "brain damage," are often used to pigeonhole factors that are not understood.

In many states there are no special qualifications for remedial teachers, and each teacher develops his own pattern of instruction. A subject so complex as remedial teaching should not be done haphazardly by the retired schoolteacher or by one who is disenchanted with general responsibilities in teaching. It is, perhaps, regrettable that many local school principals are completely free in directing the choice of remedial therapy. Educators should promulgate some guidelines to reduce the chaotic state that envelops reading clinics throughout the United States. There should be an association of reading therapists who are licensed to teach reading.

PERCEPTION

It is important to gain better understanding of the word *perception*. The lack of sufficient medical interest in the reading problem has been unfortunate and has left a vacuum between teacher and physician into which certain groups lacking in critical scientific understanding have intruded. This result will require years to disavow not only with tremendous funds and effort but also at the sacrifice of many students involved. An authority as learned as Hans-Lukas Teuber[40] admits there is neither an adequate definition of perception nor an adequate neurophysiologic theory to explain it. With this uncertainty as my background, I would like to recount what is being said about perception with reference to the remedial reader.

The phenomenon of perception takes place in Brodmann's areas 18 and 19, which surround the visual cortex (area 17) and communicate with the angular gyrus in the area of the parietal lobe. This is the area where objects are interpreted in a meaningful manner. A four-legged animal assumes identity; i.e., a horse becomes meaningful and is no longer just a four-legged animal. Similarly, three lines become a triangle if they are arranged properly. Likewise, in this area a word acquires meaning, as s-t-o-v-e becomes stove. The physiologic act of perception is influenced by (1) attention, (2) experience, (3) emotion, (4) duration of excitation, and (5) method of stimulation.

Visual perception is the ability to recognize and use visual stimuli and to interpret these stimuli by relating them to previous experiences. Perceptual development is a function of maturity, and it is important in enabling the child to detect in the printed word clues which will enable him to read with speed, fluency, and understanding. Perception is different from vision or sight. When one reads the Snellen Test Chart, he sees it with varying degrees of resolving ability. A child may have 20/20, 20/30, or 20/70 vision as a measure of ocular acuity or resolving power within the eye. This, however, is not what we mean by perception. After the focused image leaves the retina, it continues as an electrical chemical change by way of the optic nerve to the lateral geniculate body and from the lateral geniculate body along the optic radiations to the occipital cortex. From the gray matter of the occipital lobe the impulse continues, with many synapses and cross connections, into the angular gyrus which is in the parietal lobe. It is in this area that we intellectualize, or develop the connotation of visual images. This is perception. From the parietal lobe the visually derived stimuli continue to the frontal lobes, where conception and understanding occur. In summary, three definitions are used to describe our input from the symbols or visual pictures of the printed word: *vision, perception,* and *conception.*

Visual perception can be stimulated. Perceptual skills develop from birth

Fig. 10-2. Illustration of the Gestalt, or completion, phenomenon by which a series of dots are interpreted as a square and a triangle. (From Bender, L.: A visual motor gestalt test, 1938. Copyright, the American Orthopsychiatric Association, Inc., reproduced by permission.)

Fig. 10-3. Series of disconnected lines indicating how people read by cues.

and reach a peak of development at the age of 8 years. If such skills are still absent at this period, the child is destined for a difficult educational career. At this time a more direct attack in the perceptual areas must be attempted by the remedial therapist. It is hoped that, once the diagnosis of perceptual deficiency is made, the child will be transferred to the care of the remedial therapist. The fact that a child shows some deficiency in one area of perception does not indicate that the child cannot learn successfully. The chief method of perceptual stimulation is done by what is familiarly known as VAKT, or visual, auditory, kinesthetic and tactile stimulation. Frostig[16] has outlined five chief areas of perception as attributed to reading. They are: (1) visual motor area, (2) figure-ground perception, (3) perceptual constancy, (4) perception of position in space, and (5) perception of spatial relationships. A child who suffers from a reading disability, in which there is some perceptual difficulty, will profit by stimulation in any of these areas. But it must be remembered that a well-grounded reading-readiness program contains all of these methods of stimulation. Success in reading is most likely to be achieved if these areas of perception are well indoctrinated in the reading-readiness program, rather than after the child has failed and reading difficulty has become associated with secondary frustration.

Fig. 10-2 illustrates the Gestalt, or completion, phenomenon in terms of a square and a triangle. Isolated dots are put together in the mind to establish familiar patterns of a square and a triangle. This applies to the reading process, and the child who is successful in this area can use sight reading or total word teaching as a means of learning. The child who has poor perceptive qualities as evidenced by failure on the Benton Visual Memory test or the Bender Gestalt test[3] will have difficulty with sight reading and should, perhaps, be taught by phonetic methods.

Fig. 10-3 shows a series of lines that have already been put together to form the word "lab." This is how people read by clues. Accomplished readers do not read entire words or break down each word; they scan and pick up clues as they skim along.

The phenomena of perception are influenced by a number of factors: symmetry, tendency to organize into a configuration, the influence of Gestalt in supplying missing words or parts, and the importance of experience.

Likewise, certain laws of perception are involved in the conceptualization of reading.

John Money[26] speaks of three laws underlying the harmonious development of reading. The first is the law of *object constancy* in which an object is the same regardless of its position. That is, we see a rocking chair regardless of the position in which the chair is placed. However, this law is modified by the law of *directionality*. That is, a "b" has to be a "b" if it is facing in the proper direction; it is not a "b" but is a "d" if it is facing the opposite way or breaking the law of directionality. The law of *form constancy* points out that a "C" may be small or large, but it must be without the little hook that makes an "e" or "G." If we can differentiate these three laws, we can apparently become good readers.

In some subgroups of cases, a relationship apparently exists between dyslexia and impaired directional sense. Money, however, reported seventeen cases[2] of Turner's disease; all had impaired directional sense and loss of space-form perception. Turner's disease is seen in children, usually females, who have precocious sexual development. They have difficulties in direction and a loss of space-form perception. However, in all these seventeen cases, reading was normal or above normal.

The work of Marianne Frostig[16] represents one of the major forces in remedial education, and her techniques concerned with teaching of reading to children with perceptual disturbances are widely recognized. She has developed a test of visual perception, yielding the P.Q., which is related to perception somewhat as intelligence is to the I.Q. P.Q. stands for perceptual quotient. Her test involves five areas of information listed previously.

Unfortunately, Frostig entered into the area of eye movement and described a homemade metronoscope designed to help focus attention and to improve eye movement. These movements represent synchronous but searching activity in the process of reading. A good reader comprehends the content of written matter by one to three fixations along each line. Reading is generally done by obtaining clues from the printed words; if the clues are correct, reading is smooth, rapid, and easy, with few regressions and few fixations. If the printed sentence is difficult or incomprehensive, there are more regressions and more fixations. These fixations can be charted by a device called an ophthalmograph, which consists of a camera focusing on the cornea. As the subject reads a card placed before him, a movie camera charts the course of his binocular movement. The resulting graph is a record of fixations, but its interpretation by many individuals leaves much to be desired.

Faulty eye movements do not generally cause poor reading, but usually the converse is true. The faulty eye movements and inefficient fixations are the result of poor understanding of the printed word.

Recently, using a more refined apparatus called an oculonystagmograph, I have charted movements of the eye by measuring changes in retinocorneal electric potential. The oculonystagmograph is also used by neurologists and otologists in neuro-otologic diagnosis. It entails no apparatus on the eyes, not even glasses. It is an unencumbered method of analyzing ocular movements, including physiologic and pathologic nystagmus and reading movements. It avoids

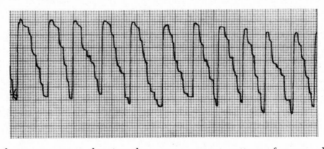

Fig. 10-4. Oculonystagmogram showing the eye-movement pattern of a normal reader.

complex photographic cameras and actually measures differences in electrical potentials between the retina and the cornea. Each clue is charted as an impulse.

Figs. 10-4 to 10-8 illustrate recordings from the oculonystagmograph. Fig. 10-4 shows the oculonystagmogram of a good, normal reader with an appropriate number of fixations. Rapid and hesitant fixations are quantitated. When this child read silently, he did better than when he read aloud.

Figs. 10-5 to 10-8 show oculonystagmograms from retarded readers, varying from low-grade deficiency to those with extreme brain damage. Fig. 10-5 shows a difference from the normal reader as characterized by long hesitations or missed words. There is normal reading, but a sudden cessation of rhythm occurs when the child encounters an unfamiliar word.

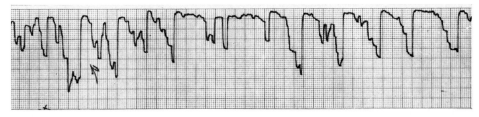

Fig. 10-5. Oculonystagmogram showing long hesitations (horizontal tracing) over unfamiliar words.

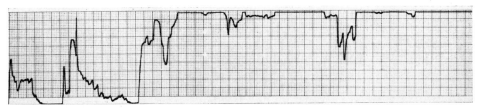

Fig. 10-6. Oculonystagmogram of a brain-damaged child, groping and grasping for understanding.

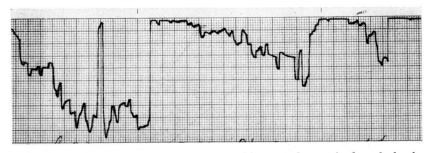

Fig. 10-7. Oculonystagmogram of a child who is able to read at a third grade level, while attempting and hesitating over sixth grade material.

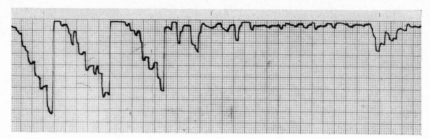

Fig. 10-8. Oculonystagmogram of the child in Fig. 10-7 being assisted over unfamiliar or difficult words in the first three lines (left portion of tracing). Right portion of tracing shows reversion to abnormal pattern when the assistance is stopped.

Fig. 10-6 shows an oculonystagmogram of a brain-damaged child. The long hesitations represent groping and grasping for the understanding of words. This confusion is happening in the brain, not in the eyes.

Fig. 10-7 shows an oculonystagmogram of a child who could read at third grade level fairly well but on sixth grade passages could not proceed. To confirm the central need rather than bulbar limitation of movements, I asked him to read the same sixth grade passages, and I helped him over difficult words. Fig. 10-8 shows a normal tracing, indicating that this child can accomplish normal eye movements. His comprehension was bad. When I stopped helping him, he reverted to a hesitant pace of repetitive fixations.

By studying these figures we can draw the following conclusions:
1. A good reader has fewer fixations, but only because he can make better use of the clues.
2. Regressions are due to the inability to understand written words.
3. Silent reading is easier and faster than oral reading.
4. Clues come from individual letters, syllables, and words; although each clue is registered individually, it is rapidly reconstructed to make a general pattern. The better the reader, the fewer clues he needs.

A blind patient will generate similar impulses from his finger movements as he reads Braille. The usual adept Braille expert reads the left hand and then the right hand. The forefingers are the fingers of best ability, and the Braille reader receives sensory impulses by both fingers and centrally sorts them out. Critchley wrote about this in 1953.[10]

Smith[37] recently reported a study of 190 subjects, indicating that by teaching scanning, reading improves and there are fewer fixations and fewer regressions. Interestingly, there was no improvement in comprehension. Movement patterns were improved but without improvement in comprehension. Unless comprehension improves, the type of movement matters little. A good reader will have synchronous eye movement, but it is incorrect to think that by changing eye movement one will overcome symbolic confusion and improve comprehension.

In summary, perceptual disturbances in children may be associated with a maturation lag, or they may be due to varying degrees of brain damage or even to severe emotional disturbances.

BRAIN DAMAGE

The brain-damaged child represents another area of vagueness in identification and treatment. I do not refer to the grossly brain-damaged child but rather to the child in whom there is confusion between the immature brain (maturational lag) and subminimal brain damage. The first difficulty is that of identifying this child. Ford has described the brain-damaged child as follows:

> In most cases, there is no marked reduction of intelligence, but personality changes of a profound nature frequently result. Physical signs are absent or trivial, but these children are destructive and impulsive. Impulses which occur to them are at once translated into action. Their misdeeds are not planned, but are the result of the temptation of the moment. The natural inhibitions of fear or consequence which restrain us all from injudicious behavior seem to be lacking in these children. Without thought of punishment they will steal, lie, destroy property, set fires, and commit other offenses. They usually make no effort to evade detection, but when reproached with their conduct will reply that they could not help it. They may be quite indifferent to punishment, or may exhibit exaggerated remorse for their offense, which however, does not prevent further misdeeds. An important factor in the behavior disorders is emotional instability. The child's mood changes in response to the slightest stimuli. These patients are very restless and overactive, going from one form of mischief to another throughout the day. The child is often impatient of any restraint.*

Factors in the brain-damaged child are hyperactivity, awkwardness of motor coordination, impaired perceptive ability as demonstrated with Bender Gestalt tests, and psychologic tests showing a wide scattering of results. The child may do especially well in one area but fail miserably in other areas. Unfortunately, the line of differential diagnosis is not absolute; the child with maturational lag can exhibit some of these signs but not as completely in all areas as in the brain-damaged child.

The keys to diagnosing subminimal brain damage are the EEG and the results of the psychometric tests.[19] However, there has been confusion concerning the significance of the EEG in reading retardation, largely because of the manner in which it has been done. In order to determine the relationship between reading retardation and brain damage, I have compared a group of children with severe reading difficulty with children of the same age and intelligence but not retarded in reading.[20] Electroencephalograms were made on each of the students, and the results were interpreted by Dr. Curtis Marshall. The tracings were seen by Marshall without his having any knowledge of the patient's history. Without exception the EEG showed evidence of brain damage in those children with reading retardations. The reason for some of the differences of opinion regarding EEG testing is probably in the technique of testing. In some clinics, only one or two leads are examined, leaving considerable possibility that an area of damage could be missed. Marshall used an eighteen-lead type of electrode and, thus, took a complete cross section of the brain. The predominant EEG abnormalities were, in general, disorganization with

---

*From Ford, F. R.: Diseases of the nervous system in infancy and childhood, ed. 4, 1966, Springfield, Ill., Charles C Thomas, Publisher, p. 110.

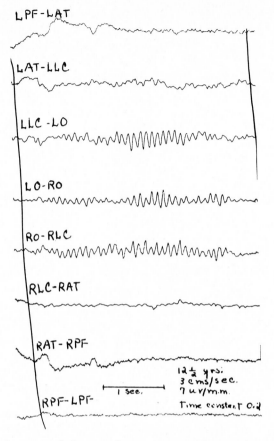

Fig. 10-9. Normal electroencephalogram showing tracings from eight representative leads.

asymmetry, abundant, slow activity, and occasional sharp waves in the parietal area. There were no seizure disturbances or discharges (Figs. 10-9 and 10-10).

Correlation of psychologic tests and EEG findings in such patients is helpful. In all of these cases, defects of perception were present. Psychologic examination of the visuomotor functions of these patients showed that they could copy simple designs but were unable to represent perspectives. Drawing from memory showed characteristic disarticulations and piecemeal procedure. Designs were poorly copied, and the patients were slow and awkward in tying knots, often being satisfied with mere twists of the string.

Reading retardation is more frequent in boys than in girls. There are a number of reasons for this observation. Biologic and maturation differences favor the female.[33] Roentgenograms of bones show the epiphysial centers to be more developed in the female. Motivation is greater in the female child. There is a tendency for the boy to play outside, but the girl is more apt to be content with household chores or reading. Of importance is a recent finding of

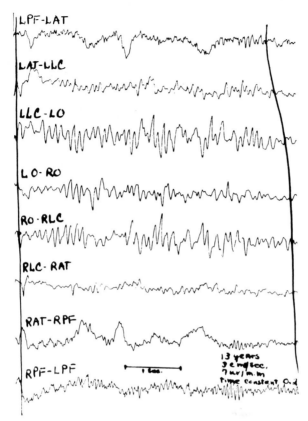

Fig. 10-10. Abnormal electroencephalogram showing disorganization, asymmetry, slow activity, and occasional sharp waves in parietal area.

Khoudadoust[24] at Johns Hopkins Hospital. He has examined 1,000 newborn children in the first 24 hours of life. The deliveries were normal. Twenty percent of the children examined showed evidence of retinal pathology, characterized by hemorrhage (Fig. 10-11), choroidal rupture, and venous thrombosis. Schenker[31] and Krebs[25] in separate studies have recently published confirmations of the high incidence of central nervous system involvement noted immediately after birth. The findings were similar to the findings of Khoudadoust. Walsh and Lindenberg[41] have noted the effects of hypoxia on the optic pathways. These are transient signs, but possibly subsequent follow-up will reveal that these patients have reading problems or evidence of minimal brain damage. Emphasis is lent to this report by the late Jonas Friedenwald, who found 18 percent of stillborn babies with evidence of retinal hemorrhage. This coincides with the work of Kawi and Pasamanick[23] who found that in 205 cases of reading retardation 16.6 percent had been exposed to two or more maternal complications as compared to 1.5 percent of a similar group without reading disorders. The complications were such that would lead to fetal anoxia.

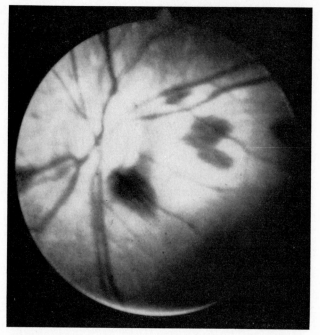

Fig. 10-11. Photograph of the fundus of the eye in a newborn infant showing flame-shaped, superficial retinal hemorrhages.

VISION

Generally, too much emphasis is placed on the importance of good vision as it affects children with reading problems. The simple fact is that there is little evidence of any relationship between visual ability and the reading problem of symbol interpretation.[18, 27, 35] Many schoolteachers and reading specialists assume that when a child has a reading problem, compensation for visual limitation with glasses or muscle exercises will be a substantial aid. In fact, some highly respected reading specialists have, on the basis of tenuous evidence, suggested the use of eye exercises as an aid to reading problems.

Certainly schools should give visual screening tests to detect visual disorders, and such conditions should be made known to the parents. Poor lighting and visual handicaps contribute to ocular fatigue and slowness in reading. In order to affect the child's learning ability, particularly in the near-reading range, vision must be reduced by at least 50 percent. Frequent studies have agreed on this point. The Los Angeles and Dartmouth studies,[22] the analysis by Park,[27] and my series of cases at Johns Hopkins Hospital, all indicate that poor vision is not a cause of the child's reversing letters or reading "saw" for "was." To illustrate how reading specialists may be misled by claims that eye exercises, or visual training, aid in reading retardation, the following case report is outlined.

The patient was sent to a "visual specialist" for a 10-week summer session. Each morning the refractionist saw this child for visual training, and each afternoon the child went to a reading clinic for remedial therapy. The refractionist apparently stated that the youngster could use both eyes effectively at a far distance, but he could read at near distance with only one eye. The refractionist asked that one eye be covered for a period of 15 minutes, then the other eye covered for the same length of time during the hours when the child was under care in the reading clinic. After 4 weeks the refractionist informed the reading tutor that the child could now use both eyes together at reading distance for ½ hour each day. After 6 weeks, the refractionist informed the teacher that there should be no limitation to the child's reading, except that he be permitted short periods of relief from near activities whenever he requested them. During the last 4 weeks of the course, relief periods became less frequent and were finally eliminated. This report concludes that as a result of the "visual training program," the child was able to improve his reading as much as any other child in the clinic. This case is an example of misinterpretations that can be made and for which reading specialists and parents must be on guard. No supporting evidence can be mustered to claim that one of a series of activities was responsible for the improvement in this child's reading. It is unlikely that the exercises described could have been of any value to the child's problem.[30] Improvement was more likely the result of other factors. In this case a warm, personal, one-to-one relationship between teacher and child was probably enough to increase motivation and, thereby, enable the child to improve at the same rate as the others in the class.

The value of exercise, as on the trampoline, is not in learning how to represent bilaterality. It is more likely the result of learning under conditions of relaxation, in which learning is done at the top of the attention span. The average normal classroom schedule consists of reading from 9:00 to 10:00 A.M.; arithmetic from 10:00 to 11:00 A.M.; science from 11:00 to 12:00 A.M.; etc. For the immature or slow reader, this schedule is frustrating and little is accomplished. There is more relief from tension and sustained pressure if the schedule consists of reading from 9:00 to 9:30 A.M.; play from 9:30 to 10:00 A.M.; arithmetic from 10:00 to 10:30 A.M.; play from 10:30 to 11:00 A.M., etc. Trampoline activity does not enhance desk posture, crayon control, attentiveness, running posture, and walking posture as claimed by some authors. To overlook the influence of normal development and maturation and to attribute to the trampoline any development of bilaterality of the two eyes demonstrates a lack of understanding of the neurophysiologic organization of human development.

Accommodative rock, the Van Order Star, the use of the stereoscope, and the use of the trampoline are fringe benefits, perhaps increasing motivation and lessening anxiety but certainly not changing perceptive or motor coordination.[17] Changes in perceptive ability and increased learning are more commonly the result of continuing maturation, a helpful relationship between teacher and child, and increased motivation.

In support of these statements, I wish to review examples from a series of 200 cases examined in detail and under careful control at the Wilmer Institute in Baltimore. Gratitude is expressed to Mary Argue, an exceptional orthoptic technician, who did visual studies, fusional studies, muscle studies, and accommodative convergence ratios on these patients with reading difficulties. Her findings indicated no statistically significant difference in frequency of eye disorders among the group of dyslexics in comparison with a normal control group of the same size.

In summary, if visual acuity is reduced 50 percent or more, a child will have difficulty seeing details. Visually, this leads to slowness in reading but not to a disabled reader. Reading is *visual* (retino-occipital), *perceptual* (parieto-occipital), and *conceptual* (frontal lobes). The muscles of the eye really do not affect perception at all. If a child has a refractive error, it should be corrected because it will help to make him more comfortable. If he has a muscle imbalance, it should be corrected. On the other hand, glasses are not indicated for most patients with minor refractive errors, and surgery should not be done for low degrees of phoria. Some nonmedical workers in vision claim to give 90 percent of patients glasses "even though they don't need them." This is sometimes stated to be for psychologic effect. This cannot be supported by analysis of the gaussian distribution of refractive errors in the population nor by psychiatric studies.

DOMINANCE

The relationship of dominance to reading is unproved,[36] but limited conclusions about dominance can be made.[42] First, cerebral maturity and dominance are directly proportional. If a child has strong right-handed tendencies early in life, he usually presents with evidence of good motor coordination. Conversely, cerebral immaturity and poorly differentiated laterality are correlated. The less dominance is established, the greater are the signs of immaturity. Second, left-handedness is not simply the converse of right-handedness. There are at least two types of left-handedness[4]: (1) physiologic, probably influenced by environmental conditions and by genetic determination, and (2) pathologic, which may be the result of brain damage. Hand dominance begins to differentiate at 18 months of age, when language begins to develop.

Evidence for the role of pathologic left-handedness is provided by Gordon,[21] who studied 219 pairs of twins and showed that when one twin is right-handed and the other twin is left-handed, the left-handed twin frequently shows some evidence of mental abnormality. Others have found a greater frequency of left-handers among retarded children.[42] Gordon found a 7.2 percent incidence of left-handed children attending schools for normal children as against an 18.2 percent incidence attending schools for handicapped children. The relationship between handedness and eyedness is interesting. Ajuriaguerra[1] states that left-eyedness occurs in from 25 to 30 percent of individuals but is not necessarily related to left-handedness. Eye preference for monocular sighting is usually established at from 3 to 4 years of age. Eye preference is usually, but not necessarily, associated with preferential visual acuity. In those persons whose vision is affected, the better eye need not be the preferred one. In fact, the optically weaker eye may be preferred for sighting. There was a conflict of handedness and footedness in 16 percent of 316 children examined by Subirana.[39]

Further confirmation is obtained in the excellent book by Katrina de Hirsch. For the first time a comprehensive, accurate, and much-needed predictive reading analysis has been recorded in her book, *Predicting Reading Failure*.[12] Of the thirty-seven tests which were originally used, ten were found to be effective. Lateralization was tenth in the order of frequency of predictive value, and the data demonstrated that ill-defined lateralization at the kindergarten age did not preclude equal or better reading by the end of the second grade. Sixty-six percent of the subjects in de Hirsch's series who had well-established hand dominance did not read better than those who had poor hand dominance.

Shift in dominance is brought about by two conditions: (1) a peripheral lesion interfering directly with the use of the dominant part, or (2) a central lesion affecting the dominant hemisphere.[11] One fact remains clear—injuries to the dominant hemisphere incurred in childhood can be compensated for by a shift of dominance to the opposite hemisphere. This transfer of dominance can rarely occur in adults but is facilitated in one who, as a child, might have had pathologic left-handedness.

Russell Brain[6] and Subirana[39] both state that poor dominance or ill-defined laterality is not a cause of language difficulty; rather, it is a concomitant symptom reflected on a parallel level. The basic deviation of brain function is responsible for both language and laterality disorders. In other words, if there is cerebral immaturity, there will be disorders of laterality and of learning. It is not the loss of laterality that produces the disorder of language, but if there is a delay in the acquisition of language, most often it is accompanied by other signs of cerebral immaturity, including delayed or incomplete establishment of laterality. The anomaly of handedness is a corollary and not a cause of dyslexia. There is little purpose in using one hand or covering one eye in an effort to establish dominance of one hemisphere.

It is generally recognized that when a right-handed person has a cerebral stroke affecting the left hemisphere, he develops right hemiplegia; if it affects the right hemisphere, the patient develops left hemiplegia. However, he suffers disorganization of language functions only when the pathologic disturbance is located in the left hemisphere. Thus, there are two groups of individuals: (1) the right-handed group, whose language centers are situated in the left hemisphere; and (2) a smaller group of left-handed persons, whose language centers are located in the right hemisphere. But left-handed persons are not simply the mirror image of right-handed persons. Among right-handed persons, with the lesion in the left hemisphere, apparently 94 percent would have some form of aphasia and language difficulty. On the other hand, among left-handed individuals with involvement of the right hemisphere, only about 35 percent would have language difficulties. This indicates a higher incidence of ambicerebrality in those persons who are left-handed or ambidextrous.[29] Presumably most human beings prefer the right hand, but this might not always have been true. Subirana believes that the human species was originally ambidextrous. His opinion is based on Stone-Age paintings found on the walls of caves. The priority of the right hand appeared in the Bronze Age.

Of the children who have come to me with reading problems, 65 percent have some disturbance in laterality on evaluation of foot, hand, and eye dominance. They might be right-handed and left-eyed or might have other combinations. Foot and ear seem to be the least significant of the dominance tests. Hand and eye are more significant, and the eye the most significant. Hand preference can be changed by environmental influences more frequently than eye preference, since it is more easily and earlier recognized as being unusual.

Many surveys have failed to support crossed dominance as a consistent link with reading problems.[9] In a study of a class of seventy-seven pupils, who were tested in reading in the first grade and again in the third, 49 percent of the students favored the right hand and right eye; 30 percent favored the right hand and left eye; and the remaining 21 percent exhibited other combinations of hand-eye coordination. Tests in the third grade revealed that students with mixed eye-hand coordination read as well as students with consistent right-sided dominance. Some children with crossed dominance have no reading difficulties, while others with corresponding laterality exhibit the entire chain of reading difficulties.

Blind people learning Braille use the left hand, which is most frequently the better sensory receptor. The blind person rapidly reading Braille "sees" with both his right and left hands. He receives sensory impressions from both the right and left sides of his body at the same time. This compares with the eyes, where such bilateral reception is recognized as the phenomenon of retinal rivalry. Unequal retinal rivalry may lead to suppression and amblyopia, but these physiologic disturbances do not result in dyslexia. A child can recognize clues in space with one eye or two, and thus far reversals are not proved to be an abnormality of retinal rivalry.

Fig. 10-12 illustrates retinal rivalry. In *A*, we expose the left eye to diagonal

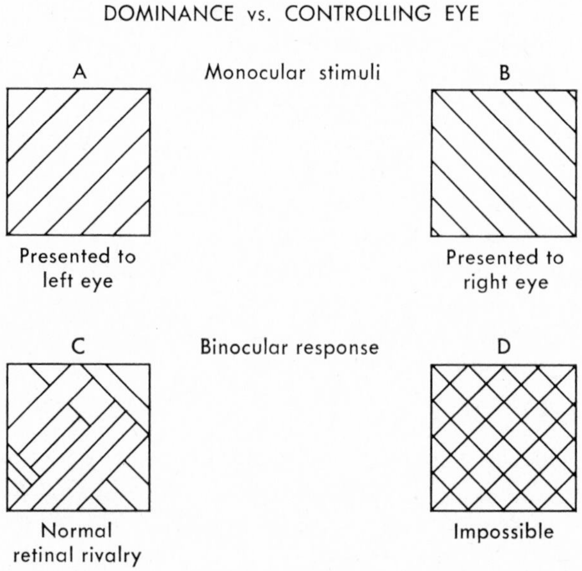

DOMINANCE vs. CONTROLLING EYE

Fig. 10-12. Demonstration of retinal rivalry in binocular response to monocularly presented targets as a factor in ocular dominance.

lines in the right-left direction. In *B*, we expose the right eye to diagonal lines in the left to right direction. When these stimuli are seen simultaneously, there is no fusion into a cross hatch as *D*. What is really seen is an alternating degree of *A* and *B*. If ocular control is greater in one eye, more of the pattern from that eye will be seen, but the overall effect will be similar to *C*. This is not dependent on dominance.

A differential may be made between the controlling eye and the dominant eye. The dominant eye is usually the sighting or fixing eye, perhaps selected because it is optically better and, therefore, produced a clearer image on the retina. However, if the image produced by the dominant eye is significantly reduced by pathology, refractive errors, or any other impediment of focusing, then there could be a transfer of visual control or lead, and the fellow eye becomes the "controlling eye."[5, 8, 14, 34] There is no immediate shift of the sighting eye, because this is a corticovisuomotor relationship that has been established by years of usage.

SUMMARY

The teaching of reading should not be made a battleground. These dyslexic youngsters are entrusted to us with, essentially, a full lifetime of problems and are accompanied by distraught parents who are both dedicated and emotional. It is necessary to provide an understanding of known facts without bias. The educator, under great public pressure to explain the high incidence of reading failure, deserves full understanding but is often ready to accept a simple explanation, even without real logic or factual basis. This is a tragedy when misconceptions are fostered in relation to vision and the child with the reading problem.

Defective vision and muscle imbalance do not have a significant role in the etiology of a condition that is influenced by cognitive learning. Reversals are neither the result of poor vision nor the result of weakness in near-point activity. The significance of low degrees of refractive error is minimal. Muscle imbalance and strabismus do not affect the interpretation of symbols by the brain. Parents, however, rely heavily on the physician's advice when a child is academically inept. The physician who knows little of reading difficulties may fail to be of assistance to disturbed and bewildered parents or to the educator, who is in need of help with medical factors that have a bearing on the child's reading problem.

The problem of reading disability is one that cannot be understood on the basis of partisan assumptions. It is difficult to evaluate the work of others in areas in which there is no final acceptable proof. For the future successful solution of the reading problem, I wish to quote the advice of two great teachers. One is from Russell Brain: "Their facts are often valuable, but their interpretations suffer from the ignorance of the work of other experts in equally important fields." The second is the "Four Stumbling Blocks to Truth" by Don Tarquinio, Baron Corvo and espoused by the great Dr. Alan C. Woods as follows:

"1. The influence of fragile or unworthy authority

2. Custom
3. The imperfection of undisciplined senses
4. Concealment of ignorance by ostentation of seeming wisdom"

REFERENCES

1. Ajuriaguerra, J., and Hécaen, H.: Left-handedness; manual superiority and cerebral dominance, New York, 1964, Grune & Stratton, Inc.
2. Alexander, D., and Money, J.: Studies in directional sense, Arch. Gen. Psychiat. **10:** 337, 1964.
3. Bender, L.: A visual motor gestalt test, Research Monographs, no. 3, New York, 1938, American Orthopsychiatric Association.
4. Benton, A. L.: The problem of cerebral dominance, Bull. Orton Soc. **16:**38, 1966.
5. Berner, G. E., and Berner, D. E.: Relation of ocular dominance, handedness and controlling eye in binocular vision, Arch. Ophthal. **50:**603, 1953.
6. Brain, W. R.: Speech and handedness, Lancet **2:**837, 1945.
7. Castner, B. M.: Prediction of reading disability, Amer. J. Orthopsychiat. **5:**375, 1935.
8. Crain, M.: Binocular rivalry, J. Gen. Psych. **64:**259, 1961.
9. Critchley, M.: Doyne Memorial Lecture. Inborn reading disorders of central origin, Trans. Ophthal. Soc. U.K. **81:**459-480, 1961.
10. Critchley, M.: Problem of developmental dyslexia, Proc. Roy. Soc. Med. **56:**209, 1953.
11. Critchley, M.: Developmental dyslexia, Springfield, Ill., 1964, Charles C Thomas, Publisher.
12. de Hirsch, K., et al.: Predicting reading failure, New York, 1966, Harper & Row, Publishers.
13. Dejerine, J.: Contribution a l'étude anatamo-pathologique et clinique des differentes variétés de cécité verbale, Memoirs de la Societe de Biologie **4:**61, 1892.
14. Enoksson, P.: An optokinetic test of ocular dominance, Gotteburg, Sweden, 1964, Elanders Boktryckeri Aktiebolag.
15. Ford, F. R.: Diseases of the nervous system in infancy and childhood, ed. 4, Springfield, Ill., 1966, Charles C Thomas, Publisher.
16. Frostig, M.: An approach to the treatment of children with learning disorders, vol. 1, Seattle, Wash., 1965, Special Child Publications.
17. Getman, G. N.: How to develop your child's intelligence, Luverne, Minn., 1958. (Published by author.)
18. Goldberg, H. K.: The ophthalmologist looks at the reading problem, Amer. J. Ophthal. **47:**67, 1959.
19. Goldberg, H. K.: Neurological and psychological aspects of reading disabilities. In Dyslexia in special education, Bull. Orton Soc. **1:**91, 1964.
20. Goldberg, H. K., Marshall, C., and Sims, E.: The role of brain damage in congenital dyslexia, Amer. J. Ophthal. **50:**588, 1960.
21. Gordon, H.: Left-handedness and mirror writing among defective children, Brain **43:** 313-336, 1920.
22. Henry, A.: An evaluation of visual factors in reading, Hanover, N. H., 1938, Dartmouth Publications.
23. Kawi, A., and Pasamanick, B.: Association of factors of pregnancy with reading disorders, J.A.M.A. **166:**1420, 1958.
24. Khoudadoust, A.: Examination of 1,000 newborn, Presented at Wilmer Institute Annual Meeting, April, 1967.
25. Krebs, W., and Jager, G.: Retinal hemorrhages in newborn, Klin. Mbl. Augenheilk. **148:** 483, 1966.
26. Money, J. (editor): Reading disability, Baltimore, 1962, Johns Hopkins Press.
27. Park, G. E.: Functional dyslexia vs. normal reading, comparative study, Eye, Ear, Nose & Throat Monthly **45:**74, 1966.
28. Rabinovitch, R. D.: Reading and learning disability. In Arieti, S.: American handbook of psychiatry, vol. 1, New York, 1959, Basic Books, Inc.

29. Rasmussen, A. T.: Lateralization of cerebral speech dominance, J. Neurosurg. **23**:900, 1964.
30. Robbins, M. P.: Study of the validity of Delacato's theory of neurological organization, Exceptional Children **32**:517, 1966.
31. Schenker, J.: Retinal hemorrhages in the newborn, Obstet. & Gynec. **27**:521, 1967.
32. Schiffman, G.: Reading problems, Presented at Maryland State Health Council Meeting, November, 1962.
33. Schiffman, G., and Clemmens, R.: Observations on children with severe reading problems, learning disorders, Seattle, Wash., 1966, Special Child Publications.
34. Selzer, C.: Lateral dominance and visual fusion, Harvard Monographs in Education, no. 12, Boston, 1963, Harvard University Press.
35. Shearer, R. V.: Eye findings in children with reading difficulties, J. Pediat. Ophthal. **3**: 47, 1966.
36. Shepherd, E. M.: Reading efficiency of 809 average children, Amer. J. Ophthal. **41**:1029, 1956.
37. Smith, B.: Changing patterns of eye movements, J. Reading **9**:379, May, 1966.
38. Spache, G.: Toward better reading, Champaign, Ill., 1962, Garrard Publishing Co.
39. Subirana, A.: Problems of cerebral dominance, Bull. Orton Soc. **14**:45, 1964.
40. Teuber, H.-L.: Handbook of physiology, Washington, D. C., 1965, Waverly Press.
41. Walsh, F. B., and Lindenberg, J. G.: Hypoxia in children, Bull. Johns Hopkins Hosp. **106**: 100, 1961.
42. Zangwill, O. L.: Cerebral dominance and its relation to psychological function, Edinburgh, 1960, Oliver & Boyd.

Chapter 11

Acquired dyslexia and related neurologic lesions

Ralph D. Rabinovitch, M.D.

Acquired dyslexia is a term used to describe patients who had adequate reading function but have lost it following head trauma, vascular accident, or malignancy: e.g., Critchley's cases in his 1953 monograph, *The Parietal Lobes.* Acquired dyslexia is the loss of a skill already attained. We do not see acquired dyslexia in children except in the rare case of a child with a major head injury who loses reading ability that had been established early.

The classic description of acquired dyslexia is detailed in the British literature by Sir Henry Head (1861-1940). In his two volumes[1] on aphasia (1926), he devotes a chapter to a specific case of a 30-year-old man. He was a highly intelligent man, an excellent reader and able scholar, before sustaining a severe head injury with parietal lobe damage, after which he became alexic. In Head's description of this case and others like it,[2] there are great similarities between the severely dyslexic child and the acquired alexic adult. Neither patient can read.

The specific technique deficiencies were outlined in previous chapters. Among the points of difference, however, alexic adults tend to do a little better on sight vocabulary than on phonetic analysis, which is reversed in the dyslexic children. Obviously, both have other associated language difficulties, such as severe anomias and other specific deficits.

In acquired alexias, there is often a right hemiparesis and sometimes a right hemianopia, which are rare in children. Although the basic process of the acquired and the congenital disturbances may be similar, the expression of the difficulty differs in relation to the age factor. The adaptability and flexibility of the brain within the developmental years facilitate compensations in childhood that do not occur in the more rigidly set adult brain.

I will not pursue the details of acquired dyslexia extensively because the functional patterns are not highly relevant to the congenital or developmental dyslexic. I will, however, describe a recent study we have done, relative to the neurologic status of children who have severe reading problems.

In Hawthorne Center we see about 1,200 new patients a year, and approximately 15 percent of them are children with learning disabilities. We have collected information on well over 1,000 dyslexics, many of them severely retarded in reading age relative to mental age. For this discussion I compared the histories of fifty children with severe reading retardations with the histories of fifty other disturbed children (called the adequate readers) seen in the clinic. These cases were selected completely at random, and I was interested and surprised in the findings.

Since Hawthorne Center is large and attracts much pathology, we are inclined to see very severe problems. We are not involved with cases such as an 11-year-old child who is in sixth grade but reads at a fifth grade level. He survives; his school should provide some kind of help for him, but he does not have the degree of problems seen in most children treated at Hawthorne Center.

The age range (from 9 to 16 years) was quite similar in both groups. The age range began at 9 years because at this age we are sure we have a true and severe reading problem; otherwise the cases are selected without reference to age. The sex distribution is fairly typical of our clinic. In a large group of severe reading problems, our ratio of boys to girls is 94 to 6. This ratio may be a little high, but we do not have more than 10 percent in our entire group who are girls. In terms of possible encephalopathy, this raises more questions than it answers.

On the other hand, the high predominance of boys referred to our clinic is also the experience of other clinics. Our total distribution of boys versus girls, under the age of 16 years, is about 3 to 1.

Basically, although there are exceptions, the general pattern is for the dyslexic child to have his greatest difficulty in spelling. His next greatest difficulty is in oral reading or in reading, and the third difficulty is in arithmetic. Ninety percent of the dyslexic children we see have deficiencies in all three areas. They vary, however, in proportions. In a large group past the age of 10 years, spelling ability is usually one grade below reading ability. Arithmetic ability is perhaps one grade higher. For example, a 10-year-old child, who should be in the fifth grade, may read at first grade level, may not score in spelling, and may do arithmetic at second or third grade level. Each of the fifty children with severe reading disability had deficiencies in all three subjects.

Having a child write to dictation is helpful diagnostically because it corresponds in most children to the reading situation. The exceptions, presenting isolated defects (referred to as specific disabilities) such as perfectly adequate reading ability but gross spelling deficiency, are rare. On response to dictation, the dyslexic who has ability to write initial consonants is certainly better than some children and is prognostically better than if he did not have that ability. The child who writes in almost total confabulation is a child with no capacity to express in symbols. When the writing includes initial phonics and initial consonants (but beyond that almost nothing), the child has some visual memory, probably for the word. He has remembered that "saw" has something to do with seeing, but he writes "see" instead of "saw," which indicates a need for pure and simple hard-work memory drill in a child who has no capacity to symbolize but has some approximations.

There are frequent examples of very bright boys with severe, total language and reading problems who may sit in regular sixth grade classrooms at the age of 12 years, obviously able to participate in a lot of discussion but still desperate with this reading problem.

Some observers are impressed with graphic aspects of dyslexia, but in dyslexics I am not certain of the interpretations. Handwriting is not good or of a high level, but it does not appear too bad in most dyslexics. Some of these children have never written and may have a motor defect, although quantitatively the motor defect is not as great as the symbolic defect.

The gestalts on these children vary tremendously and are difficult to predict. Some are grossly bad, but others are relatively good. Perhaps some of these represent a more dysgraphic kind of motor component, but many of these children have never written. They have not known anything to write, and writing is a new experience for them.

Comparative studies of verbal achievement versus performance, using the Wechsler Intelligence Scale for Children, which gives a performance I.Q. and a verbal score, confirm our previous findings of a great difference between verbal and performance functions. A consultant from the Harvard Clinic went over our material blindly and found the same thing. Whether the Michigan dyslexic child has a greater difference between his verbal and performance functions than others, I do not know. It is again likely that our series represents more severe cases.

We included no child in the dyslexic group with a performance age or mental age under 9 years, yet many scored in the retarded area in verbal testing. The mean verbal score was 8.5, and the mean performance score was 10.4, a tremendous difference. The crucial scoring level is about 7, which approximates an I.Q. of 80. Anything under 7 is in the retarded zone.

In our control group of disturbed children, some were schizophrenic, some were encephalopathic, some were neurotic, and others were neglected. They were selected at random from out-patient referrals. They all read well; they had a mean verbal score of 10.8, a mean performance score of 10.5, and a mean difference score of 2.8. When comparing these scores with the scores of the fifty dyslexic children, there is no question that whatever the process of disturbance in dyslexia, a language disturbance beyond reading affects capacity for verbal skills. Seventy-eight percent of the fifty dyslexic cases had a borderline or retarded score on the arithmetic test. In the intelligence tests, information was 58 percent and digit span was 55 percent. All the children had to do here was repeat numbers forward and backward. Although 45 percent of the children in the dyslexic group were in an average range, we found that those who did have trouble were equally poor at both information and digit span.

Comprehension is fairly typical of our whole clinic population. In this test, the children may use any word they wish to express a social concept, without premium on the mode of expression. The children were asked, "What would you do if you found an envelope stamped and addressed on the street?" They could say "drop it," "put it," or "take it over there," or they could draw a simple box or mailbox and be given full credit for the answer. The dyslexic has no

major problem in social comprehension. Much of the information test is orientational on the Wechsler Intelligence Scale for Children, such as "Where does the
sun set?" or "How many pennies in a nickel?" These number concepts are generally thought to be good, but the impairments are typical of our case load. Our
severe dyslexics have difficulties in language at almost every area, reflected in
retarded functioning in many areas.

We carefully reviewed the histories of these one hundred children, but we
did not concern ourselves, as Kawi and Pasamanick[3] did, with the gestational
history. Pasamanick, in his long, large epidemiologic study in Baltimore and elsewhere,[4] related most problems in children to what he terms "the reproductive
casualty," i.e., the concept of some cortical or cerebral insult to the fetus or some
nutritional or other supporting lack in prenatal care of the mother. He believed
there was a biologic factor emanating from deprivation or poor prenatal care and
producing brain damage in a great many problem children with conduct debili-
ties. He has also related this factor to reading disability.

Of our fifty children with severe reading retardation, 46 percent showed, on
the basis of hospital record or history, either definite or suggested evidence of
brain damage, leaving 54 percent with no evidence of brain damage in the prenatal history and raising the question of at least two etiologic groups. Interestingly, in our fifty adequate readers, who were presumably equally disturbed and
sent to the clinic for a variety of problems, only 16 percent had a history of prenatal insult.

Among the dyslexics were several outstanding neurologic defects. For example, a totally illiterate 9-year-old boy came to us with a diagnosis of severe
dyslexia. During his hospital studies, it became apparent that he had rage reactions and periodic clouded consciousness, which the neurologist believed probably
represented both psychomotor and akinetic seizures. The EEG showed a focal
lesion in the left parieto-occipital region. Skull roentgenograms indicated the
presence of an abnormal vascular shadow in the temporoparietal region, posterior
to the coronal suture. The size, the prominence, and the location of this shadow
suggested either a vascular shunt, a hemangioma, or a meningioma. The pneu-
moencephalogram was normal. This young man is now 27 years of age. He
turned out to have a congenital anomaly of arteriovenous communication. He has
remained totally and completely illiterate, despite great effort to help him. Looking at these cases, one wonders if a number of these children have not had something that has affected the occipital, parietal, or temporal region.

Another dyslexic boy was particularly interesting because of gross perinatal
hypoxia. He had nearly fatal breathing difficulty at birth and was transferred
from a small hospital in Michigan to the University Hospital, where he was kept
in oxygen for 2 weeks. He had periodic anoxic episodes with convulsions during
his first few days of life. He recovered, but he is totally aphasic and absolutely
alexic. He has a verbal I.Q. of 52 and a performance I.Q. of 104, but he cannot
talk sensibly. His speech is semigibberish. He has gross language deficits. The
diagnosis at the time of the hospitalization in Ann Arbor was brain damage secondary to anoxia. Why does anoxia lead to this specific symptom pattern? Motor-
wise this patient appeared adequate. Socially, he is quite comfortable. In cases

with this kind of history, one cannot be positive of the cause-effect relationship, but the probability is suggested.

We want to repeat this study with a larger group. Any one of several types of brain damage will yield, in some children, a severe impairment in reading.

There is no question, however, of another subgroup in which the genetic history of family pathology in this area is so obvious that it would be unrealistic to discredit the existence of a congenital and hereditary type of dyslexia or to presume gestational insult over several generations and in many sibs. There are a number of subgroups. Perhaps there are developments in a particular child that make him more vulnerable. Zangwill[5] of England discussed the problem of mixed dominance, which he believes makes the child more vulnerable to stress. His interesting concept needs additional proof. Unfortunately, it is difficult to differentiate the children in these subgroups by any motor behavior patterns.

When dealing with dyslexic children, one must remember that they come to the physician for just one reason; they cannot read. They come not because they cannot walk a board, not because they have a minor, unusual eye movement, or not because they are anything but nonreaders. If, in the course of study, we find other problems, we surely give them attention, but the basic need for help is in learning to read, regardless of etiology.

At present, the best therapy for the nonreader appears to be hard daily work in reading, which is slow and costly of time, effort, and patience for both child and teacher. If working with peripheral objects aids the child with symbolization, fine. There is no substitute, however, for giving a child with a symbolization problem help in the specific area of his needs.

REFERENCES

1. Head, H.: Aphasia and kindred disorders of speech, vols. 1 and 2, London, 1926, Cambridge University Press.
2. Head, H., and Holmes, G.: Sensory disturbances from cerebral lesions, Brain 34:102-254, 1911.
3. Kawi, A., and Pasamanick, B.: Association of factors of pregnancy with reading disorders, J.A.M.A. 166:1420, 1958.
4. Pasamanick, B., and Knobloch, H.: Syndrome of minimal cerebral damage, J.A.M.A. 170: 1384, 1959.
5. Zangwill, O. L.: Cerebral dominance and its relation to psychological function, Edinburgh, 1960, Oliver & Boyd.

Questions and answers: Third session

MODERATOR: VIRGINIA T. KEENEY, M.D.

Dr. Virginia Keeney: Dr. Rabinovitch, have you ever seen a true mirror reader?

Dr. Rabinovitch: Yes.

Dr. Virginia Keeney: Does patterning, as used in some institutions, play any role in rehabilitation of a child with perceptual or dyslexic problems?

Dr. Goldberg: I have visited such an institute and have seen patients crawling and creeping. Staff members have pointed out patients presenting convergent strabismus who appeared better when crawling and creeping. These patients, who show increasing ocular convergence or esotropia in the down position or even the horizontal position of gaze and who show much less ocular deviation on looking up or in elevated gaze, were examples of V esotropia. A second point, as mentioned in one book from such an institute, is that microphthalmus, or underdevelopment in the physical size of the ocular globe, can be improved in excess of average growth changes by crawling and creeping. This is without support and has not been reproduced elsewhere.

Dr. Virginia Keeney: What is the difference between the controlling eye and the dominant eye?

Dr. Goldberg: The dominant eye is the preferential eye, which we use for aiming or sighting. This dominance is manifested at the age of 18 months. It is true, however, that under certain monocular test conditions (as with the checkerboard on the Orthorator) the nondominant eye shows more enhancement of acuity than does the fellow eye and thereby identifies the other or controlling eye, which may be the lead eye in binocular tasks.

Dr. Virginia Keeney: Dr. Rabinovitch, please say a few words on neurophysiology, that is, changes taking place at synoptic junctions as part of the learning process. Do enzymes for remembering exist at birth, or do they come later? When?

Dr. Rabinovitch: Actually, there have been suggestions that some reading retardations in children stem from a thyroid deficiency. There was a school developed in Ann Arbor, Mich., on the basis of giving thyroid to these children. A good many of the children were incompletely studied prior to the institution of hormone therapy; nothing happened to their reading. Later, there was the concept of an acetylcholine deficiency. Then someone talked of calcium deficiency, leading to disturbances of eye movements that were described. At the present, I

115

know of no specific neuropharmacology or pharmacologic approach aside from the pemoline group of so-called memory enhancers recently under study. However, one word on neurophysiology. In these conditions that have extensive familial background, the enzymes should be studied through electrophoresis or tissue culture. Genetic enzyme studies are very much in order here, and we are hoping to do some in our laboratory.

Dr. Virginia Keeney: Thank you. Dr. Cruickshank, how can the I.Q. of a dyslexic child be accurately assessed?

Dr. Cruickshank: I doubt that we can accurately evaluate the I.Q. of any neurologically handicapped children. But I never worry about this. If by accurately diagnosing we mean merely obtaining an I.Q. figure, I do not think it makes a significant difference whether the I.Q. is 108, 118, or 98 in terms of planning for the child. We take a lot of comfort in figures and hide behind them. When I work with a child in what appears to be a reasonably normal range or a subnormal range, these are useful functional groupings. Far more importantly, at whatever level the child is functioning, I want to have a detailed blueprint of what makes up the intelligence he demonstrates. I want to have a dissection, and this should be done carefully and analytically to determine the specific characteristics. Only when I know this can I then complement them by an individual plan.

Dr. Virginia Keeney: Dr. Cruickshank, are speed-reading techniques of any practical value for the dyslexic child or even for the normal child? How about the normal adult?

Dr. Cruickshank: They might be, although I have never used them because I have never worked with a child who could attain what my definition of speed reading would be. In order to utilize a technique such as speed reading one first has to know how to read. I am dealing, as is Dr. Rabinovitch, with children who have a long way to go to get the initial mechanics of reading out of the way. I would not confuse the issue by exposing seriously handicapped children to gimmicks of this sort—gimmicks which are intended to be superimposed on individuals who already have achieved certain skills and to improve those skills.

Dr. Virginia Keeney: Dr. Goldberg, abnormal occipital discharges on the EEG are often associated with amblyopia ex anopsia. Is it not possible that these discharges develop secondary to a visual deprivation syndrome and are not primary to it?

Dr. Goldberg: Amblyopia ex anopsia is really part of a brain dysfunction, a central suppression. Therefore, it could be a manifestation of brain dysfunction. Electroencephalographic records are irregular in children under 5 and 6 years of age, and interpretation is difficult, but abnormal potentials are frequent.

Dr. Virginia Keeney: Dr. Rabinovitch, please distinguish between the concept of delayed maturation and Dr. Critchley's implication that recovery never takes place although compensation does occur.

Dr. Rabinovitch: I do not think Dr. Critchley said that. Is he here?

Dr. Arthur Keeney: He is shaking his head horizontally.

Dr. Rabinovitch: Dr. Critchley did not say it, so that part of the question is settled.

Although we also see many children with delayed maturation, some of the children Mrs. de Hirsch describes are children that she has uniquely followed through the second grade. Some will improve by the fourth grade, sometimes spontaneously. The more help they receive, the more comfortably they can live with their maturational difficulty, and the more they may improve. Some do and some do not. The old idea that all children with reading problems or other learning problems will, in time, grow out of them was erroneous for many cases. Too many parents have been told, "Don't worry, there is nothing wrong. He'll probably grow out of it." A lot of children do not. The truly dyslexic child has a relatively poor prognosis for high level reading. However, with good re-education methods, with individual or small group remediation, many dyslexic children move from near illiteracy to, perhaps, fifth, sixth, or seventh grade functional reading.

The earlier you start working with a child, the better the prognosis will be. We sometimes start very late. We see some illiterate youngsters who are 16 years of age; someone is still waiting for growth to compensate. That is too late. An important part of the answer is early diagnosis. I give each child all help possible, realizing that some will not compensate spontaneously. The true dyslexic child always remains language impaired to some degree, but we are interested in functioning. We must evaluate not in terms of cure but in terms of social, functional, and educational rehabilitation.

Dr. Virginia Keeney: Dr. Cruickshank, is there evidence that motor-sensory techniques will definitely override the dyslexic condition?

Dr. Cruickshank: Dr. Rabinovitch has spoken of this, and I would say "Amen." Perhaps this question refers to other things that we have done. A multidisciplinary approach has been effective in some groups of youngsters in returning them to their regular grades, able to compete reasonably at age and grade level.

In the data that we have, the effectiveness is slightly less than 50 percent of the group. Dr. Rabinovitch said that the earlier we see these youngsters the better. I have never had the privilege of working with children less than 6 years of age in groups large enough for generalization. If we could see these children, at from 2 to 3 years of age, we would be able not only to adjust to a preventive concept but also to be more than reasonably effective, beyond 48 to 49 percent of the group.

Dr. Virginia Keeney: Dr. Goldberg, what evidence do you have that trampoline, board walking, and pursuit are not valuable?

Dr. Goldberg: Actually, they are valuable as fringe benefits. It is wonderful to work in a relaxed classroom. The child's attention span is rather limited, and when lessons go on in a concentrated manner, the child does not learn and becomes frustrated. If such a child is given periods of relaxation, whether by trampoline, board walking, basketball shooting or whatever, his span of attention is more or less restored, and he is better able to learn. In this way it is beneficial but not for the reasons frequently stated.

Dr. Rabinovitch: May I add one comment? In present clinical work we are seeing some major tragedies. When we hold out the promise of hope for a child and his family, we had better be on solid ground. It is a terrible thing to tell a child to jump this long or take this much eye exercise or take these pills and you will read. Many bright children in the last few years have come to us depressed and frustrated because they had expected to wake up one morning and find they were reading. Some of these children had devoted themselves with tremendous energy to these techniques. If the techniques are not relevant, it is a major tragedy to hold out false hope. Certainly the trampoline is great, if you have coordination. If a child comes to us because he has a gross motor problem and says, "I'm too tight," or "I'm too tense to move smoothly," we would send him to Martha Graham for training or give him a trampoline or something of that sort.

But if the child comes to us because he has a major symbolization problem, then we need assurance that what we recommend will have relevance to this problem.

There is another thing that, as physicians, we have to remember. If we have misled patients and they have worked hard, the next person who wants to work with them in a reasonable way will have a lot of trouble. There will be a negative psychologic set, which I think is inevitable. This is clinically of great importance to all of us.

Dr. Virginia Keeney: There seems to be general agreement to that statement. Dr. Cruickshank, do you wish to comment?

Dr. Cruickshank: I agree with Dr. Rabinovitch. I am a little concerned, however, that since we have no quantitative data we do not rule things out too abruptly, simply because the advocates do not fall within our professional field. I agree with the other panelists that we have no evidence to show that motor development as it is described in our literature in a number of cases is specific to the improvement of reading. But there is some evidence accruing that before a child can learn to read or to do anything of an abstract nature, such as number concepts, he must have a well-integrated body image and self-concept. There are people who believe that motor training can help a child develop an appropriate and well-integrated body image, out of which more abstract concepts related to learning can accrue. If these people are correct, we need to integrate motor training appropriately, in the total life experiences of a child in a good educational or psychotherapeutic regime.

Dr. Virginia Keeney: Dr. Rabinovitch, are there forms of neurologic therapy that can improve a dyslexic child?

Dr. Rabinovitch: There is no surgery, there is no prosthesis, and there is no standard neurologic help available. Medication? Possibly. Particularly in the young, driven, or hyperkinetic child, Dexedrine, paradoxically, may be very helpful in increasing concentration. There are times when the side effects of Benadryl or some other antihistaminic drugs may be useful. I like to offer a child all possible avenues of help. We follow what Dr. Bender has for so many years advised—looking for help for children from anywhere you can find it without bias and giving them whatever they need.

Although medication may help, our own experience has been that the basic need for the dyslexic child is a long, gradual, slow exposure to reading skills. If the child has no phonetic analysis skill, then he needs to learn sounds of letters first, letter naming, and then gradual blending. If he has no visual memory, the training should be directed there. If there is an associated dysgraphia or major motor difficulty, he will need training for that. If directionality is lacking, then he will need training in that. One would want to define with the child his specific symbolization defect or learning defect, and then carefully plan according to his clinical situation. Each case has to be clearly individualized.

Years ago, Paul Schilder pointed out that a good remedial therapist, who is usually a teacher with special education background, learns what is needed as he works with the child and draws out of this knowledge specific techniques for that child. There is no one method or one book, because there are no two children quite the same. You have to adapt the approach to what you see and feel in that child, and then move along with him.

Chapter 12

Therapy and therapeutic advice

Part 1: Methods and systems for teaching dyslexic pupils

Morton Botel, Ed.D.

THE NEED FOR COMPREHENSIVE STUDIES OF OUTSTANDING DEVELOPMENTAL READING PROGRAMS

Well over 90 percent of the theory, reporting, and research concerning dyslexia is in the areas of definition, etiology, and diagnosis. Relatively little attention has been given to comparing and testing methods of treatment. And only a fraction of this meager effort has been given to preventive or developmental programs.

At the University of Pennsylvania Reading Clinic, our research associate, Jane Levine, who is engaged in the mammoth task of summarizing and indexing all the available literature on dyslexia in the United States and other countries, includes in her index of treatment methods such diverse procedures as psychotherapeutic treatment, medical treatment, perceptual training, gross motor training, kinesthetic reinforcement, eclectic educational methods, group and individualized methods, and extrinsic reward. Names such as Fernald, Orton, Gillingham, Spalding, Delacato, and Barger and techniques such as the Initial Teaching Alphabet appear in her index.

However, most of this limited literature on methods and systems is clinical or remedial in nature. None of the material we have found thus far reports reliable evidence on the extent of success of various procedures. This is not to say that such diverse methods as the Fernald[8] or the Gillingham[11] system have not produced some gratifying results. However, we do not have answers to the following two fundamental questions:

1. Which of the reading methods or combinations of methods are superior in clinical and in classroom situations?
2. Which of the reading methods are peculiarly appropriate for dyslexic pu-

pils as compared with normal pupils or those with minor reading disabilities?

Having worked for 15 years as reading consultant for a number of school systems that have developed exemplary programs, I suggest that one way to find the answers to these questions is to study the reading and spelling performance of all pupils who have gone through a good school system, perhaps through the sixth grade, and to examine the rationale and elements of the program that produced the results found.

I will present such information for one school system I have recently served: the Pennridge Schools* in Bucks County, Pennsylvania.

Since estimates of the incidence of dyslexia in the total population vary from 1 percent[18] to 25 percent,[20] studies I propose would also provide data upon which to reach more valid conclusions on incidence. If a definition of dyslexia requires that we rule out poor instruction as a possible cause of reading disability,[6, 16] we must select for incidence study those school systems that have a demonstrated record of outstanding reading instruction. Data from randomly selected school systems cannot be used because the typical school system is doing a mediocre job of teaching reading, according to a recent national survey of reading practices in our public schools.[1]

An example of a poor practice, not uncommon in typical schools, is the *overplacement* of pupils. Schools overplace many pupils when they are assigned to books based upon the grade or the performance on standardized silent reading tests rather than on oral reading fluency and mastery of easier levels of the program. The frustration that accompanies overplacement produces disfluency, poor comprehension, reversals, poor spelling, poor word attack, etc., which are usually given as characteristics of dyslexia. I have estimated elsewhere that from 10 to 15 million pupils in the United States are probably overplaced[3] in their readers.

Until we are certain that schools are personalizing reading instruction for each pupil over an extended period, we must regard reading disability in these schools as a function of poor instruction in some indeterminate measure.

READING AND SPELLING PERFORMANCE
OF PENNRIDGE PUPILS

Before analyzing reading and spelling performance, it is helpful to know about the population we are studying. We should know (1) the kind of community the pupils come from, (2) the intellectual level of the pupils, (3) the average class size, (4) the average cost of educating each pupil, (5) whether these pupils are all products of the school system, (6) the amount of extra-class help provided in reading, (7) whether all pupils have been included in the

---

*The Superintendent of Pennridge Schools is Robert Rosenkranz, and the Administrative Assistant in Charge of Elementary Education is Patricia Guth. These educators have main responsibility for organizing the program and for collecting data used in this report. One of the most significant features of the program is the in-service aspect, which provides for continuous growth of teacher understanding of pupils and of teacher competency in using media as tools of instruction.

study, (8) the extent of pupil retention, and (9) the grouping pattern of classes. Following are the facts as regards Pennridge Schools:

1. The Pennridge school system is in a semirural, white, middle-class community and is largely Pennsylvania German in heritage.
2. The average I.Q. of the pupils is approximately 106. This estimate is based on the performance of all first grade pupils over the past 3 years on the SRA Primary Mental Abilities Test (K-1) 1963. A better estimate would have been established if similar results were available for all pupils at the first grade level and at their present grade level. However, school administrators believe that this is a fairly accurate estimate of the average I.Q. level in the school system.
3. The average class size is twenty-seven pupils.
4. The median cost of educating a pupil over the last 5 years is $370.82, somewhere around the national average. (The corresponding figure for many school systems on Long Island, N. Y., during the same period was over $1,000.)
5. The 772 pupils in this study have attended Pennridge Schools continuously. Seventy-five percent of these pupils began school in kindergarten and 25 percent began in grade 1.
6. Special small-group (average, 5 pupils) instruction is provided for the lowest 10 percent of pupils in the summer. Five-week, two-hour-per-day programs are available, beginning the summer following grade 1. The program is a more personalized version of the program throughout the year. In addition, similar instruction was provided last year only for the pupils in grade 6.
7. The performances of eighteen pupils in the two Opportunity Classes were not included in the tables. These pupils (2.3 percent of the population being studied) are slow learners as determined by certified psychologists using individual Binet or Wechsler-Bellevue intelligence tests and by their teachers and supervisors. (The reading performance of the ten pupils in the older Opportunity Class shows that there are two pupils reading at preprimer level, one at primer level, two at first reader level, one at beginning second level, three at high second level, and one at high third level.)
8. Approximately 10 percent of the pupils repeat one grade level by the time they finish grade 6. Repetition almost inevitably occurs in the primary years. No one repeats more than one grade level.
9. Beginning in grade 1, each classroom is organized according to reading instructional levels so that no classroom has a range greater than three reader levels.

With this background we can analyze the data in Tables 12-1, 12-2, and 12-3.

Table 12-1 is a record of the reading placement of pupils as estimated by the Botel Reading Inventory[2] on September 12, 1966. This test purports to place a pupil at his instructional level. At this level the pupil's performance characteristically must be *at least 95 percent fluent* in oral reading and *at least 75 percent correct* as measured by percentage of comprehension in independent study in

Table 12-1. Percent of pupils in grades 2 to 6 achieving various reading instructional levels on the Botel Reading Inventory on September 12, 1966

No. of pupils	Grade	Reading levels											
		Pre-primer	Pri-mer	First reader	Beg. sec-ond	High sec-ond	Beg. third	High third	Fourth	Fifth	Sixth	Jr. high	Sr. high
176	2	5	23	15	28	10	7	8	3	1			
150	3	1	2	3	7	19	20	22	18	8			
160	4			1	1	1	6	21	39	31			
165	5					1	1	9	27	52	6	5	
121	6							2	13	47	12	22	4
772													

reading workbooks. The actual placement of pupils was checked by Patricia Guth, Director of Elementary Education. Mrs. Guth estimates that the levels given by the tests are valid in at least 90 percent of the cases and vary only slightly from the pupil's true level in the remainder.

The following facts may be observed from Table 12-1:

1. There is an average range of approximately 6 to 7 levels of pupil performance at each grade level.
2. The following percentages of pupils are reading more than 2 years below grade placement: 2 percent of fourth graders; 1 percent of fifth graders; and 2 percent of sixth graders.
3. By fifth grade no pupils are reading as low as beginning second reader level and by sixth grade no pupils are reading as low as beginning third reader level. Thus, in this population, after completing fifth grade no pupils with I.Q.'s above 80 appear to be reading at levels commonly associated with dyslexia, i.e., preprimer through beginning second reader levels.

Several other facts are important: first, practically every pupil reading more than one grade level below grade placement has an I.Q., as measured by a certified psychologist, of between 80 and 90; second, only one pupil, a fourth grader reading at the first reader level, is judged by the professional staff to have a low reading score attributable largely to emotional factors; and third, only one pupil in this total population is in a special class for pupils adjudged to be minimally brain damaged.

These findings certainly suggest that dyslexia can be anticipated and minimized within the framework of a fine developmental reading program based on fundamental principles of child development, linguistic research, and learning theory.

Tables 12-2 and 12-3 are presented as further confirmation of the performance of the pupils. Table 12-2 shows the performance of the 596 pupils in grades 3 to 6 on a standardized reading test; Table 12-3 shows the performance of these pupils on a standardized spelling test. Standardized tests are useful in showing

Table 12-2. Percent of pupils in grades 3 to 6 achieving various grade equivalent scores on the SRA Reading Test* (total score) on September 30, 1966

No. of pupils	Grade	Reading grade equivalent scores										
		1.0-1.4	1.5-1.9	2.0-2.4	2.5-2.9	3.0-3.4	3.5-3.9	4.0-4.9	5.0-5.9	6.0-6.9	7.0-9.9	10.0+
150	3	1	5	3	29	21	17	15	7	2	Highest possible score	
160	4		1	1	5	6	20	37	10	20		
165	5				5	8	18	18	23	21	7	
121	6						6	15	21	42	16	

*Part of the SRA Achievement Series, Multilevel Edition.

Table 12-3. Percent of pupils in grades 3 to 6 achieving various grade equivalent scores on the SRA Spelling Test* on September 30, 1966

No. of pupils	Grade	Spelling grade equivalent scores										
		1.0-1.4	1.5-1.9	2.0-2.4	2.5-2.9	3.0-3.4	3.5-3.9	4.0-4.9	5.0-5.9	6.0-6.9	8.0-9.9	10.0+
150	3	1	5	17	15	27	24	8	1	2	Highest possible score	
160	4		1	2	3	10	13	34	14	23		
165	5				3	6	12	17	17	32	13	
121	6				1	2	8	8	23	25	33	

*Part of the SRA Achievement Series, Multilevel Edition.

Table 12-4. Comparison of pupil performance on reading and spelling tests with grade levels and expected scores

Grade level at which test given	Expected median based on I.Q. of 106	Achieved median		Lowest score		Highest score	
		Reading	Spelling	Reading	Spelling	Reading	Spelling
3.1	3.3	3.5	3.2	1.2	1.2	6+	6+
4.1	4.3	4.5	4.6	1.3	1.3	6+	6+
5.1	5.4	6.0	6.7	3.2	3.2	11+	11+
6.1	6.5	7.2	7.4	4.2	3.2	11+	11+

the general standing of groups of pupils with respect to the standard population (theoretically this represents the total population).

Some of the main features of Tables 12-2 and 12-3 can be seen in Table 12-4, in which pupil performance is compared with average expectancy at each grade with the norm and a corrected norm based on the estimate that this pupil population has an average I.Q. of 106.

By the fifth and sixth grades, these pupils, on the average, score approximately 1 year above expectancy in reading and spelling. No child in fifth or sixth grade achieved a score lower than 2 years below grade placement.

THE PENNRIDGE INSTRUCTIONAL PROGRAM

The instructional program in reading at Pennridge Schools is based on fundamental principles of child development, linguistic research, and learning theory. The system of reading instruction might be described in four categories: (1) respect for each pupil's unique pattern of maturation in personalizing his instructional program, (2) provision of broad oral and written language experiences, (3) provision of multisensory experiences to enhance language perception, and (4) provision for the learning principles of structure and discovery. Let us examine our beliefs with respect to each of these dimensions of the program and note the instructional practices that make these beliefs operational.

Respect for each pupil's unique pattern of maturation. It is essential to place each pupil at his *instructional level* in a scaled reading or spelling program and to adjust the program to the *individual learning rate* of each pupil. To accomplish these goals we take the actions outlined in the following paragraphs.

1. We require that each pupil's performance be fluent in oral reading and show high comprehension in silent reading. A breakdown in fluency, comprehension, or both, accompanied and identified by inevitable symptoms of disorientation, disfluency, and vague understanding is regarded as overplacement and leads to frustration. Such performance signals the need for helping pupils work for mastery of simpler material before going on to more complex work. The Botel Reading Inventory is used to place each pupil at his instructional level. This is the first step in continuous appraisal. Reliability and validity of placement derives from the oral and silent reading performance in the classroom on a day-by-day basis. Needed adjustments may then be made.

2. We systematically teach high-yield subskills so that each pupil can advance as quickly as possible. These subskills include word attack, vocabulary, oral reading, and silent reading.

3. We encourage each pupil to read widely among books of his choosing. By the efficient use of the school library and classroom library, by providing time during school hours for this pleasure reading, and by commitments to cultivate lifetime reading habits, we completely individualize the pupil's independent reading program to his level, rate, and interests.

Provision of broad oral language and written language experiences. Language skills are interrelated, and they reinforce one another. Two major aspects of this principle involve (1) the need to build reading and writing instruction on experience with oral language, and (2) the need to help pupils understand at the outset of reading instruction that writing is a record of speech and that reading converts the alphabetic code back into oral language.

To accomplish these needs we attempt to provide the following advantages for each pupil:

1. Listening, speaking, and dramatic experiences designed to improve and extend control over vocabulary, articulation, syntax, intonation (the melodies of speech), paralanguage (the sounds of emotion), and kinesics

(the use of facial expression and body movement). (Since the only sounds which we record systematically are vowel and consonant sounds, we must help pupils appreciate and reconstruct the other missing structural elements.)

2. Opportunities to see his speech or oral sentences represented immediately by written sentences as the teacher records what he says on chalkboard or paper
3. Systematic help in learning to recognize and write the alphabet
4. Opportunities to write his own ideas and read (really speak) them back again from the written record
5. Specific, continuous help in learning that consonant and vowel sounds are represented by letter patterns

Provision of multisensory experience to enhance the perception of language. Learning takes place by way of our sensory apparatus. Wepman[21] has suggested that individuals may differ in modality maturation and that they may be genetically visile or audile. If this is true, then we must provide instruction sensitive to these different types. Even if this theory is true, it is possible that the meaning for instruction is not that different emphases be provided for different types but rather that all sensory modalities, including tactile and kinesthetic, be cultivated and brought to bear on learning.

One area of consensus, among the various (and very different) approaches for teaching reading to dyslexic pupils, appears to be the support for a multisensory approach to learning. These are provided in three major ways.

First, pupils who are apparently unready to begin formal reading are helped to develop gross muscle and fine muscle control through perceptuomotor experiences like those recommended by Kephart,[12] de Hirsch,[7] Maney,[15] and Frostig.[10] Such activities are concerned with the development of increased awareness of body image, coordination, and laterality. They include unhurried but structured opportunities to throw, skip, jump, ride a bike, hop, walk a plank, handle materials and toys (including geometric forms and letters), build blocks, finger paint, play rhythm games, engage in general calisthenics or muscular fitness activities, copy designs (including letters and other geometric shapes) write on the chalkboard or blank paper, and use stencils to produce letters and geometric shapes.

Second, pupils are helped to see and feel speech as well as to produce and hear it. Attention is focused on the speech mechanism as the teacher produces and contrasts sounds in word pairs that have minimal contrasts in various positions, such as *hat-cat, at-it, pat-pot, pan-pat.* Pupils study their own speech mechanism in articulatory exercises, sometimes with the help of mirrors.

Third, pupils are helped to learn letters, words, and sentences by looking at, saying, tracing, copying, and writing from memory *from the beginning.* Tracing and copying are generally dropped for most pupils within a few months or a year, as they demonstrate ability to master work readily without such tactics. Such instruction is regarded as spelling and handwriting as well as reading. Dyslexic pupils whose progress is significantly slower than their general aptitude would suggest should continue tracing until *they themselves* realize they no longer need this reinforcement. Pupils are the best guide in making this decision. It is an individual matter.

Provision for the learning principles of structure and discovery. We believe, with Bruner,[5] that teaching the *structure of a subject* rather than limiting study to facts, rules, and manipulations is important in learning. Emphasis on structure simplifies a subject, makes it more understandable, ensures greater recall, and increases pupil interest. The structures of language and communication (sound-letter pattern relationships, intonation, syntax, etc.) are presented in such a way that pupils will better understand the logical interrelationships of the elements under study. Further, these interrelationships are presented by a discovery method: pupils are challenged to look for patterns and clues and are guided to draw logical conclusions and rules for themselves. (Explication of this use of *structure* and *discovery* in teaching requires more space than the other three aspects of instructional design. This does not imply that the topic is of greater moment than the others. Rather, it is because of difficulty in making the ideas clear without the use of more illustrative material.) Examples of application of the ideas of structure and discovery are found in two categories of content: sound-spelling pattern study and sentence pattern study.

1. *Sound-spelling pattern study.* In the sound-spelling pattern aspect of vocabulary study, we move from regular spelling of words to the less regular and then irregular spellings. Words in such study are presented in patterned sets.

   Examples of some early patterns that we teach in the instructional design and that foster discovery are as follows:

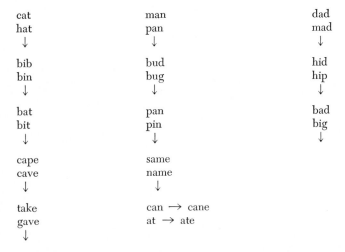

The arrows suggest that the patterns can be extended to include more words. As pupils examine the patterns, or *structures,* to see how they are alike and different with respect to sound and letter patterns, they will be able to discover for themselves how they can be extended. Telling the child the words is not out of the question, but whenever possible, teachers should foster discovery by adding additional clues. Study of the rule in the formal sense is postponed until pupils have studied the pattern and extended it in this intuitive manner. Actual emphasis on the statement of the rule is minimal until the upper grades.

Later patterns become more complex, revealing the alternative ways of spelling given sounds and structural changes in the root elements of words that have endings added, such as the following patterns:

/ ā /				
ate	rain	may	run →	running
cake	paid	stay	hop →	hopping
↓	↓	↓		
come →	coming		penny →	pennies
hope →	hoping		baby →	babies

The scope and sequence of such patterns are set forth by several authors such as Fries[9] and Botel.[4]

2. *Sentence pattern study.* In the study of sentence patterns, we utilize certain patterns that occur with great frequency in English. For example, sentences having the following basic structures and their variations, elaborations, and combinations make up perhaps from 80 to 90 percent of the sentences in the speech of typical Americans:

Noun	*Verb*	*Noun*
The boy	plays	the piano.
The engineer	builds	the highway.
The _____	_____s	the _____.

Noun	*Verb*
The lion	growled.
The boy	whistled.
The _____	_____ ed.

Noun	*Linking verb*	*Noun*
The man	is	an engineer.
The flower	is	a rose.
The _____	is	a _____.

Noun	*Linking verb*	*Adjective*
The flower	is	very beautiful.
The boy	is	very unhappy.
The _____	is	very _____.

These patterns suggest many activities that help pupils get the feel for written sentences and their relationship to oral sentences. As pupils explore structure sentences such as

Those _____s are _____ing my _____.

they see how structure serves as a vehicle for meaning. They begin with structural elements only: word order, structure words (the, those, are, and my) and word endings (s, ed, and ing) and, using these clues, create sentences by adding words to make the sentence sensible. They then experiment with adding words, phrases, and clauses in various positions before, after, and within the sentence.

This experience helps pupils see how modification of the meaning of sentences is affected by elaborations of basic patterns. Moreover, it helps pupils learn to express their ideas better both orally and in writing. By thinking of the work with such sentences, not as filling in the blanks, but rather as a way of thinking about and saying total utterances, we work with intonational structures as well. In this way we encourage pupils to read these sentences aloud with the melodies of speech.

The scope and sequence of such syntactic patterns are set forth in books by Roberts,[17] Lloyd and Warfel,[14] Lefevre,[13] Strickland,[19] and Botel.[4]

Clearly, this description of the Pennridge reading program suggests a broadly based flexible developmental program, which from the beginning is sensitive to the level, rate, and motivation of each pupil. The results of this report suggest that with similar populations as in Pennridge Schools, few pupils, if any, need be reading lower than fourth grade level by the *end* of sixth grade.

Similar studies of total pupil populations in different regions of the United States and in different communities—urban, suburban, and rural—where good programs have been in force for extended periods should delineate high-yield elements and alternatives in the design of a reading system that will serve all pupils, including dyslexics.

REFERENCES

1. Austin, M., and Morrison, C.: The first R, New York, 1963, The Macmillan Co.
2. Botel, M.: Botel reading inventory, Chicago, 1966, Follett Publishing Co.
3. Botel, M.: Guide to the Botel reading inventory, Chicago, 1966, Follett Publishing Co.
4. Botel, M., et al.: Spelling and writing patterns, pupil's books and teacher's editions, levels A to F, Chicago, 1965, Follett Publishing Co.
5. Bruner, J.: The process of education, Cambridge, 1960, Harvard University Press.
6. Critchley, M.: Developmental dyslexia, Springfield, Ill., 1964, Charles C Thomas, Publisher.
7. de Hirsch, K., et al.: Predicting reading failure, New York, 1966, Harper & Row, Publishers.
8. Fernald, G.: Remedial techniques in basic school subjects, New York, 1943, McGraw-Hill Book Co.
9. Fries, C. C.: Linguistics and reading, New York, 1963, Holt, Rinehart & Winston, Inc.
10. Frostig, M., and Horne, D.: The Frostig program for the development of visual perception, Chicago, 1964, Follett Publishing Co.
11. Gillingham, A., and Stillman, B.: Remedial training, Cambridge, 1960, Educators Publishing Service, Inc.
12. Kephart, N. C.: The slow learner in the classroom, Columbus, O., 1960, Charles E. Merrill Books, Inc.
13. Lefevre, C. A.: Linguistics and the teacher of reading, New York, 1964, McGraw-Hill Book Co.
14. Lloyd, D., and Warfel, H.: American English in its cultural setting, New York, 1956, Alfred A. Knopf, Inc.
15. Maney, E. S.: Reading readiness program, Elizabethtown, 1958, The Continental Press, Inc.
16. Money, J. (editor): Reading disability progress and research needs in dyslexia, Baltimore, 1962, Johns Hopkins Press.
17. Roberts, P.: Patterns of English, New York, 1956, Harcourt, Brace & World, Inc.
18. Stauffer, R.: Certain psychological manifestations of retarded readers, J. Educ. Res. **41:** 435-452, 1948.

19. Strickland, R. G.: The contribution of structural linguistics to the teaching of reading, writing, and grammar in the elementary school, Bulletin of the School of Education, Indiana University 40(1): 1964.
20. Walker, L., and Cole, E. M.: Familial patterns of expression of specific reading disability in a population sample, Bull. Orton Soc. 15:3-15, 1965.
21. Wepman, J. M.: Dyslexia: its relationship to language acquisition and concept formation. In Money, J., editor: Reading disability, Baltimore, 1962, Johns Hopkins Press.

Part 2: Treatment needs of the child with developmental dyslexia

June L. Orton

The treatment needs of the dyslexic child are largely *educational,* requiring the skills of a specially trained reading therapist, and are based upon diagnostic studies to determine the areas and extent of the language defect, the nature of the learning impairment, and the child's reaction to it.

By definition, specific dyslexia excludes the presence of gross physical, mental, and emotional defects or environmental deficits and implies an innate developmental delay or deviation in the child's ability to acquire the meaningful use of graphic language symbols—reading, spelling, and writing. This peculiar learning difficulty may appear in children of superior intelligence from superior homes and has been noted in other countries in about the same proportions as in the school population of the United States. Certain families seem predisposed to language problems, boys much more so than girls. The effect of such a learning block upon the personality and emotional development of these children has long been recognized, as has their urgent need for early recognition and adequate remedial training. The development of predictive tests of kindergarten children's later reading ability, primary group screening tests, a few special classes for dyslexics, and experiments with flexible, differentiated methods of teaching reading are all encouraging. In general, however, the needs of dyslexic children are still unrecognized, and facilities for diagnosis and remediation are limited. Teacher-training courses are few, and when remediation is attempted in the schools, it is usually "too little and too late."

The treatment of dyslexic children is complicated by the fact that they are by no means all alike and, therefore, require not only a very specialized type of education but also a highly individualized one. This limits the public schools in attempting to provide adequate programs, since public schools seldom have enough regular classrooms and teachers to keep up with the increasing population. Even the attempt to meet every pupil's special needs suggests a paradox. As Robert M. Hutchins stated in a recent press article: "Since education means the development of the highest powers of the individual, the idea of mass education involves a contradiction in terms."[3a] This applies especially to the problem of educating dyslexics, since many of them cannot profit from group instruction. They usually will gain most from individual lessons in which the teacher can choose whatever procedures are indicated at that particular time for that particular child and, most important, can establish and maintain a therapeutic relationship.

This individual approach, which presupposes a diagnostic study, may be called a clinical approach, but the services offered by so-called reading clinics vary greatly. Some clinics give a limited range of tests; some give many tests but with little correlation or interpretation and a blanket recommendation of remedial reading with no specifications as to what remedial reading should include or how it could be implemented. Other reading clinics are organized more like child-guidance centers and provide diagnosis and treatment through the coordinated services of a language disability team.

The team approach is desirable because dyslexia exists *in the child* and the child exists *in* his own particular environment. For an understanding of the reading difficulty, the whole child, his whole environment, and the interaction of the child with his environment must be evaluated and often "treated," which is more than can be expected from any one member of a clinic staff. Preliminary examinations require the skills derived from specialized training and experience not only in pedagogy but also in medicine, clinical psychology, social work, and counseling as related to the understanding of developmental language delays in children. A comprehensive medical-developmental-social-educational history provides information as to the findings that have been obtained by ophthalmologists and other specialists and points up the areas requiring further investigation. Before remedial teaching can be started, or along with it, there may be need for medical correction of visual or other physical defects, psychotherapy for the child and/or his parents, and changes in the child's environment. There will certainly be need for an able arranger to supervise and schedule the program to suit the school, the parents, the therapist, and the child. Successful treatment also involves continued enlightenment and support of the classroom teachers and the parents, who may be disappointed at first when no miracle occurs but who can often be drawn into active participation; e.g., the classroom teacher may be willing to substitute oral examinations for written examinations and arrange for the parents to help the pupil at home by reading parts of his assignments to him or letting him dictate his compositions to them.

The therapists must understand these correlates of their pupils' reading problems but must be free to focus their activities upon the teaching itself, which is their area of special competence. This includes understanding the normal development of language in children (oral language, "thinking" language, and written language) and its auditory, visual, and motor components and temporal and spatial elements. The remedial teacher should be familiar with the history and current methods of teaching the language arts, the research studies that support or discredit them, and the methods to which the pupil has been exposed. Training in speech pathology, and particularly work with adult aphasics, is helpful but does not in itself prepare a teacher to be a reading-spelling-handwriting therapist. This specialist must know much more about the history and development of *graphic* language; the alphabetic English code with its rules, regulations, and exceptions; modern grammar; semantics; linguistics; and the newer theories of learning from animal studies, programmed and machine teaching, and computer experiments. The education of the reading therapist is never finished!

Unfortunately, most schools of education do not provide even the foundations, and little mention is made of specific dyslexia in special education texts or courses. To qualify as a reading therapist, the teacher is also expected to be a paragon of virtues: highly intelligent, imaginative, resourceful, observant, objective, sensitive, sympathetic, experienced in work with children, and still very fond of them!

After all of the preliminaries and accessories to an individualized retraining program have been arranged and a qualified therapist has been secured, how and what is the dyslexic child to be taught? The answer can be expressed in three words: "That all depends." The type and method of remediation will depend on many factors: the child's chronologic age, his mental age, his emotional maturity, his hyperactivity or passive resistance, the academic demands upon him, his goals, and his parents' goals for him. More specifically, the child's teacher will take into account the *quality* of his reading, spelling, and writing as disclosed in the initial testing and an analysis of the visual, auditory, and kinesthetic fractions of his language processes. The dyslexic child's understanding of the spoken word, his ability to express ideas in speech, and his level of concrete and abstract thinking must also be considered by the therapist, and a unique program must be devised to meet each pupil's specific needs. The pupil himself will furnish additional clues to the alert instructor in every subsequent lesson.

The therapist must work, however, from some organized conceptual background, and even those therapists who pride themselves on being eclectic must follow some general plan and have a reason for it. From our studies and experience, based upon earlier training with Samuel T. Orton, we have found that the chief difficulty of dyslexic children seems to be that of forming dependable, retrievable *associations* between sound patterns, which constitute the spoken word, and symbol patterns, which represent the printed word. In most of our school cases, we do not see evidence of a primary distortion in perceptual processes per se, and the children may have had no difficulty in the development of oral speech, motor skills, or even handwriting. They do have a specific difficulty in *remembering* whole printed words as presented visually in the sight method of teaching, and they do not know how to use phonetic associations as a guide to reading and spelling.

Orton pointed out one characteristic symptom of the specific reading disability, confirmed by many other observers, which contributes to the associative, integrative difficulty. This is the children's confusion during early school years in recalling the direction of reversible letters like "b" and "d" and words like "on" and "no." Later, they have trouble remembering the correct order of letters in words and may read "left" as "felt," spell "snow" as s-o-w-n, or reverse syllables in a word. (One of our third grade pupils recently wrote "is" as "si" and read "who saw" as "how was.") Orton's term "strephosymbolia," meaning twisted symbols, is useful in describing this pervasive characteristic of the dyslexic child. His hypothesis that this symptom and other findings might indicate an inconsistency in the normally unilateral control of the language function by the dominant brain hemisphere, genetically determined, suggested a new physiologic approach to word blindness in children. Such studies could profitably be carried much further by the neurophysiologists and the geneticists, who now have more data and improved techniques to investigate normal and deviant language development.

Orton's envisagement of the dyslexic problem as one involving the cerebral integrative processes and the establishment of dependable associations between visual and auditory language symbols led directly to retraining procedures that correct the directional confusions and establish the desired linkages between spoken sounds and the written letters that represent them. An important contribution was his use of simultaneous finger tracing or writing to reinforce the visual and auditory associations through another sensory channel. This visual-auditory-kinesthetic technique was later systematized by Anna Gillingham and Bessie Stillman in their comprehensive and well-known manuals for remedial training.

Another important aspect of remedial teaching is that it must be a carefully programmed, step-by-step process of building associations, starting with the simplest language units and proceeding systematically to the more complex language units in a hierarchy of learning tasks. We usually begin with a few selected consonant sounds and their letter symbols and the short-vowel sound of "a," teaching the pupil these individual phonic units and how to blend them to form a recognizable word, which is "reading." We also teach him to hear the separate sounds in a spoken word sequentially and write a corresponding series of letters, which is "spelling." In individual work, repetitions can be given as long as needed, with immediate quiet correction of mistakes and immediate smiling approval of the correct response. Activities adapted to the pupil's interests are introduced to provide practice and to maintain effort. It is rewarding to see the pupil's own confidence in his learning ability steadily increase as he is helped to master each step before advancing to a more difficult one.

It is often hard for adult readers and even for many teachers to realize that retarded readers and poor spellers require this specific training in our alphabet code and that they must be *taught* the sounds represented by the letters singly and in combinations and *shown* how to blend them together to form a word pattern. It is not necessary for most of us to understand the mechanisms underlying the various media of communication—the telephone, radio, or television—or to analyze the mechanics of our own speaking and writing habits. But when there is a breakdown at any point we must have the help of the trained communications expert. I doubt if many very able readers could produce the short sounds of all the vowels promptly and accurately; and it does not matter at all if a good reader can or cannot do so. Most retarded readers and spellers cannot, but it is very important that *they* be taught these particular letter-sound associations, the keystones of most syllables. The remedial teachers must know and teach the English phonemes as precisely and as accurately as they would the notes in a musical score, and they must often begin their own professional training by relearning the English language analytically and thoroughly, as if it were Russian or modern Greek.

As the pupils progress and their reading techniques become internalized and automatic, the remedial program is extended to increase their understanding of word meanings, sentences, and paragraph patterns and to facilitate their written expression. They will need long-continued remedial work to improve their spelling and writing, which will always show some traces of the earlier dyslexia if the condition has been at all severe. The amount of time that should be allotted to remedial work and its duration will vary, but an estimate of the hours per week and the months or years that will be needed can usually be forecast. This should be understood by the parents and the student. The program may be interrupted sometimes for periods of rest and assimilation, but it should be available to meet any marked change or increase in academic requirements, which may be expected at the fourth grade level, upon entering junior high school, upon taking up a subject with a new vocabulary, or upon beginning a foreign language. The latter should be most carefully selected and presented, if attempted at all. Several of our dyslexic students have had particular difficulty in meeting the foreign language requirements for a Ph.D. degree. It is encouraging to know, however, that many have successfully completed college and postgraduate professional training, although some have required extra time to do so.

We have been emphasizing the individual differences among dyslexic children and their need for individualized remedial training, but comprehensive programming in a public school system necessitates some group instruction. The same techniques that we have described for individual dyslexics have been applied successfully to selected pupils in small groups or special classes, sometimes with the entire curriculum adapted to their reading limitations. (This is very different from the practice of placing all poor readers together in a slow reading group or a remedial reading class which is taught by the same classroom methods with the same materials only more slowly or at a lower reading level.) Several states have passed legislation establishing special classes for children of normal intelligence with specific learning disabilities, federal funds are becoming available for the training of more special teachers, and the future is beginning to look more hopeful for the public education of the dyslexic child.

Some younger pupils with the diagnosis of specific dyslexia learn to read later without special instruction, but since every child is expected to learn to read and write in the first grade, regardless of his physiologic or emotional maturity, the late bloomer is subjected to devastating experiences in his early school years, which may retard his learning rate and his personality development. A suitable remedial program may accelerate his progress and forestall the damaging effects of frustration and failure which will follow if he has to wait for maturation to solve his problems.

We, therefore, recommend for all children with the symptoms of developmental dyslexia an early, active, constructive, enlightened, sympathetic, individualized, and specific educational attack upon the language disability itself, in a suitable education setting, as the best approach to meeting their treatment needs.

REFERENCES

1. Bender, L.: Specific reading disability as a maturational lag, Bull. Orton Soc. 7:9-18, 1957.

2. de Hirsch, K.: Predicting reading failure, New York, 1966, Harper & Row, Publishers.
3. Gillingham, A., and Stillman, B. E.: Remedial training for children with specific disability in reading, spelling and penmanship, eds. 5 and 6, Cambridge, reprinted 1964, Educators Publishing Service.
3a. Hutchins, R. M.: Machine age in education, Journal and Sentinel (Winston-Salem, N. C.), 1966.
4. Masland, R. L.: Brain mechanisms underlying the language function, Rockefeller University, Oct. 28, 1966, The Orton Society, Inc.
5. Orton, J. L.: A guide to teaching phonics, Winston-Salem, N. C., 1964, Orton Reading Center.
6. Orton, J. L.: The Orton-Gillingham approach. In Money, J., editor: The disabled reader, Baltimore, 1966, Johns Hopkins Press.
7. Orton, J. L., and Karnes, L. R.: A history of specific dyslexia in relation to special education. In Karnes, L. R., editor: Dyslexia in special education, monograph no. I, 5-22, Pomfret, Conn., 1965, The Orton Society, Inc.
8. Orton, S. T.: Reading, writing and speech problems in children, New York, 1937, W. W. Norton & Co., Inc.
9. Orton, S. T.: Visual functions in strephosymbolia, Arch. Ophthal. 30:707-713, 1943.
10. Rawson, M. B.: After a generation's time, Bull. Orton Soc. 16:24-37, 1966.
11. Saunders, R. E.: Psychotherapy with remedial reading, Bull. Orton Soc. 11:46, 1961.
12. Slingerland, B.: Screening tests for identifying children with specific language disability, Cambridge, 1964, Educators Publishing Service.
13. Slingerland, B.: A public school program of prevention for young children with specific language disability. In Karnes, L. R., editor: Dyslexia in special education, monograph no. 1, Pomfret, Conn., 1965, The Orton Society, Inc.
14. Sperry, R. W.: The great cerebral commissure, Scientif. Amer. 210:42-52, 1964.
15. Subirana, A.: The problem of cerebral dominance: the relationship between handedness and language function, Bull. Orton Soc. 14:45-66, 1964.
16. Thompson, L. J.: Reading disability: developmental dyslexia, Springfield, Ill., 1966, Charles C Thomas, Publisher.

Part 3: Responsibilities of the ophthalmologist

John V. V. Nicholls, M.D., F.R.C.S.

Dyslexia is a complex problem. It is complex in etiology, complex in its manifestations, complex in the analysis of cause in any particular case, and complex in treatment.

Only infrequently is dyslexia primarily an ocular problem. Solution of the problem requires the coordinated efforts of people of many disciplines. The general physician, neurologist, psychiatrist, pediatrician, otologist, and ophthalmologist, together with the psychologist and educationalist, all play important and correlated roles in the diagnosis, investigation, treatment, and education of dyslexic patients. Visual disturbances are so wide ranging, so variable in their significance, and so dependent on other systemic health factors that each patient must be assessed on his own merit.

The interplay of physical and emotional factors—not only in the assessment of the significant visual aberrations found, such as refractive errors, neurologic deficits, and ocular incoordination, but also in the modes of treatment—makes examination of affected children by an eye physician, or ophthalmologist, essential. As unrelated problems, these children, of course, may have any ocular defect or disease seen in the general population.

The ophthalmologist, for his part, must not only diagnose and treat specific ocular disturbances exhibited by the patient but also knowledgeably and dependably segregate and relate any fraction of ocular disturbance that is caused by, associated with, or subsequent to the central nervous system defects. As the physician often initially consulted, the ophthalmologist acquires major responsibilities relative to the subsequent and total investigations. He must be prepared to direct proper and responsible studies, seeing them through to a logical conclusion. In order to do this with intelligence he must be fully aware of the contributions to total diagnosis and therapy that may be expected from other disciplines. The ophthalmologist must have a working knowledge of the other possible factors involved. He must exhibit the attributes of the complete physician. A merely technical attitude is not enough. Proper counseling and even eugenic advice should be expected. Nowhere in the practice of medicine or ophthalmology is this function more evident.

These multiple approaches, requiring as they do the close collaboration of many disciplines, can be carried out particularly well in some sort of group practice or clinic. The group should contain members representing neurology, psychiatry, ophthalmology, otology, and pediatrics. The ophthalmologist will be aided in his duties by the service of an orthoptist. Also, there should be a clinical psychologist, experienced and interested in psychometric evaluations, so that such quantitative data can be provided to teachers. Far from least, there should be an expert group of sociologists or social scientists.

Current treatment of dyslexia, in the last analysis, is largely a matter of education through the use of modified training techniques. Therefore, the diagnostic and medical groups or clinics must work with the understanding cooperation of the school authorities. There must be easy and free channels of communication between teachers and associated personnel in the field on the one hand and among medical workers, psychologists, and educational researchers on the other hand.

Ophthalmologists must enhance such developments through their patients, at parent-teacher meetings, and at conferences with educational authorities. At present integration is far from being achieved in most areas of the United States and Canada.

In the absence of formal organizations, each ophthalmologist must develop such coordinations and be prepared to take the helm sooner or later. It is often to the ophthalmologist that these patients turn. Not infrequently, the parents have sought help elsewhere, in an undirected and uncoordinated way. They often have received conflicting or pseudoscientific information. Frequently, there has been great expense with no benefit. Ophthalmologists must equip themselves as knowledgeable and compassionate advisors.

In order to advise, ophthalmologists must identify and evaluate places in the community where the kinds of needed assistance may be obtained at reasonable prices. Channels of referral and communication must be set up beforehand. Time and effort must be expended to push matters to a decision.

Following the patient's first visit, the ophthalmologist must obtain from the child's teacher impressions as to the exact type of difficulty the child is having. Then, a psychometric assessment is most helpful. Many school boards supply this kind of survey and advice from within their own systems. Otherwise, it must be obtained from private psychometricians. Information concerning the level of intelligence and the area of perceptual deficiency is vital. It is in this context that any visual deficiencies must be assessed.

Then, depending upon the general medical history, diagnostic assistance must be sought from the pediatrician, neurologist, otologist, or psychiatrist, and treatment must be instituted as indicated. For this type of assistance the ophthalmologist must choose people who he knows are interested, self-critical, and well motivated. Also, the school authorities must be given a complete report.

This is a great deal of work indeed, but proper care demands no less. In actual fact, after referral channels are set up, it often turns out to be less work than expected. In the majority of children, little work is needed after the initial consultations, programming, and conferences with the teacher.

In reviewing my 20 years of experience with dyslexic children, I find that approximately 15 percent of children in each of the early year classes can be expected to have a significant reading difficulty. Of this number, about two-thirds usually can be adequately corrected in the average school system, providing the ophthalmologist and people from other disciplines cooperate with the teacher. Perhaps the teaching techniques require modifications. Maybe parental pressures should be reduced and emotional disturbances corrected. Then the teaching progresses relatively well, and by the time the child is in the sixth or seventh grade, he has pretty well caught up with other children of his age.

This leaves one-third of the children who are not so easily handled. Special training on an individual basis is needed. Within this group, one will find about one-third forming a hard core, children who are little helped by any known technique. It is easy to think of these children as having an organic defect of the parietotemporal lobe, and certainly looking over my own clinical records, I support this. These children often exhibit evidence of organic brain disturbance by physical signs and electroencephalographic changes. The ophthalmologist must know the facilities and programs of this type the school system itself provides or where assistance may be obtained elsewhere.

For what, more specifically, is the ophthalmologist responsible? He is responsible for a detailed history and a complete, painstaking ophthalmic and neuro-ophthalmic examination using cycloplegic drops for refraction. Where there is hyperopia or esophoria (crossed eyes), it is strongly recommended that atropine be the cycloplegic agent. Many youngsters have hidden or latent hyperopia of high order, which may be unknown if a proper cycloplegic agent is not used.

There is no valid defense for prescribing spectacle corrections for small refractive errors or bifocals in the absence of motility problems.

A detailed ocular motility study, both motor and sensory, is required. An experienced orthoptist may be of great assistance. Orthoptic training occasionally may be indicated when there are fusional difficulties, i.e., disturbances in the sensorial side (afferent area) of the motor coordinational mechanism. Surgical correction of extraocular muscles may be required if there is a significant motor problem, or heterotropia. This is an area in which meticulous surgical technique should be used, with minimal handling of the tissues and most careful control of bleeding.

There is no valid defense for surgical correction of *small* motor imbalances. The topical use of miotic drops for excess convergence in esophoria and esotropia, under periodic medical supervision, may avoid extraocular muscle surgery by helping the young child until facial growth and increased neuro-ophthalmic stability are achieved. Like any other medical treatment, the occlusion of the better eye for correction of amblyopia, or lazy eye, is a medical responsibility, although it may be delegated, under supervision, to an orthoptist. Ocular occlusion for any reason is a medical responsibility.

Finally, I wish to emphasize statements made previously. We are dealing with a complex problem. This very complexity and the emotional tension engendered in the parents and in the child contribute to confusion, frustration, and even panic. This is fertile soil for the promoter, the pseudoscientist, or the charlatan. The ophthalmologist has an inescapable duty to assure that intellectual honesty and good sense prevail and to protect the patient. The patient and public welfare are our first concern.

Part 4: Facilities and their evaluation

William M. Cruickshank, Ph.D.

Interdisciplinary tolerance and respect in regard to reading problems are greatly needed. No one of the professions related to the treatment of dyslexia is so penetrating as to be considered omnipotent. In terms of the complex problem (dyslexia) that we face, an understanding of the other professions is essential; this involves empathy. Neither neurology nor psychology can give all the answers, yet many psychologists are doing high level work within the construct of their philosophic orientation. Educators should listen to the counsel of physicians, and physicians to educators in this related field.

No single field of investigation can probe the entire biologic spectrum in which we are forced to work. In this light and in this feeling, which is very deep seated on my part, I hope we can now consider the evaluation of facilities available for the treatment of dyslexia.

Recently, I made a detailed survey of all facilities in an eastern state that purported to be serving brain-injured children. This survey went beyond the immediate topic of dyslexia. Within the facilities of this state's departments of education, health, and welfare (in a large state of many millions of people), we found sixteen remedial facilities. Six of the facilities were public school systems. One was a state school and hospital. Nine were private schools, but one of these was not discovered until 2 days before the survey was completed and is not included in the survey.

In evaluation of facilities, we should consider what Botel has stressed in the need for good studies of teaching methods and diagnostic techniques. Interprofessionally, what makes a good facility for these children?

Perhaps there is need for extensive federal, state, and municipal funds for the establishment of modern regional service and training programs to fill the tremendous gap in this field. This survey, in reasonable depth, exemplifies the situation in a state that proudly is one of the wealthiest states in the nation.

The fifteen facilities studied vary from those providing free (tax-reimbursed) tuition, as in the six public school centers, to one private school that costs $10,000 per annum per child. This is not an unusual figure, and during the next few years most private schools providing across-the-board services will have put their cost at about this level.

These institutions were studied on the basis of ten areas, and in each area the institutions were awarded a point ranking of from one to one hundred somewhat arbitrarily. This was done by competent personnel not only working from materials that the agency provided but also actually working within each institution for 6 full days.

A prime area of appraisal is the staff. To what extent is there interdisciplinary representation and to what extent does the staff meet the qualifications of their own professions? Were the ophthalmologists certified by the American Board of Ophthalmology? To what extent were the psychologists looked upon as diplomates in their own professional organization?

In fifteen highly publicized programs, called, in many instances, leaders, ratings ranged from 12 to 90, with an average rating of the fifteen institutions less than 50. In other words, we see that less than 50 percent of the staffs meet the professional standards of their own profession. This was in 1965.

To what extent are ancillary services utilized? In almost every chapter in this book, the authors have emphasized the need for interdisciplinary structure. In two institutions the rating was 1, which meant that some worker passed through an office, once upon a time, representing something other than his discipline. Interestingly, these were two of the public school systems. As an educator, I believe that one of the greatest needs within our own profession is the demonstration that public schools and educators cannot stand alone. We must expand our frame of reference to a broader professional spectrum. Ratings of 1, 1, 3, 4, 12, and 60 were received by the six public schools in the area of utilization of consultants.

In the area of diagnostic and follow-up services, ratings spread from 8 to 91, with an average of 42.

In the evaluation of pupils themselves and their periodic reassessments, nine of the fifteen agencies rated less than 10 on a possible score of 100. To what extent do we know how children change as time goes on? A number of times, when we looked at public school records, the last diagnostic evaluation was 4 years earlier. Children do change, and they change rapidly. Even educational assessments are often more than 3 years old.

In the scope of the educational program, we see similar negative findings in these fifteen agencies, findings which, I suspect, are typical of the United States as a whole. In the area of educational methods we did not make judgments of the adequacy of one method over another. We were concerned with the concreteness of a working philosophy. We sought philosophies that were structured. Eight of the institutions studied could not define the philosophy on which they worked. The others could.

In the area of parent contacts or integration of parents into the activities of education, we found the lowest rating of the ten areas. Not one of the agencies received a rating of higher than 61 from our evaluators. Parents have their children far more clock hours than anybody else; yet, frequently we, as professional people, leave them at the end of a limb and frequently we saw it off by saying we do not want parents to tamper. If parents are made a part of the interdisciplinary team and provided with the counseling they often need, they can become one of the most important factors in behalf of the children's development.

What about in-service training of the staff in this uncharted but ongoing field? Eleven of the fifteen agencies carried on no consistent in-service program. Only two of the remaining agencies had an in-service program in an interdisciplinary setting. On the contrary, it was usually the physicians meeting alone, the psychologists meeting alone, or the educators meeting alone. This meeting exemplifies the necessary cross fertilization of ideas.

I am concerned about the sizable number of agencies, in a wealthy state such as this, in which out of a possible 1,000 points in rating there is an average of only 178. The endowment of one institution is 14 million dollars. Another is operating in a building that has been condemned by the fire department. Still another has a rating of 295 with a $7,500 per annum tuition.

In three other public schools in a large metropolitan area populated by professional people (physicians, lawyers, merchants, etc.), in which integration problems are few, everybody lives very comfortably, tax rates are low, and educational facilities are low, there were ratings of 357, 401, and 412. Can we tolerate this?

This statistical data indicates pressing need for more and improved remedial facilities. I do not think the parents or the children who are caught in this situation need tolerate such professional service. I do not blame people for being rebellious. As a matter of fact, I urge them to be rebellious in behalf of their children. As professional people, we cannot be content with mediocrity in this field. If we do not join these parents and offer them the kind of guidance that they require and that the federal legislators say they will support, we may not have an opportunity to try again.

Part 5: Management of dyslexias associated with binocular control abnormalities

Curtis D. Benton, Jr., M.D.

If we define dyslexia in its broadest sense, as a selective retardation of reading skills resulting in an observable gap between a child's progress in reading and his progress in other areas of learning, then dyslexia is one of the most common and important problems in primary education today. The necessity of a multidisciplinary approach to the study of dyslexia has been stressed,[10] but contributions from ophthalmology have not answered enough questions.[12, 17, 19]

A 7-year study was made in an attempt to evaluate the role of binocular control abnormalities in dyslexia. Examination of 1,500 school children because of specific reading problems showed some new and interesting findings. About 200 other slow readers were rejected because their problems were judged to be caused by a low I.Q., with poor achievement in all subjects. These 1,500 children all came from middle-class or upper-class families who were interested enough in their children to seek private medical care. Factors such as poor home environment, inadequate motivation, frail health, and substandard schools were eliminated by this accidental case selection.

Seventy-seven percent of the total, or 1,155 children, were found to have a binocular control abnormality. Management of 700 of these children has extended for periods long enough for evaluation—from 9 to 24 months, with follow-up observations up to 4 years in many cases.

BACKGROUND

Initially I found that most dyslexic children had normal eyes on routine examination. Many had distinct environmental learning advantages but failed to improve under psychiatric or psychologic treatment or remedial reading programs. At this point I began to find some unusual binocular patterns in many of these children and reported them at the annual meeting of the Florida Society of Ophthalmology and Otolaryngology in 1960.[2] Then I discovered similar work had been reported 22 years earlier.

In 1938, Berner and Berner reported on binocularity in 376 patients with reading problems.[4] They found that 75 percent of their patients showed a pattern of control in binocular reading by the eye on the side opposite the master hand. They managed 373 patients by reversing this control pattern and noted improvement in all cases.

The concept of a dominant eye influencing reading progress was not widely endorsed. Crider, Walls, Fink, and others gave reasons why it was unlikely.[5, 9, 18]

143

Many investigators, however, have reported a high incidence of left-handedness, ambidexterity, or right-left confusion in dyslexics.[1, 15]

In 1959, Delacato (and Fay) advanced a theory involving cerebral hemisphere dominance as a factor in reading.[7, 8] Their explanation was that the optimally developed brain is strongly lateralized, with one side dominant over the other. Language, man's last acquired and most intricate cerebral accomplishment, is the first skill affected by minimal brain damage or incomplete neurologic organization. Dyslexic children with improper or inadequate lateralization were trained in (1) making the hand, foot, and eye on the same side preferentially used, (2) using neck, body, and limb muscles in rhythmic coordination by exercises of gross muscle groups and positioned sleep, and (3) restricting music (tonal) stimulation of the nondominant hemisphere. This theory seemed so easily understandable to the lay public and to workers in nonmedical fields dealing with vision, mental functions, neuromuscular performance, and education that a wave of enthusiasm was germinated across the United States.

EVALUATION PROCEDURES

After another 4 years of study, I reported results of treatment on 250 dyslexic children.[3]

Complete evaluation of dyslexic children by the ophthalmologist now includes the following:

1. Careful history of the nature and severity of the reading disorder and questions to the parents about these symptoms of symbolization difficulties:
   a. Defective ability to recognize symbols
   b. Difficulty in constructing complete symbols from partial representations
   c. Poor handwriting
   d. Rotations and reversals ("saw" for "was" or "won" for "now"; "b" for "d" or "p" for "q")
   e. Mirror writing
   f. Transpositions ("past" for "part" or "gril" for "girl")
   g. Mistakes with words that look similar ("these," "those," "this," "them," "they," "their")
   h. Omission of short words in sentences ("an," "on," "a," "the")
   i. Hesitations and regressions
   j. Slow reading speed
   k. Difficulty with separation of syllables
   l. Difficulty with prefixes and suffixes
   m. Dislike of reading
   n. Headaches after reading
   o. Weakness in grasping the meaning of a new word from its context in a sentence
2. Associated details commonly observed and helpful in classification of dyslexia:
   a. Family history of poor readers (parents or siblings)
   b. Confusion of right and left or a tendency to ambidexterity

    c. Speech defects (lisping, lallation, stuttering, perseveration)

    d. Poor body-motor coordination

    e. Distorted handwriting

    f. Behavioral problems (hyperactivity, excessive talking, short attention span, failure to complete assigned classwork)

    g. Birth complications

    h. Unusual trauma in childhood

    i. Severe infections in childhood

3. The usual routine ophthalmologic examination, including refraction (cycloplegic agent, age 10 years or under; mydriatic agent, age 11 years and over) is done. Convergence is measured as the ability to converge the visual axes on a fixation target that approaches to 5 cm. from the base of the nose, held for a count of 5.

4. Tests for hand, foot, and eye dominance:

    a. Hand preference is noted in writing, throwing, batting, using scissors, brushing teeth, combing hair, eating, turning pages of a book, shooting guns, and picking up small objects. Classification is then:

        (1) Right-handed

        (2) Left-handed

        (3) Mixed (nearly equal, mostly right, or mostly left)

    b. Foot preference is noted in stepping forward, stepping backward, stepping off a step, stepping onto a step, kicking a ball, hopping, and skipping. Classification is then:

        (1) Right-footed

        (2) Left-footed

        (3) Mixed (nearly equal, mostly right or mostly left)

    c. Special tests for ocular preference:

    (The patient should have normal and equal visual acuity, with or without correction, in both eyes. Binocular fusion should be present, as found on the Worth 4-dot test, the Wirt polaroid test, fly, or other fusion tests, on the stereoscope or major amblyoscope.)

        (1) In *sighting tests,* the child is given a card with a 5 mm. hole in the center. He holds the card at arm's length from his face and sights a small light source across the room. The child is given a toy pistol and is watched as he aims it at an object. For near sighting, he finds a pen light 33 cm. from the card through the hole in the center.

        (2) *Controlling-eye tests* are done with the Keystone DB2-D and DB3-D cards in the Telebinocular or the Benton Eye Dominance Test Card in the hand stereoscope (Figs. 12-1 and 12-2). Both eyes must be open and fusing the cards. The test is first done with the right eye seeing the acuity marks and the left eye seeing the blank (side A on the Benton Card or the DB2-D Telebinocular Card). When the child reaches the limit of his ability to identify correctly the position of the black dot, this number is recorded and the left eye is occluded. If the child can go any further correctly, the last

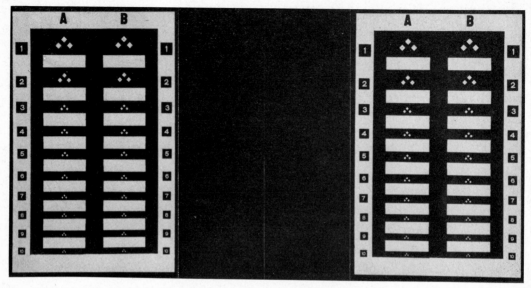

Fig. 12-1. Binocular test card used to determine controlling eye.

Fig. 12-2. Child observing test card in hand stereoscope for evaluation of controlling eye.

correct number is recorded. The left eye is then tested (side B on the Benton Card or the DB3-D Telebinocular Card).

A difference of two acuity levels is counted as significant. The controlling eye scores better than its mate on the first, or binocular, part of the test. The noncontrolling eye shows a greater gain when the controlling eye is occluded than in the reverse situation. For example:

Fig. 12-3. Monkey and cage test card used in hand stereoscope to evaluate alternate intermittent macular suppression or retinal rivalry.

Binocular: right eye scores 8
Left eye occluded: right eye scores 8
Binocular: left eye scores 6
Right eye occluded: left eye scores 8

The right eye is the controlling eye. If both eyes score to 10 in the binocular test or score equally below 10, this suggests no definite controlling eye; then the test for Alternating Intermittent Macular Suppression (AIMS) is done.

(3) In the *AIMS test,* retinal rivalry targets, such as the lion and the cage pair are placed in the stereoscope or the amblyoscope (a suitable card is being tested and developed for use in the hand stereoscope) (Fig. 12-3). The child is asked to report if part of the animal or the cage disappear and reappear from his sight. At a certain speed this is normal for retinal rivalry, but if it occurs rapidly, it is of diagnostic and prognostic importance. Suppression of the macular images (AIMS) is graded as follows:

Slowly or once in 4 seconds   1+
Once in 3 seconds   2+
Once in 2 seconds   3+
Once in a second or more   4+

Findings of 1+ or 2+ are normal. Findings of 3+ or 4+ are considered positive.

(4) The *Keystone Tests of Binocular Skill* adapted from the Gray Oral Reading Check tests are used to check reading ability. A manual for test administration and interpretation is available from the manufacturers. It is usually apparent if one eye performs better alone than binocularly.

5. Auxiliary tests commonly needed:
   a. Medical work-up
   b. Psychiatric evaluation
   c. Psychometric measurements (including tests of visual perception and auditory perception)
   d. Neurologic consultation (including EEG)

INTERPRETATION OF RESULTS

1. *Sighting eye.* Since the sighting eye is often a learned phenomenon rather than an inherent strength, it is not significant enough to be used as the main criterion for diagnosis (with the possible exception of the right-handed child who sights with his left eye). This may be the reason some researchers have discredited the role of eye dominance in dyslexia.
2. *Controlling eye.* The test for the controlling eye may show one or neither eye in strong control.
3. *AIMS test.* If 3+ or 4+ AIMS exists, this is called mixed dominance or mixed control.

TEST RESULTS

1. The incidence of birth complications, childhood head trauma, and severe infections was about 20 percent. Many investigators believe these incidents occur more frequently in dyslexic children, but most dyslexics experience a routine childhood.[11, 16] If minimal brain damage is an underlying factor in a significant group of dyslexics, it is too subtle for detection by the tests used in this study. Neuromuscular coordination aberrations were noted in about 22 percent of the series and fell into two main groups: clumsy and hyperactive. Patients of the hyperactive type were often classified as suffering from the "organic neurologic behavior syndrome."[14]
2. Handedness and footedness tests resulted as follows:

   Right-handed 70%
   Left-handed 10%
   Mixed handedness 20%
   Dominant foot on side of dominant hand 75%
   Mixed foot dominance 15%
   Dominant foot on side opposite dominant hand 10%

3. Sighting tests resulted as follows:

	1,500 dyslexics	300 good readers
Sighting eye on same side as dominant hand	62%	80%
Sighting eye on side opposite dominant hand	23%	10%
Mixed or inconsistent	15%	10%

4. Controlling eye tests resulted as follows:

	1,500 dyslexics	300 good readers
Controlling eye on same side as dominant hand	25%	78%
Controlling eye on side opposite dominant hand	42%	8%
Mixed or no certain control	33%	14%

5. AIMS (Alternating Intermittent Macular Suppression) tests resulted as follows:

	1,500 dyslexics	300 good readers
1+ or 2+ (Normal)	20%	92%
3+ or 4+ (Abnormal)	80%	8%

6. Convergence insufficiency:

Dyslexics 22%
Good readers 4%

CLASSIFICATION OF DYSLEXIA

1. *Primary dyslexia,* the congenital word blindness of Hermann,[13] or the developmental dyslexia of Critchley.[6] Eye tests in patients suffering from primary dyslexia are similar to the controls, except in perceptual functions. Most of these children apparently have poor perception. They display an inability to learn to read by all usual teaching methods and are difficult to treat. There is variation in severity, and the diagnosis rests with the history, the degree of the impairment, and tests of perception.

2. *Dyslexia associated with "organic neurologic behavior syndrome,"* as developed by Morris and Dozier.[14] These are often hyperactive children who cried frequently and slept fitfully as infants and who cannot sit still in school long enough to learn to read. Evaluation by the pediatrician or neurologist is helpful. Eye findings are unrelated and compare with the controls. Treatment must include drugs (tranquilizers or psychic energizers) and is of long duration and limited effectiveness.

3. *Dyslexia associated with binocular control abnormalities.* These are children with crossed control (right-handed–left-eyed or left-handed–right-eyed) or children with mixed control and 3+ or 4+ AIMS (Alternating Intermittent Macular Suppression).

4. *Dyslexia secondary to functional or environmental factors* (cultural deprivation, lack of motivation, overcrowded schools, phonetics versus "look-say" methods of teaching, hearing and speech defects, emotional problems, and conventional ophthalmologic factors. The number of my patients in this category may be unusually small because of case selection. Few children from low income groups seek this care in the office of a physician in private practice. Retarded reading due to low I.Q. is not true dyslexia and, therefore, does not appear in the classification.

The 1,500 children I have examined were classified as follows:

	Estimated incidence in unselected cases
Type 1— 150 (10%)	20%
Type 2— 120 (8%)	15%
Type 3—1,155 (77%)	30%
Type 4— 75 (5%)	35%
1,500(100%)	100%

OTHER OBSERVATIONS

Other observations regarding binocular factors in dyslexia are as follows:

1. Dyslexia is rare in monocular children. I have studied fifteen children who lost one eye (or the sight thereof) in infancy. All were good readers, regardless of the side of the remaining eye.

2. A group of ninety-seven children with constant convergent strabismus and one amblyopic eye contained 8 percent dyslexics. A group of twenty

children with intermittent exotropia and fusion for near vision had 30 percent with reading problems. After correction of the strabismus in the ninety-seven esotropes, the incidence of dyslexia rose from 8 to 19 percent.

3. Some dyslexic children appear to read faster when one eye is occluded. I have found about fifty children who show all the preceding binocular irregularities but who perform well because they have discovered they could read faster by closing or suppressing one eye.

4. I have seen three dyslexic children improve rapidly after an injury impaired the vision of one eye.

5. Adults may show similar patterns. I have examined two hundred adults for eye control. When abnormalities were found, these patients often reported they had done poorly in reading in school and in adult life rarely read books or magazines for pleasure. It would appear that untreated dyslexia persists in adult life, has a tendency to spontaneously improve, and in some persons may be completely overcome. Much more needs to be known about the natural history of dyslexia.

MANAGEMENT

Management of dyslexia depends on the type of abnormality present. Dyslexic children showed either (1) crossed control (crossed dominance) or (2) mixed control (incomplete dominance) with a rapid Alternating Intermittent Macular Suppression (AIMS) of 3+ or 4+.

Convergence. The 22 percent of dyslexic children who had convergence insufficiency were treated by pencil-to-nose approximation drills, physiologic diplopia recognition at near vision, and overcoming of base out prisms, or vergence stimulation on the amblyoscope (synoptophore) to bring the near point of convergence to 5 cm. with steady holding for 5 seconds. By itself this does not improve symbolic confusion or dyslexia, but it does reduce asthenopia and headaches from reading.

Handedness. When either hand is definitely and strongly dominant, I do not attempt to change it. When there is a tendency to ambidexterity, it is discouraged and the child is encouraged to be fully one-sided.

Rarely, I find a child who seems to perform equally well with either hand. If possible, I encourage the use of the hand on the side of the controlling eye. If neither eye is dominant, then I try to make the right hand and the right eye dominant, but in a few instances I have abandoned this when a trial proved unsatisfactory. For this, the child is trained in all the listed activities in the handedness test.

Footedness. The only foot activity apparently associated with dominance is kicking. This is encouraged on the same side as the dominant hand.

Eyedness. Children with Type 3 dyslexia had normal and equal visual acuity in the two eyes. If a difference of two or more lines on the acuity chart exists between the two eyes (e.g., 20/20 and 20/40), it is not possible to program for dominance control. Children with large heterophorias should not be treated for dominance. They often belong to Type 4 dyslexia and should be treated by conventional ophthalmic means.

If a Type 3 dyslexic child shows a complete lack of one-eye control (mixed dominance) or shows control by the eye opposite the dominant hand (crossed dominance), training is directed to the eye on the same side as the dominant hand. Between ages 5 and 10 years, I prescribe constant occlusion of the eye which should be nondominant. In a right-handed child, the left eye is patched as much of the waking day as possible for from 9 to 24 months or until the control shifts to the right eye. When tests suggest that control is changing, wearing time of the patch is progressively reduced.

Children from 10 to 16 years of age usually will not wear a patch for social or emotional reasons. In these older children, one drop of 1% atropine may be instilled each morning in the eye which should be nondominant. This is done for 3 weeks each month. Progress testing is done every fourth week when the atropinization effect has worn off. Atropine causes little problem, except light sensitivity in some patients. Duration of management is the same as with the patch.

Adjunctive programs. In addition to fostering homolateral eye and hand dominance, I carry out adjunctive programs in six other areas.

1. *Remedial reading.* Since dyslexic children are, by definition, behind their grade level in reading, they need help to catch up in reading. About 30 percent of the children in this series had been tutored, enrolled in private schools, or attended special reading classes in public schools with little or no improvement. After attention to these binocular dominance problems, progress became apparent. On the other hand, I always urge the parents of children under my care to provide extra help in reading by any or all facilities available. It appears that stressing of phonics and word analysis is the most rewarding assistance.

2. *Neuromuscular coordination exercises.* I have used exercises of crawling, creeping, and walking as an adjunct and have the impression they are helpful in those children with coordination problems. It is not without difficulty, however, that parents get their dyslexic children to perform them regularly. Most consistent results are obtained in group exercises under leadership of an interested parent. I had an active group meeting every afternoon for 30 minutes in a large vacant store. Their success was rewarding.

I spend little time on crawling and move quickly to creeping and walking. The child is instructed to exercise for 30 minutes daily for the first 3 months; then gradually cut down over the next 6 to 9 months, after which time the exercises are usually discontinued.

3. *Drugs.* Parents frequently ask for tranquilizers for the hyperactive dyslexic. A third of all dyslexic children have superimposed or underlying emotional disturbances. The agitation is primary in dyslexia Types 2 and 4 but usually is secondary in Type 3. I have seen dozens of children who have spent months under intensive care by psychologists and mental health clinics with little improvement until their eye dominance abnormality was corrected.

The dyslexic child does not complete his classwork at reading time in school and becomes frustrated. He then disturbs the class by getting out of his seat, talking, interrupting the teacher, or other unacceptable behavior. Usually tranquilizers fail to help this problem. The child usually continues his behavior with the added difficulty of not being sensitive to his irresponsibility. Tranquilizers are helpful in children who are withdrawn, shy, or difficult to get along with at home or school.

For children with reading difficulty who try but become frustrated or have trouble concentrating, I prescribe deanol acetamidobenzoate (Deaner), 50 or 100 mg. each morning, methylphenidate hydrochloride (Ritalin), 10 or 20 mg. each morning, or sometimes dextroamphetamine sulfate with amobarbital (Dexamyl). Ritalin has given the best results.

Drugs are prescribed only after consultation with the pediatrician and discontinued as the situation improves.

4. *Music.* Music, or tonal simulation, is said to evoke a response in the nondominant cerebral hemisphere. As part of my program, I eliminate background radio, television, or phonograph music during study periods.

What other part music plays, I cannot say, since I have done no controlled studies on this subject.

5. *Skill games.* I encourage dyslexic patients to play games requiring skillful eye-hand coordination. Some common examples are archery, tennis, target shooting, dart throwing, ping pong, etc.

6. *Sleep position.* The child is taught to sleep in a prone position with his face turned toward the nondominant hand. For a right-handed child, the left arm is at a right angle with palm down opposite the face. The right arm is alongside the body and the right leg extended. The left leg is flexed to a right angle. Left-handed children are urged to sleep in the opposite position.

Parents place the child in the proper position at bedtime and must reposition the child if he moves before the parents retire. The position becomes habitual after a few weeks.

CONCLUSIONS

I have worked with 700 dyslexic children for periods of from 9 to 24 months and observed many up to 3 years. *Excellent improvement* means attaining grade level in reading, reading for pleasure, disappearance of behavior problems, and gain in bodily coordination skills. *Moderate improvement* means some gains in reading achievement sufficient to earn promotions to the required level and some improvement in behavior. *Failure* was lack of improvement in the reading problem.

Sometimes immediate change results when one eye is occluded, as in the following example:

> *Case report 1.* S. C., 10 years of age; trouble reading since starting school; in fourth grade and reading at first grade level
>
> Examination: left-handed, except for batting a ball and using scissors; right-footed; right-eyed for sighting
>
> Dominance test:
>
> | | |
> |---|---|
> | OD binocular 5 | OD monocular 7 |
> | OS binocular 7 | OS monocular 8 |
>
> Alternating Intermittent Macular Suppression: 3+
>
> Interpretation: dyslexia with poor binocular stability (AIMS 3+)
>
> Management: right eye occluded; practice sighting with left eye; coordination

exercises; schoolteacher called in 3 weeks to report improvement in reading; improving rapidly while wearing eye patch

With most patients, improvement is slower but rewarding, as the following case illustrates.

Case report 2. S. B., 9 years of age; in fourth grade but reading on third grade level; I.Q. a little above average

Dominance test (left eye controls):

OD binocular 7   OD monocular 9
OS binocular 9   OS monocular 9

Alternating Intermittent Macular Supression: 4+

Interpretation: dyslexia with crossed dominance; fully right-handed; sights with left eye

Management: occlusion of left eye; sleep pattern; coordination exercises; remedial reading in summer: October, 1964, treatment started; January, 1965, teacher reports working 50 percent better; October, 1965, in fifth grade, doing much better; June, 1966, control test—right eye dominant; supervision stopped; reading for pleasure; B average student

The results in the 700 cases were as follows:

Excellent improvement	336	(49%)
Moderate improvement	280	(39%)
Failure	84	(12%)

Tests on the 336 children with excellent improvement reveal that approximately 50 percent changed their dominance pattern to homolaterality. Fewer children showing moderate improvement exhibited this change (30 percent), and none of the failures changed dominance patterns.

CONTINUING STUDIES

Present studies are proceeding on the following points:

1. Is the dyslexia associated with binocular abnormality predictable on the basis of tests in young children (first graders)?
2. Are the eye findings repeatable by other examiners or by the same examiner when not supplied with previous findings?
3. How important is the psychologic element in treatment? The child finds acceptance and interest by the physician and technician a stimulating factor in itself. The parents better understand the child's frustrations and begin to help instead of criticize. The schoolteacher becomes sympathetic and gives more assistance and closer observation. These are all strong success factors and cannot be divorced from the total picture for separate evaluation.
4. Can tests with greater reliability be developed?

Meanwhile, we labor empirically. The dyslexia problem is so great and so urgent that it cries out for closer attention and help.

REFERENCES

1. Benton, A.: Right-left discrimination and finger control, New York, 1959, Harper & Row, Publishers.

2. Benton, C. D.: Ophthalmological approach to the problems of retarded readers among elementary school children, J. Florida Med. Assoc. 47:1123-1125, 1961.
3. Benton, C. D., McCann, J. W., and Larson, M.: Dyslexia and dominance, J. Pediat. Ophthal. 2:53-57, 1965.
4. Berner, G. E., and Berner, D. E.: Reading difficulties in children, Arch. Ophthal. 20: 829-838, 1938.
5. Crider, B.: The importance of the dominant eye, J. Psychol. 16:145-151, 1943.
6. Critchley, M.: Developmental dyslexia, Springfield, Ill., 1964, Charles C Thomas, Publisher.
7. Delacato, C. H.: The treatment and prevention of reading disability: the neuro-psychological approach, Springfield, Ill., 1959, Charles C Thomas, Publisher.
8. Delacato, C. H.: The diagnosis and treatment of speech and reading problems, Springfield, Ill., 1963, Charles C Thomas, Publisher.
9. Fink, W. H.: The dominant eye: its clinical significance, Arch. Ophthal. 19:555-582, 1938.
10. Flower, R. M., Fogman, H. F., and Lawson, L. L.: Reading disorders, Philadelphia, 1965, F. A. Davis Co.
11. Fowler, I.: The relationship of certain perinatal factors to behavior, speech, or learning problems in children, South. Med. J. 58:1245-1248, 1965.
12. Goldberg, H. K.: The ophthalmologist looks at the reading problem, Amer. J. Ophthal. 47:67-74, 1959.
13. Hermann, K.: Reading disability, Springfield, Ill., 1959, Charles C Thomas, Publisher.
14. Morris, D. P., and Dozier, E.: Subtler organic factors in behavior disorders of childhood, South. Med. J. 58:1213, 1965.
15. Orton, S. T.: Reading and writing and speech difficulties in children, New York, 1937, W. W. Norton & Co., Inc.
16. Pasamanick, B., and Knoblock, H.: Syndrome of minimal cerebral damage, J.A.M.A. 170:1384, 1959.
17. Schubert, D. G.: The doctor eyes the poor reader, Springfield, Ill., 1957, Charles C Thomas, Publisher.
18. Walls, G. L.: Theory of ocular dominance, Arch. Ophthal. 45:387, 1951.
19. Weisbach, P. T.: The ophthalmologist's role in the management of dyslexia, Amer. J. Ophthal. 59:265, 1965.

Chapter 13

Anxiety and learning

Herman Krieger Goldberg, M.D.

Many years ago I realized that children with reading problems often exhibit a great deal of fear and anxiety. If the tendency becomes progressive, this anxiety often leads to "block" and "panic." When this happens to the beginning reader, an immediate and severe learning disability or late failure as a result of being a high-anxiety student may be produced.

I shall not discuss psychiatric complications with reference to reading disability. However, one facet of the psychiatric problem does interest me. It relates to anxiety and learning, and I will outline some of my experiences involving these areas.

A series of personal experiences emphasized the role of anxiety in learning. A few years ago I interviewed a young boy who had been referred with a diagnosis of brain damage. This diagnosis was based mainly on psychometric tests and the electroencephalogram. This youngster's alertness and his excellent coordination made me question the diagnosis. Although he was reported to have failed the Bender Gestalt and the Benton Visual Memory tests, on repeating these tests I found, to my surprise, he could perform them all easily. I asked the child's mother to enter the office, and I repeated the tests in her presence. This time the child failed all of the examination. This procedure was repeated, with the same results; failure occurred when the mother was present, and success, when the mother was absent. The presence of the mother was sufficient to have raised the anxiety level of the child to the point of failure. These findings have been frequently present in other dyslexic children.

A second impressive occurrence is the loss of comprehension by some patients in a situation of high anxiety. In discussing a series of diagnostic possibilities, one may suddenly find the patient not understanding what is being said, unfortunately remembering only what is ominous, and forgetting the benign statement of the conversation. The words "cataract" or "detached retina" need only be mentioned to such a patient, and suddenly there will be a complete tuning out. He may tune back in at any subsequent moment, but this might be two to three sentences later.

My third experience occurred in a learning atmosphere. There are two kinds of anxiety: first, the normal anxiety needed for extra incentive and, second, the pathologic anxiety, which is intellectually crippling and prevents productivity. All of us have had the experience of tensing up before a competitive situation. This tension before a game, an examination, or a speech is normal. In fact, our attitude might be flat if this tension were not present. On the other hand, too much tension can result in disaster. Fumbling, stuttering, and blocking are results of too much tension. Occasionally, this block occurs in the presence of specific teachers. If anxiety is overcome, learning becomes easier, answers are facilitated, and conversational flow is simple.

It is understandable and natural to transpose the feeling of the adult who reacts to tension in this way to a child in a new learning experience. With this background, I have analyzed pertinent reports and would like to review some of this data.

Anxiety, as a powerful influence in contemporary life, is increasingly recognized, since this phenomenon is constantly reflected in many facets of our culture. Anxiety[5] seems to be an accepted problem of modern living. It influences college students because of the draft, and it clatters from Wall Street tickers. The adjustments necessary when beginning school are more taxing than most other periods in a child's life. While it is well known that a moderate amount of tension and motivation are of assistance in learning, I would like to differentiate the debilitating effect of high anxiety as opposed to that of low anxiety, which can be stimulating.

The high-anxiety group is characterized by a tendency toward ego decompensation under stress, by the presence of body sway under pressure, by a feeling of loneliness, by easy embarrassment, and by general nervous movements. Physiologically, there may be an increase in systolic blood pressure, rapid respiration, and heart rate and a decrease in the alkalinity of the saliva, a decrease in 17-hydroxyketosteroid, and an increased flow of digestive juices.

Anxiety may be either acute or chronic. The overly anxious child may fail to learn in the very beginning, or anxiety may evidence itself later in a high-anxiety group, having a marked incidence of failure in later stages of adult life. This was demonstrated by an experiment at Duke University,[5] showing a large number of failures in a high-anxiety group.

It is difficult to predict when an emotional problem will undermine academic learning. Many factors may alter the specific emotional problem. The degree of protection afforded to the student is measured by his contacts with teachers in the classroom, by sibling relationships, and by parental attitudes. Anxiety, depression, preoccupation, and personality disorganization all may interfere with the child's classroom functioning.

There may be some symbolic associations that affect isolated learning areas. Rabinovitch[3] cited a child who functioned well in all areas except spelling. During the course of psychotherapy, it was revealed that when the child learned to spell he was taught some obscene words, which he repeated to his mother.

She became belligerent and harshly punished the child, who thereafter associated spelling with something unclean and something to be avoided. This was the reason for failure in this area.

Anxiety is important because it affects motivation.[4] This motivation can be of two types: (1) the extrinsic, in which concrete awards are the goal, or (2) intrinsic, in which an inner satisfaction is the goal. Some children have little interest in learning and apply themselves minimally; they do just enough to get by. There are a number of reasons for lack of motivation. Some parents are permissive, make no demands, and avoid all possible frustrations. Some children have no sense of values by which to be guided and are, thus, passive and uncertain. They may gravitate to a group or gang identification. It is important to offer these children personal relationships that will generate intrinsic motivation for learning. Children who are anxious have greater difficulty with tests than their nonanxious counterparts.[4] Performance of high-anxiety students is poor as measured by a variety of standards.

Mothers, as compared to fathers, are inadequate in estimating the anxiety level of their children and tend to increase the anxiety in a male relationship as compared to that of a female relationship. Some investigators have found that maternal rearing produces a higher anxiety level in boys than in girls. This is an additional factor that may contribute to the greater frequency of reading problems in males than in females.

If teachers could recognize the children whose anxiety levels are high and, therefore, are going to have greater interference with productivity, much would be saved. Unfortunately, this is often not possible. It is unfair to expect teachers to also be diagnosticians, therapists, and administrators. Yet, we are demanding this today. If we could identify the high-anxiety child, the teachers' problems would decrease and the productivity of the child would increase. Teachers vary greatly in the degree by which they create an atmosphere of security and pupil self-esteem. Too often this atmosphere is established only by the child's success in performance. In some classes the reaction of the teacher to failure will heighten the child's inadequacy, while in other classes the teacher's response to failure is such that it will not make the child feel inadequate or rejected. The teacher's opinion is of great moment to the child, particularly when he wants to be liked by the teacher because *he* likes the teacher.

Spielberger,[5] in a series of studies, demonstrated the effect and influence of anxiety on learning. The first experiment showed the deleterious effects of anxiety on recall. Students reported that they were unable to reproduce answers to test questions which they felt reasonably certain they knew. Frequently, a high-anxiety student subconsciously misinterpreted a test question and wrote copiously about the question, only for it to be wrong. One reason for this reaction is that misinterpretation is considered less traumatic than blocking, because it is not generally discovered until some time after the examination.

Spielberger[5] studied the effect of anxiety on academic achievement. High-anxiety students were inferior to low-anxiety students. Twenty percent of the high-anxiety students dropped out of school, as compared to 5.8 percent of the low-anxiety students. A follow-up study to evaluate long-term, high-anxiety effects showed that academic failure was four times as great in high-anxiety groups.

A group of patients studied by Diethelm at the Payne-Whitney Clinic[1] clearly demonstrated that anxiety decreased active attention, learning, and thinking as measured by Kohs Block tests. The difference between patients of high- and low-anxiety levels was from 20 to 40 points. In high-anxiety patients, learning on the maze test was reduced, and retention ability was reduced. This probably explains why cramming for an examination might be satisfactory for the immediate future, but retention is extremely reduced in high-anxiety episodes. In a subsequent paper, Welsh and Diethelm[6] showed that anxiety has a deleterious effect on inductive reasoning. In one test, groups of objects that made a light go on were listed. The subject was asked to name the object that was the factor for making the light go on. Similarly, groups of objects on a card were presented to a patient and the question, "What made the child ill?" was asked. The patient had to determine from the cards what the isolated factor might be that caused the illness. In 187 patients tested, there were 92 failures when associated with anxiety. Inductive reasoning was adversely affected in the psychoneurotic, the psychopathic, the depressed, and the elated patients. Anxiety may prevent instruction by the teacher because of its adverse influence on reasoning.

The Draw-a-Person test[2] as a predictor of school readiness and as an indication of emotional and physical maturity is recommended in reading retardation. The test may easily be given by a secretary and should be administered without parental observation. The test gives an estimate of the developmental level from 3 to 12 years of age. It makes three demands of the subject: (1) visualization of the human figure, (2) organization and interpretation, and (3) reproduction by way of motor skills of the visualized image. Examination may indicate defects in vision, interpretation, and motor coordination, with considerable variation in detail also being related to the child's I.Q. The following three reports represent cases in which the Draw-a-Person test was used successfully. In one case the parent was advised not to have the child enter the first grade but, perhaps, to have him attend kindergarten for one more year. This was done, and the next year the school situation was most successful. The second case was a fearful child also being considered for school. The parents were advised against his attending school because the mental age showed a development of only 5.9 years, and there was great emotional instability evidenced by the drawing. This child developed well and in the following year on entrance into school gave a satisfactory performance. The third case was a child who was advised not to enter the first grade because he was delayed in all phases of development. The parents refused to cooperate, and the child began the first grade. He became completely unmanageable, cried incessantly, complained of abdominal pains, and reacted poorly to the school situation, with resulting frustration and failure.

To obtain rapid and objective evaluation of a patient's drawing, the Dale Harris norms[2] are helpful. By using the 28-point Harris Scale score of the child's drawing, one can rapidly ascertain the percentile rank of the drawing and estimate the child's maturity.

As the complicated answers to questions about reading retardation are considered, it is proper that this reason for educational failure be questioned. The wide divergence of educational opportunities among the culturally deprived families, the use of inexperienced teachers in the first and second grades, the lack of early diagnosis, and the absence of standard remedial therapy are currently grave threats to the child who begins school. Some children cannot function in a group situation, especially children with maturation lag, brain damage, or emotional disturbance. Opportunities for small classes and a one-to-one relationship of teacher and child must be made available. These opportunities can mean the difference between a successful learning experience or total failure and subsequent drop-out. In order to acquire academic learning most effectively, the child must feel free to invest maximum energy in his schooling experiences. Emotional problems of any type may impair such freedom, and therefore they represent an underlying cause of learning disabilities. When learning is blocked by anxiety, the pattern of errors is baffling. For instance, a child may complete a difficult problem and then miss a series of very easy problems. The problems that he solved yesterday cannot be understood today; but perhaps they will be understood tomorrow. Anxiety is so important and variable in test performance that it has been questioned whether intelligence test scores adequately indicate the underlying abilities of the individuals who have a high-anxiety drive in testing situations. Failure to progress in school can be due to stress, and stress, in turn, causes other emotional problems. The child, unable to comprehend what is being taught, is ashamed to display his ignorance and so remains away from class. Thus begins a vicious circle of the child's falling further behind and staying away more.

In certain children, school phobia is due to fear of an overly strict or overly critical teacher. In other children, it derives from school failure and the attending discouragement and loss of self-confidence. High anxiety is revealed in the surprisingly violent scenes that these ordinarily good children make when forced to attend school. Leon Eisenberg describes the problem of school phobia as "the umbilical cord being pulled at both ends."

Insofar as treatment is concerned, frequently the major need is patience and time. In other cases, the problems may be more deep-seated, with psychotherapy being desirable. Drugs have been useful in diminishing or abolishing the destructive effects of anxiety on learning. Tranquilizers may be successful in treating the anxiety neurosis. After success is achieved, the child's concentration, attention span, and adjustment in school may rapidly improve.

In summary, I have tried to emphasize the important area of anxiety as it relates to reading. These clinical impressions are verified by knowledgeable workers in the field of psychology and psychiatry.

REFERENCES

1. Diethelm, O., and Jones, M. R.: Influence of anxiety on attention, learning, retention, and thinking, Arch. Neurol. Psychiat. **58**:325, 1947.
2. Harris, D. B.: Children's drawings as measures of intellectual maturity, New York, 1963, Harcourt, Brace, & World, Inc.

3. Rabinovitch, R.: Reading and learning disability. In Arieti, S., editor: American handbook of psychiatry, vol. 1, New York, 1959, Basic Books, Inc.
4. Sarason, S. B., et al.: Anxiety in elementary school children, New York, 1960, J. Wiley & Sons, Inc.
5. Spielberger, C. D.: Anxiety and behavior, New York, 1966, Academic Press, Inc.
6. Welch, L., and Diethelm, O.: Effects of pathologic anxiety on inductive reasoning, Arch. Neurol. Psychiat. 63:87, 1950.

Questions and answers: Fourth session

MODERATOR: HERMANN M. BURIAN, M.D.

Dr. Burian: Have any control studies been done for your dyslexia therapy or therapies, Dr. Benton?

Dr. Benton: I have tabulated 300 controls for our 1,500 patients, but I did not take a group of dyslexic children and observe them with *no* treatment. I do not have that type of control, which is truthfully needed.

Dr. Burian: Is it not essentially impossible to refrain from all therapy in order to establish a control group within your private practice?

Dr. Benton: These private patients come willingly for help and to pay for service. I cannot use nontreatment controls except when they decline helpful steps or drift away.

Dr. Burian: Dr. Cruickshank, how often does hyperactivity occur in genetically determined dyslexia?

Dr. Cruickshank: I have not the slightest idea, and I do not think anybody else does. There are no studies that I know of on this particular question. However, in a study of 700 mentally retarded children, presumably genetically determined and all between the chronologic ages of 6 and 16 years, 28 percent were classified as hyperkinetic. That is as close as I can come in a different but, possibly, comparable group.

Dr. Benton: My figures show 22 percent.

Dr. Burian: Mrs. Orton, in your experience, have active, anxious, poorly cooperative children usually had permissive, nondisciplining, or inadequate parents? Could one solution be to take children out of such an environment to a more consistent, structured one?

Mrs. Orton: This is a type of have-you-stopped-beating-your-wife question. I do not believe that, in general, parents of hyperactive children should be condemned for their discipline or lack of it. They, in my experience, are anxious parents—anxious to do their best for this child. When they have more understanding, even the little that we can give them, they are greatly aided in their control. As we work with the child and as the child begins to derive satisfaction from the stimuli, the hyperactivity drops off quickly. The question of whether any child would be better off in a residential treatment center, again, depends on evaluation of his whole situation and of the available treatment center.

Dr. Burian: Dr. Nicholls, would you discuss the value or utility of so-called eye exercises in dyslexia?

Dr. Nicholls: This cannot be answered quickly in a few sentences. Dr. Benton has dealt with one aspect of ocular training, and I have dealt with another. In properly selected cases, extraocular muscle exercises will enhance fusional reserve and thereby help ocular fatigue and enhance the attention span in any child, whether a poor reader or not. In a significantly large cross section of children, whether they are good or bad readers, there will be a modest percentage of children with motility problems. These are legitimate candidates for help with competent orthoptic procedures according to the specific visual indications.

Dr. Burian: Dr. Botel, do you believe that you might have achieved the same results as reported in your study by merely and only reducing the teacher-student ratio, as compared to keeping the ratio at the 1 to 25 or 1 to 30 level? How sufficient is a low teacher-student ratio? What ratio do you consider optimum for learning?

Dr. Botel: Reducing class size by itself is not adequate. I have seen schools in which the average class size is considerably lower than twenty-seven pupils that are doing a very poor job of reaching individual youngsters. I favor small class size for the reason that special, personal contacts between a teacher and a child are enhanced. Those of you who have taught know that when a class gets much larger than twenty-five pupils, teachers do not really know individuals in that class. Much of the work we are addressing today must be on a personal, 1 to 1 basis. You can have a small class size and still not do the things I enumerated or even pursue equivalent steps.

Reducing class size per se will not guarantee the teacher accomplishments we are seeking. On the other hand, in the presence of our typical American public school classroom, reduction in class size tends to increase all teacher efficiency. This, by itself, however, should not be considered the determining factor.

Dr. Burian: Dr. Cruickshank wishes to comment.

Dr. Cruickshank: I would like to go a step further. Dr. Botel is talking about youngsters who fall within the apparently normal framework insofar as motor and emotional behavior are concerned. To handle the extremes in hyperactivity, discussed by several speakers, the teacher-pupil ratio should be approximately 1 to 8, with a full-time aide. Recently I scheduled a teacher to work with eight predetermined and carefully selected children, only to discover, to my horror, that she soon was almost ready for an institution herself. I had to move her back, for almost 9 months, to a teacher-pupil ratio of 1 to 4, with a full-time aide and then gradually increase the number of students assigned to her.

We must be careful about generalizing on the issue of teacher-pupil ratio, even when specific clinical or behavioral groups are described. In planning for the reasonably normal child, the teacher-pupil ratio that Dr. Botel specified is correct. But this ratio should not be translated into the abnormal clinical problems we are delineating today.

Dr. Burian: Thank you. Dr. Nicholls, are there any visual hazards in habitual television watching? May television watching be helpful in increasing the attention span of children?

Dr. Nicholls: I know of no visual hazards related to watching television.

There is an attractive therapeutic use of television in supporting occlusion. If a child wants to watch a specific program and if his better eye is occluded so that he must use the other, or lazy, eye, a strong stimulus is exerted on the lazy, or amblyopic, eye. Under these conditions, the active desire to see on the part of the child combats the amblyopia.

Dr. Burian: Dr. Cruickshank, what should be the first step in bringing together the school, the medical facilities, and the community in diagnostic procedures?

Dr. Cruickshank: The basic step is merely a firm decision to do it, to establish interdisciplinary facilities. Step two is a careful analysis of specific professional individuals from the various disciplines to be certain they are personalities that will work constructively together. Step three is a decision that an interdisciplinary team does not require every discipline in the always-busy community but only the minimum number of truly needed disciplines with the occasional use of consultation from other areas as indicated.

For example, it is not necessary for every hyperkinetic or dyslexic child to be seen by a cardiologist or an endocrinologist, but these physicians will be needed from time to time. The team needed for the dyslexic problems being discussed derives basically from seven areas: pediatrics, clinical psychology, neurology, vision, speech, hearing, and special education. Beyond these basic seven are the areas of consultative need or more elaborate administrative program decisions.

Administrators must provide contributory disciplines with ample time for these individuals to work together before results will be obvious. We have found that teams rarely function appropriately in much less than from 12 to 18 months. If we try to force programming, there are usually serious breakdowns.

I have seen five or six remarkably effective groups. The Center for the Development of Blind Children is a very small unit at Syracuse University. Here we have an ophthalmologist who certainly knows the eyes but did not know much about how the eyes were used or about the behavior of a blind child as a functional human organism. We have an educator who knows a great deal about teaching the blind but little about the eyes. We have some other people on the unit who knew their own specialties, but did not know the others.

In organizing such teams, the responsible administrator must be prepared for considerable education within the team and periods of stress between teammates, especially during the first few months. Some members may not even be able to verbalize their own problems. There must be somebody on the team who can serve as a buffer to take up the emotion and direct reorientation as each profession really learns how the others work and contribute.

When the team progresses properly, it ultimately becomes difficult to tell who is the ophthalmologist, the pediatrician, or whatever, because the members are thinking and working together in the light of acquired interpersonal insight and appreciation of one another.

Dr. Burian: Dr. Critchley, you said something about obstetric histories. How often does dyslexia occur in children delivered by cesarean section?

Dr. Critchley: I have encountered this fairly often, but I have not yet put my figures together in order to be able to reply in terms of percentages.

Dr. Burian: Dr. Goldberg, do you concur with those engaged in eye patching and techniques as devised by Delacato for treating children with so-called cross dominance; if not, should some formal statement be forthcoming condemning such practices?

Dr. Goldberg: I do not think there should be a statement roundly condemning anything. We really do not have the answer to everything. I would say that one should not patch an eye, because I believe that both the difficulty and the correction lie in other areas. If a child presents as right-handed, right-eyed, right-footed, and right-eared, he is more likely to be of good coordination and more likely to overcome language difficulties. If a child presents with left dominance or mixed dominance, there may be greater difficulty ahead. But patching or teaching dominance is not really going to overcome the basic difficulty of symbol confusion.

Dr. Critchley: I could add apropos of these techniques, quoting Voltaire, "I disagree with every word you say, but I defend your right to say it to the death."

Dr. Burian: Thank you, Dr. Critchley. Was the reputed difficulty with which Sir Winston Churchill mastered the English language really a manifestation of developmental dyslexia?

Dr. Critchley: No. I am inclined to think that his difficulties at school were a little exaggerated by himself. He played it up.

Dr. Burian: Dr. Goldberg, has any blind child with a severe primary developmental dyslexia shown this handicap in Braille?

Dr. Goldberg: I am not sure. However, the related use of kinesthetic imagery helps some dyslexics. Teaching is assisted for some dyslexics by large, raised letters, which the child traces with his finger, and this is perhaps where the Braille factor comes in.

Dr. Critchley: This almost constitutes another research project. It would be extremely interesting to see what would happen to a developmental dyslexic if you tried to teach him Braille, which is, of course, extremely difficult in itself. My guess would be that he would have just as much difficulty with Braille as he had with visual comprehension of symbols. The defect is not in the eye but in the brain.

Chapter 14

Topics worthy of research

Macdonald Critchley, M.D., F.R.C.P.

For the final chapter I have drawn up a list of seventeen projects that call for further study.

1. We sorely need an agreed definition of developmental dyslexia, i.e., the true developmental, specific dyslexia of the neurologist. A suggested definition is as follows: *A difficulty in learning to read, which is constitutional, often genetically determined, and which is unassociated with general intellectual retardation, primary emotional instability, or gross physical defects.* The last point includes gross ophthalmologic defects.

2. Every well-worked–up case of developmental dyslexia, fully and faithfully documented and recorded, constitutes a contribution to the sum total of our knowledge.

Full and detailed case recording in each patient with developmental dyslexia is important. If this were done routinely, it would multiply opportunities for verifying data, about which there have been expressed differences of opinion here and in the earlier literature.

Some of the points to be recorded are as follows:

a. Sex incidence. Please remember the caveat I made previously, namely that sex incidence may be partly determined by the fact that in some countries more attention is paid to boys than to girls who cannot read.

b. Type of inheritance. Whether it is dominant or recessive, heterozygous or homozygous, partially or fully penetrant, etc.

c. Birth order. What is the incidence of dyslexia in the first-born child, the second-born child, or the last-born child?

d. The incidence of perinatal trauma. This recording may necessitate seeking detailed information from the obstetrician, from the hospital records, and from the parents and the pediatrician.

e. Whether or not the child in his development skipped the stage of crawling, as has been postulated by some writers.

3. There is a need for some stock taking of many of the diagnostic tests

which we have taken for granted. How dependable and reliable are the commonly used tests of reading age and spelling age? Merely listing a few tests, such as the Schoenell, the Holborn, the Hagerty, the Gray, the Monroe, the Iota, the Stanford Achievement, the Neill, and the Gillmore, suggests that there is dissatisfaction and a certain lack of secure standardization. These tests should be reassessed. Of course, some of these reading tests entail comprehension, some concern silent reading, and others concern accuracy of articulation in reading aloud. Few of these tests are completely satisfactory, and many do not critically include the factor of speed of reading. Some children take these tests flightily and too quickly and make careless errors. Performance speed should be quantitated in the final picture of reading age. To a neurologist this is a fault that lies behind many psychologic tests. The mark "plus" or "minus," "yes" or "no" is incomplete. Hughlings Jackson taught 110 years ago that whether the patient succeeds in a test or not is less important than *how* the patient does it. There are important differences between a patient who gets the right answer promptly, quickly, and confidently, and another one who gets the correct answer, in an abnormal fashion, after trial, error, and hesitation.

4. There should be a close anthropometric study and careful correlation of the physical habitus in children with developmental dyslexia. This is easily done in the clinic. One should, as a routine, measure the child's height, his weight, and the circumference of his head. A record should be made of such anatomic variables as coloring. Is there a tie-up with dark hair, red hair, fair hair? The incidence of blood groupings should be noted for possible correlation. All these are vitally important, if, as we believe, developmental dyslexia is a constitutional disorder. There should also be chromosome studies, both morphologic and chemical.

5. We very much need to know the geographic distribution based upon a world survey of dyslexia. An association should be sought with many factors besides languages, because language may not actually be the major point. It is a matter of race, which ties up with constitutional, genetic, and anthropometric factors. Difficulties of carrying out field studies in undeveloped countries and backward communities vary from considerable to enormous. In places where the incidence of illiteracy is high, the whole problem is obscured. In Nigeria, the incidence of illiteracy ranges from 33 percent in boys aged from 15 to 20 years to 100 percent in women over the age of 65 years. How much of this illiteracy is due to sheer lack of opportunity and how much might be due to an innate inability to learn to read?

6. We also require biochemical studies of every child with developmental dyslexia. We have heard much about lack of maturation and late bloomers. Maturation, after all, may well depend upon a chemical factor. A mare gives birth to a foal, which very quickly gets on its legs and, after a few uncoordinated efforts, walks. Human babies do not behave like this until 13 or 14 months of age because there is a difference in the rate of myelination of the pyramidal tract between a horse and a human being. And the myelination of the pyramidal tract depends upon the action of the oligodendroglial cells, which, in turn, is a matter of brain enzymes. Thus, chemistry influences myelination and, in turn,

neural function. Any alteration in this brain chemistry might well bring about a delayed maturation, perhaps not in the pyramidal tract but in some other system.

We should search for any possible inherited metabolic dyscrasias. We might find none, but at present, we have not really investigated and, therefore, we do not know. This research should entail at least amino-acid analyses of serum, urine, and spinal fluid and a study of the electrophoretic patterns in the serum globulin. There are several good analogies of disorders in childhood, such as galactosemia, Lowe's syndrome, and celiac disease, which are genetically determined metabolic disorders, now subject to remedy. Phenylpyruvic oligophrenia (phenylketonuria) and homocystinuria are two examples of innate, inborn biochemical abnormalities, causing delayed or imperfect maturation of the brain, one of which, at any rate, can be remedied. Perhaps next year or 10 years from now, someone may identify a biochemical dyscrasia, which might supply the answer to the problem of developmental dyslexia and its rational treatments.

7. More and more electroencephalographic studies should be done. Patients with developmental dyslexia often show minor dysrhythmias. Are these dysrhythmias specific for any one group of dyslexics? What is the natural history of such changes? Do these electroencephalographic dysrhythmias gradually fade and leave a normal pattern, as in some treated cases of childhood seizure states, or do they persist throughout life? Interestingly, Oettinger and Barro of Los Angeles have tested developmental dyslexics electroencephalographically, both while resting and during the act of reading. When some of these children are tested while trying to cope with a reading text which is just beyond their competency, the electroencephalogram shows a dysrhythmia that becomes progressively worse as they continue and finally takes on epileptic qualities. These patients do not develop overt convulsions or seizures, but the dysrhythmia becomes that which is characteristic of epilepsy.

Oettinger has suggested that these cases show a subclinical reading epilepsy as opposed to the well-defined type of epilepsy in which a seizure is precipitated by reading. This interesting work needs repeating in various centers throughout the world and requires correlation with other features in the clinical field.

8. It is important to investigate dyslexic children in relation to slowness in learning to talk. Some investigators, mainly pediatricians, believe that developmental dyslexia may be just a fragment of delayed acquisition of speech. In acquired cases, there is no doubt about this. Dr. Buchanan pointed to the angular gyrus of the brain where a lesion will be followed by an aphasia, of which the outstanding clinical feature is dyslexia or alexia. Neurologists sometimes claim that in these acquired cases, this is a pure or clear-cut entity. But if the patient is examined closely from a linguistic point of view, some other difficulties entailing the manipulation, comprehension, or utilization of language will always be found. The associated defects may be quite subtle or minor, but they are always there.

But this does not necessarily apply to the child with developmental dyslexia, because both the clinical entities and the brain structures themselves are quite different. Personally, I do not believe that developmental dyslexia is just a fragment of delayed acquisition of language, although, undoubtedly, we find a slowness in learning to talk in quite a number of patients. I would very much like to know how many dyslexics belong here. If forced to hazard a guess, I would say possibly 50 percent. This is a matter that should be known for certain.

Delayed acquisition of speech may be followed by a slow acquisition of words, with a slow combining of words into phrases, and then slow evolution of sentences. In other children, however, late development of speech may be followed by rapid linguistic progress. These are the slow starters who thereafter rapidly catch up.

Inseparable from the subject of the time of acquisition of spoken speech is the question as to the clarity of articulation. Did the dyslexic child ever stammer, stutter, or show any other form of speech disorder, perhaps requiring the help of a speech therapist? In some cases there is no doubt about this. But is the proportion significant? Does it have any bearing on the etiology of developmental dyslexia? That is for us to determine in the future. Personally, I am a little skeptical about the whole matter.

These articulatory defects generally disappear quite soon, and by the time the child is brought to see me, it is rare indeed for me to find any such defects other than, perhaps, a little difficulty in pronouncing the letter "r," which is very common. Other children have difficulty with the "th" and the "f" sounds. But this may be merely a manifestation of immaturity, and by the late teens this defect is overcome in most cases.

Apart from late development of speech and the disorders of articulation which may or may not accompany it, there is the question of a very mild associated anomia. This entails a subtle difficulty in naming a presented object at a given moment. It has also been stated that some of these youngsters have difficulty in narrating a story because their phraseology is poor and their vocabulary is elusive. This suggests a latent or subclinical aphasia. This might be considered a preaphasia, because it is a disorder of language and not of speech.

I am also rather skeptical about this, even though I am very familiar with speech disorders, because much of my professional time is spent investigating patients with dysphasia. When one finds such a language disorder in children with dyslexia, one is possibly dealing not with developmental dyslexia but with symptomatic, or secondary, dyslexia subsequent to a brain lesion.

I would like to take this opportunity to recommend the abandonment of the term "aphasia" as applied to a child. A child who does not develop speech does not have aphasia. Aphasia is a word which we should restrict to adults who *had* a mature language faculty built into their personality. Each adult has his own personal language, and no two individuals speak exactly the same language. This may be confirmed statistically, so that it is clearly possible to tell the difference between what any two people have written or spoken. Each person possesses his own "idiolect," which is an extremely vulnerable faculty. As the result of brain disease, this is one of the first things to break down in the development of aphasia.

This is very far removed from the case of a child who is late in learning to talk. To speak of such a child as a congenital aphasic is an abuse of the term.

I hesitate to suggest another term as an alternative to congenital aphasia, but "congenital disorder in the acquisition of speech" is certainly far more appropriate. "Congenital dyslogia" would be shorter. But, please, never again "aphasia."

9. This point concerns the question of manual dexterity and clumsiness. How often does one find a clumsiness of the hands, the feet, or the legs? We must exercise extreme caution because this is a very deceptive evaluation, except for those who are highly experienced in developmental pediatric neurology. The amateur should avoid the problem. The term "clumsy child" has no precise meaning to a neurologist. Clumsiness may entail a number of physiologic deficits: cerebellar, proprioceptive, pyramidal, extrapyramidal, or even dyspractic. These deficits are quite different, and it takes an expert to distinguish them. No nonmedical observer should stumble into this trap and make the diagnosis of a clumsy child without obtaining the opinion of an expert as to the cause and the nature of the clumsiness.

Furthermore, all children are awkward at certain activities at certain ages, and only gradually do they achieve dexterity or manual skills. At what age do children acquire these various facilities? This, the norm, is not fully known, even to the most experienced pediatric neurologists. When one finds a persistent lack of dexterity in a dyslexic, then one probably is dealing with a case of symptomatic dyslexia due to brain damage.

Far from finding clumsiness in the majority of my patients with developmental dyslexia, I usually find the opposite. Many of these youngsters are extremely quick and active on their feet and legs. Many little girls with dyslexia are petite, dainty ballet dancers, and some might well expect to become professional ballerinas. The boys frequently find an outlet for their dyslexia in athleticism. Some of them are very good indeed at football and baseball or rugby and cricket. I have been struck by the number of dyslexic patients who are extremely clever. Most of these youngsters are quite deft at assembling and dismantling models. As they grow older one of their principal hobbies is tinkering about with hot rods. Lack of manual dexterity only comes into the picture of developmental dyslexia at an early age and is soon outgrown. But, again, we need more statistical data.

10. This point concerns proficiency in drawing and painting. Schilder and Bender reported two or three cases of dyslexia in which there was exceptional skill in drawing and painting. I have never seen this myself, and I have studied literally thousands of drawings carried out by dyslexics. As part of my routine examination, each of my dyslexic children quietly and in solitude makes for me at least four drawings. For comparison and grading, I use the same four themes: a bicycle, a house, a clock, and a man. The man can be scored by the Goodenough scale or its Harris modification, although I would ask you to exhibit a certain skepticism about the Goodenough system of marking, of which I am not too impressed. The drawings show, as a rule, a very average attainment. Occasionally, one finds an overly elaborate system of drawings, with much unnecessary added detail. I have still to find a very expert little artist with dyslexia.

11. Audiometry should be part of the routine testing of a patient with

developmental dyslexia. Gross audiometric defects are rare. Tone deafness, or lack of a musical ear, has been mentioned once or twice, but I have not yet evolved a test for tone deafness that is applicable to the consulting room: it might be worthwhile to develop one. There may conceivably be a tie-up between minor defects in auditory discrimination and developmental dyslexia.

It seems more important to develop a battery of tests for dysphonemia, something like the Wexman series. It would be useful to test children for confusion of phonemes that are somewhat similar in sound. This is one of my routine tests. When confusion of this type exists, it might aggravate the dyslexia, and furthermore, it might determine the technique of reeducation advised for that child.

12. The question of cerebral dominance is a far more difficult subject than appears at first sight. The various tests employed for dominance are very different in their individual nature. In some cases, we test for automatic activities as when we say: "Fold your arms." The right-handed way of folding the arms is with the right hand tucked under the left axilla and the right forearm under the left hand. "Clasp your hands." This is also an automatic action, and the right-handed way of doing this is with the right little finger at the bottom. These two tests are useful, but they are not 100 percent valid.

Some other tests of handedness, like writing, are cultural, whereas throwing a stone is far more automatic. Some tests entail motor skills that a younger child may be unable to accomplish with confidence, whereas an older child can do so. Of all the tests for motor skills perhaps the most reliable is the use of a nailbrush. Hand a nailbrush to the youngster and ask him to demonstrate how he would scrub his nails. A right-handed child holds the left hand still and moves the brush with the right hand; when commanded to change hands, he holds the brush in the left hand and moves his right fingers up and down the brush. This would be a strongly right-handed pattern, and it is an excellent test in an older child but not so valuable in a very young child.

The battery of tests of handedness devised by Hull, by Hurst, and by Cernacek of Bratislava are accurate but far too elaborate. They may occupy 1½ hours, and then one is not quite sure about the outcome. We badly need a more brief and more accurate battery, with perhaps a quantitative score of percentage of right versus left dominance.

Such tests should be anatomic, automatic, and independent of teaching or cultural factors. An interesting but impractical test is Wada's injection of procaine into one carotid artery and then the other to see which one temporarily ablates the function of speech. That would, at least, afford information as to which cerebral hemisphere is more bound up with the function of speech.

It may also be well worthwhile to test the preferred direction of lateral gaze because of the possible connection between the dominant eye, the lateral field, and the preferred direction of gaze. A child who is right-eyed has a greater tendency to direct his gaze toward the right field, which has more immediate attraction than the lateral field of the nondominant eye. We need to validate a test like the row of colored dots to either side of a central black cross (Fig. 5-2). Although I have not used this test very long, it already seems to be producing very interesting results.

13. The secondary emotional reactions become progressively more obvious in the latter days of the dyslexic's schooling and particularly after he enters the critical adolescent period.

Without question, there is a correlation between dyslexia, adolescent delinquency, and adult criminality. Here we already have an imposing body of figures which can be used to confront politicians, educational administrators, and governmental executives when seeking funds to support research and the care of children with dyslexia. Productive research and training might save the state millions of dollars by taking care of the predictable criminal population.

14. Can one identify discrete subtypes of cases of developmental dyslexia? Are the differences between one case and another due to innate differences in the pattern of developmental dyslexia, or are they the product of different environmental factors acting upon two children with the same reading problem? Environmental factors vary enormously from the happy understanding home with loving and intelligent parents to the opposite extreme. One school environment may comprise enlightened and affectionate teachers and another the reverse. The I.Q., which enables adaptation to environment, may also vary widely. One child may, further, be endowed with what I believe psychiatrists call egostrength, which means, in plain English, guts. One dyslexic may have strong powers of sustaining attention, but another may not. These variables sometimes make one imagine that there are different types of dyslexia, altering the prognosis. I am not yet certain about this. That is for us to determine.

Parallel to the question of subtypes is the matter of degrees of developmental dyslexia. Is it an all-or-none phenomenon? Can one person be just a little dyslexic, and another one very dyslexic? The future must answer this problem.

15. What is the natural history of developmental dyslexia? What happens as dyslexic children grow up? Follow-up studies are sparse and total far too few cases. There is need for many more and for larger series of longitudinal studies of developmental dyslexias throughout all the decades of life.

I do not believe that the prognosis is necessarily gloomy. The outlook differs from case to case. There are neglected cases that can be contrasted with favored cases. The fortunate child with developmental dyslexia is the one in whom the diagnosis had been made quite early; the one whose parents are sympathetic and whose teachers are enlightened; and the one for whom instruction has started promptly and has progressed along the proper lines.

The neglected case is one in which the child has been misconstrued as being lazy, naughty, stupid, or emotionally disturbed and has perhaps undergone psychiatric treatment, sometimes for years. Here the true nature of the disability and its organicity have almost certainly not been realized. Perhaps the parents were hostile: the father was usually more critical than the mother. Perhaps the teacher have been cruel or callous, making no real effort to teach the child at all. Such a child is all too often sent away to play or put in a corner. The end results will be quite different in these two cases of developmental dyslexia.

In the favored case, the end result is what I have called the "exdyslexic." One must not expect too much of such a youngster, apart from rather exceptional cases. The usual end product of a fortunate patient is that he can manage. He can read magazines, newspapers, and notices on the wall. But he could not possibly read Tolstoy's *War and Peace;* nor would he choose to cope with any textbook of philosophy or any technical monograph.

Many of these youngsters who eventually learn to read never read for pleasure. They would rather indulge in outdoor pursuits or modeling or manual activity than in reflective study. They read slowly and with difficulty. It is rather rare for an exdyslexic to be bookish, to be academically minded, or to attain a place in Oxford, Cambridge, or other such universities. Their principal continuing objective handicap consists in atrocious and bizarre spelling, which, as a rule, they never overcome. As I have said, few dyslexics attain university level, unless they have been fortunate enough to have had exceptional parents and exceptional teachers. One must realize that throughout their schooling, they have had time-consuming difficulty, not with all forms of instruction but certainly with textbooks and with written examinations.

On rare occasions, a child grows to an exdyslexic with semicompetency without special training, as in the case of Hans Christian Andersen, who was almost certainly a genuine example of developmental dyslexia and yet wrote most charming fairy tales. He had no problem with linguistic expression, but those of you who know Danish and will study his written manuscripts in Copenhagen will find the most fantastic errors in the scripts, errors which are easily recognized as the result of dyslexia. From his biography we know how badly he fared at school and how slow he was in learning to read. This, however, is an exceptional case of a dyslexic who succeeded in literary efforts.

16. This question deals with the optimum techniques for teaching dyslexics. Being a mere neurologist and a diagnostician, this is not within my province, but I have had enough experience with dyslexics to doubt very much whether there is any one single method for teaching them. We need to run parallel series, teaching some dyslexic children by one method and others by another method. The end result might well be the same, which would be interesting; it reminds me of the experience of physicians before the introduction of antibiotics. Careful evaluation showed that while each physician had his own private method of treating pneumonia, the mortality was exactly the same in each case.

Results may not be due so much to specific techniques as to the interpersonal relationship of the sympathetic teacher with his pupil. If there are subgroups of dyslexia, then perhaps there are different techniques of teaching that suit one child better than another. For example, the developmental dyslexic with dysphonemia should probably be taught one way, while the developmental dyslexic without dysphonemia might well be taught another way.

17. A nationwide screening among the early cases of reading retardation would be advantageous. These cases should be reassessed so as to isolate the pure cases of developmental dyslexia. Centers should be created or facilities should be developed in existing schools for special instruction of the developmental dyslexic. Also, there should be centers for the instruction of those dedicated teachers who elect to guide and aid dyslexics. I visualize these teachers

as forming a *corps d'élite* among the teaching profession, with extra pay and special privileges. They should have their own diploma and their own academy or college.

Appendix

Comprehensive classification of the dyslexias

Arthur H. Keeney, M.D., D.Sc.

Throughout this book and throughout the rapidly spawning literature on dyslexia, numerous definitions and classifications have been proposed. Characteristically, workers in each field base their classifications on the aspects that are most conspicuous in their own areas. Recently a five-member, doctoral-level working group on research concluded after 2 days of deliberation that they could not frame a definition of dyslexia. This extreme position most likely stems from not adopting a fully comprehensive classification. All classifications in medicine and biology are provisional in character, by nature of the evolving science. It is recognized that therapists or educationalists often turn to a functional rather than etiologic classification, and this can be useful at the present level of therapy by training. Ultimately, however, all classifications should be based on causative mechanisms or etiology and refined as the underlying pathology becomes better known. The following comprehensive classification is presented in the light of such limited etiologic understanding as is available at this juncture and embraces the known areas that contribute to dyslexia.

   I. Specific (primary), developmental dyslexia (strephosymbolia; dyssymbolia)

  II. Secondary dyslexias (symptomatic; secondary reading retardations)

     A. Secondary to organic brain pathology

        1. Brain damage (cerebral dysfunction; other encephalopathy; cerebral palsy; mental retardation; low I.Q.; perceptual disorders; word blindness; visual agnosia; anomia, soft neurologic stigma)

           a. Genetic

           b. Post-traumatic

               (1) Prenatal

               (2) Natal

               (3) Postnatal

      c. Postinflammatory (intrauterine; extrauterine)
         (1) Encephalitic
         (2) Meningitic
      d. Asphyxic (hypoxic) (intrauterine; extrauterine)
         (1) Placenta previa
         (2) Cord strangulation
         (3) Maternal circulatory collapse
         (4) Excessive maternal narcosis; drugs
         (5) Circulatory collapse; cardiac arrest; cerebrovascular accidents
      e. Prematurity
      f. Other specific brain lesions (aneurysm; cyst; etc.)
  B. Secondary to slow maturation (late bloomer; developmental delay) (Associated with impaired lateralization and dominance)
  C. Secondary to emotional disturbances
    1. Hyperactivity; short concentration span
    2. Depression
    3. Anxiety
  D. Secondary to uncontrolled seizure states
  E. Secondary to environmental disturbances
    1. Cultural deprivation
    2. Poor motivation (extrinsic or intrinsic)
    3. Poor instruction
III. Slow readers (handicapped without symbolic confusion), bradylexia
  A. Asthenopia; visual handicaps (hyperopia; heterophoria; astigmatism; binocular control abnormalities)
  B. Auditory impairments
  C. Hypothyroid states
IV. Acquired dyslexia (lesions of dominant hemisphere, angular gyrus, and splenium)
  V. Mixed

BASIC DEFINITIONS

Dyslexia [Gr. *dys-* difficult + Gr. *lexis* word]. A difficulty in reading understandingly due to a central lesion.

Bradylexia [Gr. *brady-* slow + Gr. *lexis* word]. An abnormal slowness in reading due neither to defect in intelligence nor ignorance of the alphabet.

Alexia [Gr. *a-* negative + Gr. *lexis* word]. Word blindness or inability to read due to a central lesion.

Index